COWBOY STUNTMAN

Horse, Sunday, sitting, with Dean standing in saddle. Publicity photo, 1983.

FROM OLYMPIC GOLD TO THE SILVER SCREEN

 COWBOY

 STUNTMAN

DEAN SMITH

WITH MIKE COX

FOREWORD BY JAMES GARNER

TEXAS TECH UNIVERSITY PRESS

This book is typeset in Scala. The paper used in this book meets the minimum requirements of ANSI/NISO Z39.48-1992 (R1997). ∞

Designed by Kasey McBeath
Cover photographs courtesy Dean Smith

Library of Congress Cataloging-in-Publication Data
Smith, Dean, 1932–
    Cowboy stuntman : from Olympic gold to the silver screen / Dean Smith [with] Mike Cox ; foreword by James Garner.
        pages cm
    Includes index.
    Summary: "Chronicles the life and achievements of Dean Smith, a Texan and Olympic gold medal winner who became a Hollywood stuntman and actor"—Provided by publisher.
        ISBN 978-0-89672-789-2 (hardback) — ISBN 978-0-89672-790-8 (e-book)
1. Smith, Dean, 1932– 2. Stunt performers—United States—Biography.
3. Olympic athletes—United States—Biography. I. Cox, Mike. II. Title.
    PN1998.3.S58585A3 2013
    791.430'28092—dc23
    [B]   2013003747

Printed in the United States of America
    14 15 16 17 18 19 20 21 / 9 8 7 6 5 4 3

Texas Tech University Press
Box 41037 | Lubbock, Texas 79409-1037 USA
800.832.4042 | ttup@ttu.edu | www.ttupress.org

To my dear young mother, Georgia Bell, who has always watched over me; my father, George Finis; and my grandmother Ollie and grandfather Pink, who encouraged my dreams.

To my darling wife, Debby, the delight of my life.

And to those who come after me, remember: You gotta have a steel backbone and a wire tail and never give up!

CONTENTS

ILLUSTRATIONS

PLATE SECTION, FOLLOWING PAGE 110

Dean and James Garner on the set of the TV series *Maverick*, c. 1978.

FOREWORD

The life story of Dean Smith reads like a Mark Twain novel; a wishful, determined, small-town boy grows up and makes good. Along the way he sets college records, wins an Olympic gold medal, plays professional football, and then accomplishes his greatest ambition of all—he becomes a motion picture and television stuntman.

When Dean asked me to help him "get into the movies," I was happy to assist but wasn't sure I was doing him any favors. Being a stuntman is a lousy way to make a living. But Dean's superb athletic ability and faith in himself enabled him to become one of Hollywood's premier stuntmen.

Dean's story is one of incredible achievement and tells us that indeed dreams can come true.

JAMES GARNER

UNSUNG HEROES
THE AUTHOR'S ACKNOWLEDGMENTS

When I first arrived in California, it was a great era—the views were majestic, the people were bigger than life, and it was not nearly as populated as today. You could actually get around and not be traffic bound.

The big studios like Republic, Warner Bros., Disney, Columbia, 20th Century Fox, and Paramount had Western streets. MGM had two, Universal had a large one, and the smaller studios had small ones. Golden Oaks Ranch, Corriganville, and Gene Autry had Western streets, too. It was a great place for a cowboy to make a living. Today, most Western streets have been torn down to make way for more modern movies, although there are a few left in the valley.

Early in the industry, the stuntman was not given any credit on film. It wasn't until the early 1960s that this started, little by little. Here I would like to recognize and give credit to some of the great stuntmen, athletes, cowboys, actors, actresses, wranglers, circus performers, and directors—all exciting men and women with whom to be associated. To get to know them and work beside them was a huge honor and thrill. The Westerns couldn't have been made without all these talented characters:

Stuntman Chuck Hayward, a Nebraska boy, was one of John Ford's favorites.

Chuck Roberson, in the John Ford Stock Co. (a big family of actors, stuntmen, wranglers, and crew that always worked in Ford's movies), worked with and doubled John Wayne.

Yakima Canutt doubled for John Wayne in the early movies and was one of the pioneering stuntmen with his sons, Tap and Joe Canutt, following in his footsteps.

Cliff Lyons, who came along after Yak, worked closely with Wayne. Cliff was a second unit director and stunt coordinator and was very helpful in my career.

Davy Sharp, a talented man, always gave me good advice, and I took it, too.

I gave Terry Leonard one of his first jobs. Terry worked his way up to being one of the premier stuntmen and second unit directors.

Glenn Randall, the great horse trainer, trained my two trick horses, Sunday and Hollywood, while he shared his training methods with me. His two sons, Corky and J. R., were successful, too.

Bob Mathias, who won gold in the '48 and '52 Olympics in the decathlon, was under contract to Batjac.

Bob Morgan, married to Yvonne De Carlo, was injured in the early 1960s in a stunt involving a train and had to have a leg removed. He was tough and continued to work for several more years.

John Epper, from Switzerland, and his family were stunt people and horsemen. His sons, Gary, Tony, and Andy, were always helping me out. I liked working with Jeannie, Margo, and Stephanie, the three Epper girls. They were excellent riders, fought well, and could mix it up.

Fred Graham did great stunt fights. Jackie Williams was the best falling horseman in the business; Jim Burke, a big man, stunt-doubled for John Wayne; Bear, Dickie, and Ace Hudkins, brothers from Nebraska, owned a great stable of horses: Hudkins Brothers Stables.

Billy and Whitey Hughes, brothers from Arkansas, were small in stature but big in heart.

Bill Hart was another fellow Texan; Gene LeBell was one tough man.

Billy Shannon, a talented acrobat; Bob Yerkes, a trapeze artist; and Polly Burson, a rodeo trick rider who doubled Kim Darby as little Mattie on *True Grit*, were all true pros.

Sharon Lucas and her sister, Shirley Juaregui, from Oklahoma, could ride the hair off any horse.

World Champion Cowboy Casey Tibbs, originally from Fort Pierre, South Dakota, was one of my heroes. Clifford and Marguerite Happy, who make quite a husband-and-wife team, work often. Their two sons, Sean and Ryan, are great athletes.

Walter, Ben, and John Clay Scott are brothers from Arizona; Dick Farnsworth and his son Diamond, along with Buddy Van Horn, worked in all the different venues of the business.

I loved doing movie fights with Chuck Hicks; Bob Minor was one of the first black stuntmen and a fine actor; Bobby McLaughlin, a Fort Worth native, is always there when I need him. McLaughlin's brother Don was a world champion roper; his brother Gene, a world champion trick roper; and his brother Lee, an actor.

Monty Montana was a famous trick roper as was his son, Monty Montana, Jr., who's still a good friend.

Rudy "It Do" Robbins, from Texas, was an actor I first met on the set of *The Alamo* and was a favorite of John Wayne's. Duke nicknamed him "It Do." He lost his battle with cancer in 2011.

Other great men and women I've had the pleasure to work with include Robert "Bob" Hinkle, a farm boy from Texas; Neil Summers, who plays a lot of bad guys; and Gil Perkins, a native of Australia and former president of the Screen Actors Guild, who did so much to help the stuntman.

Buff Brady was the greatest trick rider of our time. Bobby Hoy was an actor and a leader in our business; Gary Combs, a successful stunt coordinator, is Delbert Combs's son. Delbert was the head wrangler on *Wagon Train*.

Jimmy Sheppard had no fear. He lost his life on *Comes a Horseman*.

Joe Yrigoyen, a teamster, could drive a six-up like you could drive two, did transfers from a moving horse to wagons, as well as trains, and taught me how to do transfers. His son, Joe Finnegan, is another great teamster; his son-in-law is the inimitable Mickey Gilbert. Ed Juaregui and his son, Bob, were cousins of Joe Yrigoyen. They were all French Basque families chock-full of talent.

Some of the other notables are Al Wyatt; Dick Crockett; Troy Melton; Walt LaRue; Roydon Clark, Jim Garner's stunt double; Ted White; Bob Burroughs and his sons, Blair and Bryan; Mike McGuaghy; Jerry Gatlin; Red Morgan; Teddy Grossman; Buzz Henry; and Hal Needhan.

These people whom I worked with and grew to love came from all walks of life. I have tried to mention as many as I could; if I have not mentioned anyone, please forgive me. My time making movies was one of the most exciting in my life.

This book would not have been possible without the contributions of many who aided or encouraged me along the way. My sincere thanks to

James Garner, Dale Robertson, Debby and Finis Smith, Mike Cox, Texas Tech University Press, Judith Keeling, Barbara Brannon, Kellyanne Ure, Mark and Maye Engebretson, Carlton Stowers, Les Adams, Bob Hinkle, Anita Swift, Ethan Wayne and the Wayne family, JWCIA, Jimmy Rane, Jackie Autry and the Gene Autry Museum, Joann Hale, Sandra and Steven Herl, Bob Mathias, Michael and Kelly Carmichael, Mirus Studio, Barbara Hill, Joe Ownbey Photography, and Sargent N. Hill.

Thanks to my family, friends, and fans.

DEAN SMITH

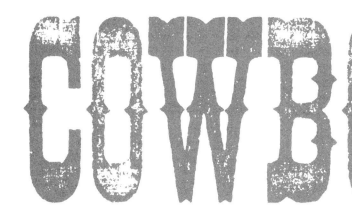

Dean doubling Steve Martin in *The Lonely Guy*, c. 1984.

CHAPTER 1

TEXAS ROOTS

As a Hollywood stuntman who got his start during the heyday of the black-and-white television Westerns, by 1983 I'd gotten pretty good at falling from horses, spinning a six-shooter, and throwing fake punches in barroom fights. But I sure never expected to end up hanging by a wire from a helicopter 200 feet over the Hudson River looking down on the Statue of Liberty.

Jack Roe, first assistant director on a movie called *The Lonely Guy*, had asked if I wanted to go to New York to double Steve Martin, the Waco-born comedian who got his big break on *Saturday Night Live*. I was older than Steve, but he and I were about the same size and both of us had pretty noticeable schnozzolas, as Jimmy Durante would say. Jack wanted me to do some running between cars on the George Washington Bridge, the double-decker over the Hudson connecting Manhattan and New Jersey. That sounded easy enough and I agreed to take it on. What Jack didn't tell me was that Neil Simon's script had one scene where Martin's double would be clutching the leading lady (well, her double) while dangling from a helicopter with the Manhattan skyline in the background.

They shot the bridge scene first. Though I was still in pretty good shape for a guy of fifty-two, breathing in all that vehicle exhaust liked to have killed me. With fourteen lanes, that big bridge is the world's busiest. The day we did that scene, it looked like every car, bus, taxi, and delivery truck in New York rolled across it.

When the helicopter scene came up, they told the crew to report to the World Trade Center, where we took off from the heliport on the top. I had stuntwoman Kerrie Cullen (doubling Judith Ivey) tied to me all the time we were in the air. I had wire and rope fastened to my harness as well as Kerrie. If the helicopter went down over the water, a guy in the chopper carried bolt cutters to cut us free so we would have at least a fighting chance at survival. We spent the whole day hanging over Manhattan, the World Trade Center, the Hudson River, Ellis Island, and the Statue of Liberty. You couldn't ask for a more spectacular view, but after a while, I would just as soon have been enjoying it sitting in first class on a jetliner approaching LaGuardia.

As I hung in the air, every hour or so my legs starting going numb. When that happened, I'd signal to the camera chopper and they'd take us down so the medics could rub my legs until I got my circulation back. We landed four or five times on the World Trade Center heliport, then we'd go back up. I'd done a lot of stunts over the years, but never anything like that. Once you're off the ground, it doesn't make any difference whether it's 20 feet or 5,000 feet; wondering whether that wire's going to hold keeps the adrenaline pumping. It wears you out. At the end of the day, I was just limp.

The next day, the front page of the *New York Post* had a picture of us in the air beneath that chopper over the city with the Statue of Liberty in the background, but that's all the exposure we got. No matter how dangerous it had been for Kerrie and me or how much it had cost to film it, that scene ended up on the cutting room floor when they came up with a different ending for the movie.

Doing that stunt had been as exciting as it was scary, and it got me to thinking that it was sure a long way from the Hudson to the Clear Fork of the Brazos, back in Texas. That's where my story starts.

✳ ✳ ✳

A beautiful piece of Texas, the Bar Double Diamond Ranch includes a one-mile stretch of the Clear Fork of the Brazos, land my family has had since the mid-1870s. On a spring morning, you can hear wild turkeys gobbling along the river. When the sun goes down, the coyotes take to howling. At night, you're likely to jump a wild hog or step on a big rattlesnake. In the fall, the hunters who lease the ranch look for heavy-horned whitetail bucks or doe for their freezer.

Most of my family's land lay in far northern Stephens County, but they traded, married, and got buried in a little town on the far southern end of Young County called Eliasville. The town's about three miles downstream from the Bar Double Diamond.

These days I run longhorn cattle on the place and enjoy walking or riding the rugged terrain, thinking of my forebears and how they survived here when the West was still wild. My cousin and his wife live on the adjoining 2,000-acre ranch, part of the original family homestead. Between us we've got six miles of river.

My family's Texas ties go as deep as a mesquite's roots, back to when Tom H. Hill and his wife, Amanda Randall Hill, made the long trek from Mississippi to Parker County in 1856, the year it was organized.

Married four years before they moved to Texas, Tom and Amanda already had two sons, John A. Hill and George William Hill, both born in Pontotoc, Mississippi. George was my great-grandfather. The Hills bought 640 acres in Parker County along Kickapoo Creek in an area known as Big Valley, about fourteen miles south of Weatherford. In 1858 Tom and Amanda had another son, a baby they saddled with one of the most famous names in Texas—Samuel Houston.

Comanches attacked Parker County frequently, killing people and carrying off their children. But the Hills managed to survive that dangerous time, the Civil War, and the worst of Reconstruction.

In January 1876, the three Hill boys—John, G. W., and young Sam—decided to strike out on their own. Borrowing money from their mother, they bought 1,300 acres on the south side of the Clear Fork of the Brazos in newly organized Stephens County, about eighty miles west of Weatherford. Back then, that part of Texas was nothing but wide-open grassland broken by an occasional clump of trees. The river bottom had thicker stands of trees along it, but the land my ancestors settled had not yet seen the invasion of mesquite or the pollution that often follows oil production.

Indians lived along the Clear Fork long before my family got here. We can find arrowheads and worked flint to this day on my land. I can also show you places on the ranch where the Indians ground holes on big rocks near the river.

Some time in the 1860s or early 1870s, there was an Indian fight on a high point above the Clear Fork on the old Lyden place just downstream from the Hill Ranch. The way I heard it, a band of Indians chased the Johnson party up the hill and they fought the Indians off. Old man Johnson got killed there, and in later years, folks started calling it Johnson Mountain.

Before the Civil War, the army had a cavalry post in the area to protect that part of the frontier—Fort Belknap in Young County. When the war began, the US Cavalry pulled out of West Texas and the people living there pretty much had to take care of themselves or go elsewhere. The military came back after the war, establishing Fort Griffin in nearby Shackelford County, and with help from the Texas Rangers they finally had West Texas clear of hostile Indians by the mid-1870s.

When the Hill boys vacated Parker County, they took their mother with them. The family story is that Tom Hill treated Amanda badly enough for her to get fed up and leave. They eventually divorced, unusual in those days. The Hills built a dirt-floor log cabin not far from the Clear Fork and started acquiring cattle and growing corn and maize. G. W. registered his brand as two diamonds side by side, calling it the Double Diamond. Sam branded a horizontal line, which is how the ranch became the Bar Double Diamond. By 1880, census takers counted 567 farms and ranches in Stephens County, one of them the Hill place. The county had 4,725 residents, but it had eight times more cattle than people.

One morning while doing the washing, Amanda watched six men wearing black hats and long coats ride up to the house. Seeing that they sat on sweaty, worn-out horses, she figured they had been riding all night. The man who seemed to be their leader said they were tired and hungry and asked Amanda if she could spare some grub. None of the men made any move to dismount. All Amanda could offer was some fresh-churned buttermilk and cold cornbread. She handed the boss the jar of buttermilk; he took a good swig and then passed it to the next man. They shared the cornbread the same way. Wiping the crumbs from his face, the man in charge took off his hat, bowed in his saddle, turned his horse, and rode off. Amanda later told my grandmother she'd fed train robber Sam Bass and his gang. Not long after that, Texas Rangers killed Bass and Seab Barnes at Round Rock, north of Austin.

When the Hills first came to Stephens County, Weatherford—fewer than thirty miles west of Fort Worth—was the closest town of any size. Because of that, the three boys continued to make occasional trips from their new ranch back to Parker County for supplies. Since they could travel only twelve to fifteen miles a day by wagon, the trip took a week each way.

Aside from raising cattle, G. W. Hill also found time for a little courting, getting engaged to a girl with the same first name as his mother, Amanda Frances Goodall. She was just a teenager, but frontier folks grew up quick. The got married on July 27, 1876, in Weatherford.

Back then, extended families often tightened their bond by marrying in-laws, and that's what happened in my family. Three years after moving to the Clear Fork country, Sam Hill married Amanda's sister, Harriet Winnie Goodall. The same preacher who officiated at G. W. and Amanda's wedding hitched up Sam and Harriet.

When the Hills came to the Clear Fork, which runs into the Brazos's main channel about three miles west of present South Bend, the nearest town was Picketville, about two miles north of what later became Breckenridge. But Picketville did not last long after Breckenridge began to develop.

About the same time, two land promoters named Elias DeLong and "Hunting-shirt" Williams settled just downstream from the Hills in Young County. Williams, always clad in a buckskin shirt, did not stay around long, but DeLong opened a store where the Hills traded.

Also in 1876, two Confederate veterans, brothers William L. and Thomas Franklin Donnell, along with their father, James D. Donnell, came to the Clear Fork with their families and took up cattle ranching. Moving to Texas from Missouri after the Civil War, they settled in Hunt County, where they ran a cotton gin and mill. Not long after arriving in Young County, they decided to resume their milling business. To power their machinery, they set about damming the Clear Fork near DeLong's store where the river spilled over a natural rock waterfall. Floods washed away their first two tries, but with help from a government engineer, they finally built a dam and gristmill that stayed put when the river got up.

Soon the Donnells enjoyed a good business turning locally grown wheat into flour and corn into meal. One of their biggest customers was the US Army, which contracted with them to supply Fort Griffin. Just below the dam lay a low-water area that served as one of the main crossings of the Clear Fork. Though normally easy to ford, it became impassable after a heavy rain, so the Donnells built a rickety suspension bridge. Folks used that until 1893, when the county put up an iron and timber wagon bridge. That lasted until 1958, when the state highway department finally replaced it.

With the mill doing well and other settlers arriving, what began as DeLong's store grew into a community named Eliasville, in DeLong's honor. Soon it had other businesses, a post office, a Baptist church, and a Methodist church. The dam the Donnells built also made Eliasville a popular place for picnics, tent revivals, traveling medicine shows, and circuses. When a couple got married in Eliasville, it became a tradition for friends and family of the newlyweds to throw the groom into the river. Supposedly that drenching made a man a perfect husband.

Eliasville was a pretty little town, but ugly things sometimes happened. One day a man accused John "Jack" Hill of letting his hogs damage his crops. When Jack denied responsibility, the man called him a lying SOB. Well, that kind of talk wasn't something many people put up with back then. Jack shot and killed him, settling the matter permanently. Figuring he'd either get lynched or have to face trial and foot the expense of hiring a lawyer, he decided it would be a good time to visit Indian Territory. To give Jack some traveling money, G. W. and Sam bought his interest in the ranch. Jack gathered his few possessions and left that night, never to return.

Tom Hill died on March 21, 1883, at age fifty-two. He was buried in the Holden Cemetery in Parker County, not far from the land he had homesteaded. Amanda never remarried, living with son Sam and his wife for the rest of her life.

G. W. and Sam each took a wagon and a ranch hand and traveled from Stephens County to Weatherford to settle their father's estate. Story goes, they were sleeping under their wagons in a livery stable one night when a gunshot jarred them awake. Groggily looking toward the door they saw silhouettes of men holding lanterns. Figuring somebody had decided to kill them, they started shooting at those lights.

That opened the ball. G. W. got hit in the arm, though the slug missed any bones. Sam caught a bullet in the stomach that lodged in his spine and stayed there the rest of his life. Supposedly the Parker County sheriff and some of his deputies had come to the wagon yard to arrest one of the Hills' hired men. The officers had no bone to pick with the Hills until G. W. and Sam cut down on them, which they naturally took personally. The whole thing was just an unfortunate misunderstanding. My great grandfather and his brother hadn't done a thing. G. W. and Sam had to hire a lawyer to keep from going to prison, spending a good chunk of their inheritance.

At least that's how the story came down to me. The *Galveston Daily News* for January 19, 1885, printed a different version of the shooting nothing like the family story. My guess is that as the Hill boys became more prominent, they whitewashed the real story and told family and friends the version I later heard. Since it came out right after the shooting, I suspect the newspaper account is closer to the truth:

> Friday night [January 17], about 12:30 o'clock, Geo. Hill, Buck Robertson and Bill S. were engaged in playing pool in Frank & Charter's saloon, when a dispute arose about the game, when Buck Robertson threatened to kill Bill S. and started to carry his threat into execution. S. struck him in the jaw with his fist, and at this point Officer Britton, a policeman, interfered, pushing the combatants away. When Geo. Hill interfered Britton pushed him back, telling him to hold on. He asked the policeman what he had to do with it? Britton told him that he had a right to do it, pushing him back the second time. George Hill then drew his pistol, Britton drawing his at the same time. Hill shot, the ball striking Britton in the side, being stopped by some papers. Britton fired, and Hill knocked his pistol up. At this time Sam Hill drew his pistol and fired at the policeman. Britton then turned and shot Sam in the shoulder, and then shot George in the arm. Then he turned again and shot Sam through the right lung, the ball passing through the body. About this time parties interfered and stopped the shooting. . . . The Hill boys live in Stephens County, and their grandfather [*sic*; father] is the oldest man in Parker County.

Sam's wife took care of him until he recovered. As soon as they got him back to the ranch, she stuffed a silk cloth into the bullet hole and then pulled the bullet out. That must have hurt like hell, but back then they thought that kept a wound from getting infected. She must have known what she was doing, because it worked.

Sam was tough as a wild hog's hide. One time after he had healed up from that gunshot wound lightning struck him inside the general store at Crystal Falls. The electricity traveled through a heavy chain used to keep the doors closed, hit Sam on the top of his shoulder, and sizzled down his back. Blowing out his boot heels and welding his spurs together, the lightning burned his back so badly he had to sleep under a quilting frame for a few weeks until he healed up enough to wear clothes again.

Starting with a son born May 24, 1877, my great-grandfather G. W. Hill and his wife had nine children (plus three others who died as infants) over the next twenty years. Their third child and first daughter was my grandmother, Ollie Elizabeth Hill, born September 2, 1881, at their ranch on the Clear Fork. She grew up on that ranch and went to school at Huffstuttle, not far from Eliasville.

By the time Ollie came along, the Hills didn't have to worry about Indian attacks. But she used to tell me that an Indian occasionally rode off the reservation in Indian Territory to return to his old hunting grounds on the Clear Fork. Her family gave bread to the begging stragglers, who by then meant no harm.

Grandmother also used to tell me how she often heard cougars screaming along the river when she was little. When her brothers or cousins worked in the fields, they always kept their horses nearby because they knew they'd start acting edgy when they caught wind of a big cat or two-legged stranger. A horse's ears will go up if something's moving toward it. And if it thinks there is a serious threat, its eyes will get big, its nose will flare, and it will start whinnying and pawing.

My grandmother also had to put up with older brothers who occasionally tormented her. One time they stuffed her in a barrel and rolled her down a hill. Like most West Texas girls, she grew up doing chores on her family's place. She had what she used to tell me I'd need in life: a steel backbone and a wire tail.

At age twenty-one, in January 1903, Ollie married Walter Pinkney Smith. "Pink," as everyone called him, had been born at Springtown in Parker County on the Fourth of July in 1871. That made him about thirty-two when he married my grandmother. He had drifted from Texas to Oklahoma and then back to Texas, where he met Ollie.

After their wedding, Great-grandpa G. W. Hill gave them 160 acres. That land was near Ivan, a small town in Stephens County on the road between Breckenridge and Graham founded in the late 1800s. J. O. Brockman, the first postmaster, named it for his son, Ivan. Besides a post office and store, Ivan had a beer joint during the oil boom.

Ollie and Pink had not been living on their Ivan place long before their first child came along. My father was their oldest son, George Finis Smith, born September 3, 1903.

Ollie and Pink Smith, Dean's paternal grandparents, 1940s.

"God ziggity damn, Ollie," my grandfather said, "he is a fine boy and we are going to name him Finis."

As soon as he was old enough, Dad started helping with the chores and got good at handling horses and mules and working cattle. Like most of the smaller land owners, Ollie and Pink farmed, keeping a few head of cattle and hogs for butchering, and raised their own vegetables. Their only other child, King William Smith, was born January 13, 1905. Later that year, Amanda Hill died, on December 9. Her sons buried her on their ranch in what's now called the Hill Cemetery.

Dad and Uncle King rode their horses to school at Ivan, making it to about seventh grade. Both could have used more education, but back then it wasn't that unusual for youngsters to decide they'd had enough book learning and drop out.

Pink and Ollie sold the land my great-grandfather had given them and bought another 160 acres between Ivan and Eliasville. Later they added seventy-six acres to that. One dry year, they managed to make just one bale of cotton, but my dad, who would have been nine or ten at the time, set fire to it. I don't know if he did it accidentally or out of meanness, but my grandfather wore his britches out for it.

My grandmother and grandfather did more farming than ranching, but G. W. Hill and his brother were cattlemen, eventually acquiring more than a thousand head. They grew a little corn and maize, but raising beef was their main livelihood.

Agriculture is how just about everyone made a living along the Clear Fork until 1916, when oil was discovered on the south side of the Brazos in Stephens County. Before long, some land man got my great-grandfather to sign a handwritten lease allowing drilling on his property. That turned out to be one of the smartest business deals the old man ever made. At one time, G. W. had six producing wells on his ranch. That brought in enough money for him to build a nice house in Eliasville in 1920 and keep his family comfortable, even through the Depression. The Texas and Pacific Oil Company also built a pump station on the Hill ranch to lift water from the Clear Fork and push it to a nearby gasoline refinery.

Eliasville really took off during the oil boom. In the summer of 1921, the Wichita Falls and Southern Railroad came through. The line ran from Newcastle in Young County through Graham, South Bend, Eliasville, Jim Kern, and down to Cisco and Eastland. The railroad company bought right of way and laid tracks through the Hill river ranch, building a long wooden bridge over one of the big draws on the place.

My grandparents did not have any oil on their property, and a bad drought made it pretty tough on them in Texas, so they moved to Oklahoma. Their new farm was at Paul's Valley near Winnywood, Oklahoma. My dad went to Oklahoma with them, which is where he met the woman who would become my mother.

In 1927, Dad married Georgia Bell Riggle in Wise County, Texas. Born April 2, 1911, in Oklahoma, she was about nine years younger than he was. They stayed along the Red River for a while but moved back to Stephens County so my dad could work in the oil fields. A horseman and muleskinner, he drove the big wagons they used to carry pipe or wrangled the mules that dragged pipe to a well location. All of that was hard, rough work, but this was during the Depression and any kind of job beat no job.

CHAPTER 2

SATURDAY WESTERNS

When my mother started having labor pains on January 15, 1932, my dad drove her from Eliasville to the hospital in Breckenridge. I weighed thirteen pounds at birth. They named me Finis Dean Smith, after my father. I always thought the name came from the Finis community, east of Graham, where the famous outlaws the Marlow brothers are buried. I was also told that we were kin to Confederate President Jefferson Davis, whose middle name was Finis. Maybe that's where it got started—I don't know. Across the street from the West Side Hospital sat the Blue Bird Inn, a beer joint where I'm sure Dad had a few drinks celebrating my arrival.

Not long after, my parents moved back to Wise County, where Ollie and Pink ran a dairy farm on the old Denton Road next to the Waggoner Ranch near Decatur. Somewhere along the way, Mother got tuberculosis. Hoping that dryer air would help her weakening lungs, they took her to a sanitarium at Carlsbad, near San Angelo, Texas. When she got worse, they carried her back to Oklahoma in early December 1933.

My mother died on the twentieth of that month in Elmore City when I was only twenty-three months old. They buried her at Elmore City and planted a pecan tree near her grave that still stands. I don't remember anything about her, but every year I try to visit her grave. After she died, my family sold the dairy in Wise County and moved back to Ivan. An outbreak of hoof-and-mouth disease helped in their decision.

For all practical purposes, Pink and Ollie became my parents after my mother passed away. In fact, for the rest of her life, I called my grandmother Mama. A petite lady who kept her hair pulled up into a neat bun, she had big brown eyes and wore glasses. She showed traces of her mother's Choctaw ancestors: her grandmother had been a full Choctaw. Mama

Dean's father, George Finis, and mother, Georgia Bell, and Dean as baby in front of a cornfield, c. 1932.

dipped Garret's snuff, which she cut with flour and kept in a tin wrapped in a handkerchief inside her purse. Of course, she never dipped in public. Though a very conservative woman, Mama had a good sense of humor and enjoyed life. She was a generous soul everyone loved.

Grandpa Pink—I called him "Pa"—was a tall, strong, but slender bald man with a reddish complexion and a Roman nose that my dad inherited and passed on to me. He could be humorous, but he had a short fuse. A fine horseman and a good teamster who chewed Brown Mule tobacco, he never learned to drive and relied on Mama to take him where he needed to go.

While Pa knew cattle and horses, he was mostly a farmer. He'd come in at lunchtime and turn his team out in our yard. One day when I was three or four, he put me on one of those old workhorses and let me start riding. The darn horse ran under the clothesline and pulled me off. Somehow, Pa caught me before I hit ground. That's the first time I remember being on a horse, but I didn't stay on long.

At that time Dad already had a drinking problem, and I'm sure the death of my mother made it even easier for him to turn to the bottle. I remember him always singing the song "Georgia on My Mind." Mama always said the reason Dad drank was that he ran around with all her older brothers and cousins and that they had a bad influence on him. I'm sure Dad wanted to be like the older men. And when it came to wrangling horses, punching cattle, or drinking whiskey, he held his own with them. But some men can handle alcohol and others can't. My dad couldn't.

On the other hand, my uncle King might have a beer every once in a while, but he did not drink enough to cause problems. Even though he was a very private person, he was just about as nice a man as ever lived. He didn't approve of my dad's drinking. Of course, my dad's disease was really hard on my grandmother. He did a lot of things that really embarrassed her.

The tragedy was, Dad was the most likeable guy you'd ever want in your life, as long as he was sober. Even though my dad drank too much, he never abused me. He'd stay on a drunk several days or even weeks and that's when he'd get mean. My grandmother was always bailing him out of trouble over this or that.

I just thank God I had my grandmother. I loved Grandpa Pink, but my grandmother was wonderful to me. As Pa got older, he had a stroke that paralyzed him on one side. It also made him unable to talk clearly and, understandably, caused him to be a little cranky. He would lie in his four-poster iron bed, and when he wasn't happy or needed some attention he would take his wooden cane and beat the iron railing, making a terrible racket. On top of that, sometimes he would take a swipe at me with it as I

Paternal grandmother, Ollie Smith, and Dean, age three, c. 1935.

walked by. When I couldn't stand it anymore, while he was sleeping, I took that cane outside and sawed it almost in two, then placed it back next to him. The next time he went to beating that cane it broke in half. Pa never knew I had done it. I guess he thought he just plumb wore it out. I still have the two pieces of that old cane.

After my mother died, Dad met a woman named Faye Duncan in Wise County and married her. In the fall of 1934 they had a son, Gerald Wayne Smith, my half-brother. Everyone called him Jerry. Faye ended up leaving Dad because of his drinking and she took Jerry with her.

Mama and Grandpa Pink in 1935 bought 345 acres near Ivan, the land I eventually inherited along with the river ranch seven miles to the north-west. They grew wheat, oats, and a little barley. Grandmother's brother

Sam Richard Hill and his wife, Manie, lived near El Centro, California, in Imperial Valley. Sam had forty acres planted in alfalfa. Mama used to tell me that he came to visit her one time and said, "I've got only forty acres in California and it's always got something growing on it." Mama said, "We cut wheat once a year." The difference was that the Imperial Valley is irrigated. On her place, they depended on rain.

At fifty-six, Mama learned to drive in a field at Ivan. Uncle King taught her in a Hudson Terraplane coupe. That was the same year I started school, 1937. You weren't supposed to start until you were six, but I was only five. It was just a little white schoolhouse with two rooms, but the Ivan school went all the way through the twelfth grade.

We had a great teacher, Stella Roach. But we tried her patience considerably. You could find a certain kind of fossil around Ivan that somebody, maybe it was one of the older boys named Johnny Kennedy, figured out was as good as a firecracker if you tossed one inside the wood-burning stove that warmed our school. It would sound like stray bullets going off and all hell would break loose. It sure made Miss Roach mad when we did it, but we always got a good laugh out of it.

A tornado hit Ivan in June 1938, after school had ended for the summer. Touching down between the front of the school and the house where the teacher lived, the twister killed three or four people around Ivan, including Volly Martin. After the storm, they found the old man's walking stick about five miles away. He owned the beer joint on the highway, back then just a dirt road. I remember the storm to this day. My grandparents were gone when the storm struck, and my dad and stepmother were asleep. First it got real still, then the wind got up, and then I heard a roaring sound. When I ran outside I could see the sky darkening. I was scared and tried to wake them up, but couldn't. We had an earthen cellar, right by our windmill, and I ran to that. I stood in the cellar with the door open and watched that tornado till it was gone. It didn't hit our place or I guess my dad and stepmother would have been killed.

When my grandfolks bought the Ivan place it had an old farmhouse on it, but Mama soon improved the property with a white, two-bedroom frame house with hardwood floors. That was the first brand-spanking-new house I ever lived in. She and Grandpa Pink slept in one room and I had the other. My father lived next door in the old house.

A dirt road that's now Farm-to-Market 717 passed by our place at Ivan, crossed Cedar Creek, and continued about ten miles to Caddo on old Highway 80 near Possum Kingdom Lake. Behind us rose a hill with a big oak tree on it. It was too rocky and the soil too shallow to grow anything on it, but I liked to go up there for the view. You could see everything in every direction. I would tell my grandmother that someday I was going to live on that hill, and she would tell me that she was afraid I would get struck by lightning. Now I live on that hill. I have a very scenic view and lightning hasn't struck me yet.

As a kid I used to scour the whole place with my two dogs, Al and Pal, searching for new adventures. If I wanted to ride I would have to race the horses to the underpass (a concrete tunnel that the highway department put under the road so livestock could move back and forth between our pastures) to catch them. If they beat me and made it to the other side I would have the worst time catching them. I didn't think much about it at the time, but I was pretty fast.

The Depression made life hard on just about everyone in our part of Texas, but Grandpa Pink and Mama managed to live off their land. We had cattle to butcher and grew enough grain to take to the mill in Breckenridge. One thing we didn't have was electricity. We had a refrigerator powered by gas from an old oil well across the road. Before that we had a real icebox, where you put a block of ice on top to keep everything cool. A wind generator sitting on top of our house ran our radio, the cable running through a pipe on the outside wall. Mama had a fig tree partially hiding the pipe. If the wind wasn't blowing we could only listen to the radio for a few hours until the battery played out. At night, we used kerosene lanterns.

Mama had a green thumb and was a wonderful cook. We ate a lot of chicken-fried steak, red beans, squash, and cornbread. Cornbread crumbled into a glass of milk was one of my favorite snacks. Of course, Mama also made sugar cookies, coconut pies, and pecan pies. She wasn't lazy and she could do anything. If a dog needed its tail bobbed, she'd stick its head in a boot so it couldn't bite her and then cut off its tail with a knife.

Whippings weren't considered child abuse back then, but Mama never hit me. If I did something I shouldn't have, she'd get me by my hair and say, "Listen, you ain't gonna do that anymore." And pretty soon, I didn't.

Mama believed she could lay hands on you and make pain go away. She had bought books to study on magnetic healing. I don't know if there really is such a thing as that, but I know this: when I went to her with a sore back or muscle, I usually left feeling better. I think that's why I always had such good health. She worked on me all my life. She'd rub her hands and then pull her hands down my back or somebody else's to cure an ache. She had a clientele who'd come to her for help with this or that kind of physical problem. Having her work on you was better than taking a damn pill. But sometimes, she'd still turn to the medicine cabinet and say, "Dean, I think you better get a pinch of Black Draught."

On the farm, my main job was watering and feeding the chickens and hauling off manure to fertilize our garden. The chickens ate store-bought feed that came in cloth sacks. Mama used the empty feed bags to make me shirts. We had thirty-five to forty white leghorns, Plymouth Rocks, and Buff Orpingtons along with three or four roosters. We also had some Japanese Bantams, but their eggs were smaller compared to white leghorns and stores didn't want to buy them.

The hens usually laid an egg a day. I'd collect eggs every evening, putting them in a straw basket and storing them in a cool place. There weren't as many coyotes in this country then as there are now, so they weren't a problem when it came to keeping chickens. Snakes were a different story. They liked to slither into the hen house and eat those eggs. Sometimes I'd find a rattler or even a water moccasin that came up from the tank, but back then all snakes were bad as far as we were concerned. I never got bit, but I sure broke a bunch of snakes from sucking eggs.

Raising poultry was good for more than just providing meat and eggs. One year during the Depression, the grasshoppers got so bad on our place it looked like a biblical plague. We were afraid they would ruin our crops. Grandpa got a friend who had 300 domestic turkeys to turn them loose on the two fields that had all those grasshoppers. Those turkeys got fatter and we got rid of our grasshoppers.

I remember a lot of things about Grandpa Pink, but not as much about my great-grandpa G. W. Hill, who died when I was only four. (His wife died before I was born.) What I do remember is that he always dressed well, wearing a black suit, white shirt, vest, and high-button shoes. He was a tough old boot, but witty. He had become a prominent man long before I came along. When he died on March 13, 1938, he left Mama some money and she bought more land with it. Mama also got some money when they settled my uncle Big John Hill's estate. (Big John was G. W.'s oldest son.)

All the surviving brothers and sisters got some of Big John's money, but the sisters spent their inheritance on houses. Mama loved the land and would not put her money in a big home. Like the old Texas saying goes, the only land she wanted was the acreage adjoining hers. Eventually, Mama put together the acreage that I own now. The river place was the biggest piece of land she owned.

After she bought the ranch, Mama ran it with Uncle King. My dad sometimes helped out. He loved horses and was a good cowboy, but they couldn't count on him because of his drinking. They raised Whiteface cattle, though those white faces sometimes got a little smudged with black. About the time the railroad came through the ranch in the early 1920s, a carbon black plant went up on acreage leased from my grandfather.

With some of the money she got when Uncle John died, Mama bought 640 acres on Hubbard Creek in Shackelford County near Moran. Twenty-two miles from the courthouse in Albany, it was called the Dumas Ranch. When I was about seven years old, Dad and my stepmother went there to live, and they took me with them. The road to the ranch wasn't paved, and if it rained and the road got muddy, it took all day to drive to town. I went to school there for only one term. About the only thing I remember about it is that two kids jumped me on the first day of school. I had to fight for my life and ended up in the principal's office. Mama bought the place for my dad, hoping he could make a go of ranching, but he didn't know what prosperity was.

I didn't like it on that ranch and came back to live with Mama and Grandpa Pink at the end of school in 1939. They leased that ranch out after Dad started acting out real bad. My grandmother did everything in the world for him, but Dad never could succeed at anything. I did not want to live with him. I wanted to live with my grandmother, the only mother I ever knew.

Going to picture shows was the highlight of my young life. Breckenridge had the National and the Palace, two movie houses built during the

1920s oil boom. In Graham they had the National, the Palace, and the
Liberty theaters. Albany had the Aztec. No matter what theater, it cost a
dime to see a movie, and popcorn sold for a nickel. They didn't serve
drinks back then, but all the theaters had a water fountain.

We'd go to town in Mama's 1939 navy-blue Ford four-door sedan.
With whitewall tires and cloth interior, that Ford was beautiful, big, and
comfortable. It had no air-conditioning so the windows were down three
seasons out of four. At some point Mama ended up selling that car to Rabbit, a black porter at the Burch Hotel. He bootlegged whiskey out of that
car. I imagine everybody in Breckenridge was wondering if my grandmother had taken up bootlegging until word got out she'd sold the car.

Driving from Ivan to Breckenridge in the spring you could smell the
freshly cut hay and sage in bloom or that wonderful fragrance of rain
from a distant thunderstorm. In the summer you could smell the hot, dry,
dusty air, and sweat would drip off the tip of Pa's nose. One time a bee
flew in the car window and stung me. I commenced to screaming, and Pa
pulled out his wad of chewing tobacco and placed it on my sting. I don't
know how, but it made it feel better. The air was clean and crisp in the fall,
but when it got to be winter, we had to drive with the windows closed. The
car had no heater, so we supplied ourselves with plenty of blankets and a
scraper for the windshield when it got covered with frost or ice.

Once we hit town Pa would usually go to the courthouse and visit the
other men sitting around on the benches. Sometimes he'd go to the Burch
Hotel, built in 1927 during the oil boom, and get caught up with his
friends. Ten stories tall, that building made Breckenridge look a whole lot
bigger than it was by the 1930s when I was a kid.

Just about everyone in the county went to town on Saturday, the busiest day of the week. We always arrived early enough to go shopping before
we went to the movie. If I needed new pants, Mama bought me Levis at
the Army-Navy store. She also shopped at Chip Greer's boot shop in
Breckenridge, a place I loved. I still smell leather when I think of that
place. Greer made saddles and boots and repaired tack. You could even get
your boots shined there. The old-timers and cowboys would go in to visit,
and I enjoyed listening to their stories.

Having a dime during the Depression to spend on a movie ticket was
another matter, but selling eggs helped me make a little pocket money. On

Saturdays, I'd gather eggs to take to town and sell at the A&P grocery. I'd usually have eight or ten dozen. One produce buyer had an apple crate with light in it and a hole drilled in one end. He'd place each egg on that hole and could tell if it was fertile by seeing how much light shined through. At the other store, the buyer would hold a candle behind each egg. Once a buyer determined that the eggs were OK, he'd pay two cents to a nickel a dozen. I'd usually end up with eighty or ninety cents and sometimes a dollar. That doesn't sound like much, but in the 1930s, that was pretty good money for a kid.

By the time we got through shopping, it would be time for dinner. (In West Texas, "dinner" is lunch and "supper" is the evening meal.) A hot dog stand next to the National in Breckenridge sold soda pop for a nickel, hot dogs with chili for a nickel, and hamburgers for a dime. Mama bought me whatever I wanted.

After dinner, Mama and I would walk next door to the movie. She enjoyed them as well as I did. The theaters in our part of Texas all operated the same. They showed dramas and comedies Monday through Thursday, with Westerns on Fridays and Saturdays. Not only did you get to see a movie, but they also showed an action serial, a cartoon, and a news reel plus coming attractions.

One of those black-and-white Westerns that really stands out in my mind is *Round-Up Time in Texas*, starring Gene Autry, who was born in Tioga, Texas. I also liked fellow Texan Monty Hale, Roy Rogers, Johnny Mack Brown, Charles Starrett (the Durango Kid), Eddie Dean, Rex Allen, Tex Ritter, and John Wayne. Tom Mix was another favorite, though a one-car accident cut short his career as a cowboy actor in 1940. Those singing cowboys along with all their great horses were my first heroes and they still are. Other than the Westerns, I enjoyed the serials like *Zorro Rides Again* with John Carroll. For laughs, I liked *The Three Stooges*. In 1941, Mama took me to see *Gone with the Wind* at the Liberty, the first color movie I ever saw. It was a bigger-than-life experience. Watching those movies sent my mind wandering, and it wasn't long before I started dreaming of getting into pictures myself someday.

Around 1940, Mama left the place at Ivan for my dad to live on, and she and Pa and I moved to Eliasville. Mama had inherited Uncle John's house on Hill Street and that's where we lived. The house was completely furnished when we moved in. When Pa needed to go out to the ranch on the river, he rode his horse from town since he never learned to drive.

Off the beaten path, Eliasville had seen its best days during the oil boom. At least it had electricity, a definite improvement over the place at Ivan. Eliasville also had shops, a drugstore, a bank (the First National), a garage, and a post office. I remember Lloyd Jones Mercantile and Stinson's Grocery Store, across the road from the post office and next to the garage.

All the churches sat on the highest hill in town. We called it Gospel Hill. On a Sunday morning, we went to church, and when the singing started, we'd tap our feet and get at it with hymns like "Shall We Gather at the River?" The red brick elementary school I attended stood at the end of the street on the same hill.

In Eliasville back then, you really had to watch where you stepped because all the town cows ran loose. One day I grabbed an old heifer by the tail and she started dragging me down Hill Street, really just a sandy road. Being pulled along by that cow was sort of like water skiing without water. I thought it was kind of cute until she kicked me under the chin. That's when I turned her loose.

When I was about nine we had a heck of an ice storm. Howard Don Evans and I skipped school one day and went down to a stock tank to go ice skating. I say "skating," but we didn't have any ice skates. We just skidded around on that frozen pond with our shoes on. When we showed up for classes the next day, our teacher said to Howard, "I want you and Dean to stay after school." We stayed and got our butts whipped with a belt. That broke me from skipping school. We could have drowned or died from exposure if that ice had broken, which is probably why the teacher seemed to swing that belt a little harder.

The first horse I remember was Old Shorty, a buckskin with a black stripe down its back. That name must have been Grandpa Pink's idea of a joke, since Shorty stood sixteen hands high, a pretty tall horse. He was also a little crazy. If you pulled the reins to the right, he'd go to the left. Pa had a high cantle-back saddle with a big A-fork. I don't know how he rode on it. It sure didn't seem comfortable. Anyway, Pa came in from the pasture one day, tied up Shorty, and went in the house. I thought I was going to do Pa a real big service and help him unsaddle that horse. I unhooked the front cinch and started pulling the saddle off, but I hadn't unhooked the flank cinch. That saddle slipped down under Shorty, which scared him, and he went to bucking. He kicked that saddle all to hell. Talk about a wreck on the main line. Pa, who was pretty fractious and agile as a jackrabbit, didn't like seeing Shorty tearing up that saddle. He came flying out of the house and as soon as he had the horse settled, he lit into me. I've been pretty careful unsaddling horses ever since.

Another time Pa came in from the ranch and left Shorty standing against the back fence with his butt toward the house. I got too close behind him and he kicked a board up near my head, just missing me. The lesson I learned: don't ever stand behind a cow or horse unless you like getting kicked.

All in all, I'd say I was a fast learner. Walking up Gospel Hill with Pa one day, I watched him take a big chew of Brown Mule as he often did. "Pa," I said, "give me some of that." He pulled out his knife and cut off a chaw, and I put it in my mouth. It wasn't long before I got sick. He wasn't very sympathetic. "Reach down and get some of that sheepshire—it'll settle your stomach," he said. I grabbed some of the grass he pointed to and put it in my mouth but I was still nauseated from the nicotine in that chewing tobacco. After that, I never chewed or dipped.

I learned to swim at the old dam at Eliasville. My introduction to aquatics came from Mack Cunningham, an older kid. Some time before, Mack had gotten his arm blown off in a hunting accident. That handicap turned him into a bully. One summer day when I was about nine, he threw me in the water. Hell, I couldn't swim, and the water was too deep to stand up in. I started dog paddling and struggling, and through plain brute strength and determination I managed to make it to shore. Standing there dripping, I told Mack that when I grew up, I was going to beat the you-know-what out of him. I don't remember what he said to that but unfortunately I never got the chance. I guess he wouldn't have let me drown, but the water pulled me under several times. About the third time I went down, I sure thought it was for the last time. I'll say one thing: it taught me how to swim.

In the late 1930s and early '40s we listened to the radio a lot. I really liked *The Lone Ranger*, but we also tuned in *Lum and Abner, Stella Dallas,*

Mr. District Attorney, and Walter Winchell's commentaries. Later I would listen to Gene Autry's *Melody Ranch*, sponsored by Doublemint. We listened to WBAP (which stood for "We Bring A Program") out of Fort Worth. One of that station's most popular programs was "Pappy" Lee O'Daniel and his Light Crust Doughboys. His touring bus passed through Ivan one time, which was pretty exciting for us kids. At night, we could pick up some of the powerful, clear-channel, 50,000-watt stations in distant cities like New Orleans and Tulsa. We'd tune to WWL to hear Vaughn Monroe play from "the ballroom high atop the Roosevelt Hotel" (as the announcer used to say) in New Orleans, and the Tulsa station would have Lem McCulloch and Johnny Lee Wills. Later, Graham and Breckenridge got radio stations, but they weren't as powerful as the big-city stations.

As a boy, I walked and rode all over our ranch. I did some fishing, mostly for catfish, at our tank, which we stocked with fish caught in the river. I never did any hunting. For one thing, up until I was about eighteen, you never even saw a deer in the Clear Fork country. They had been hunted out. Now we've got plenty, but I still don't hunt. I'd rather see a beautiful animal like that run across the road. Of course, if I was hungry enough, I'd kill a deer. But I don't believe in killing just for killing.

I was with Mama and Pa at the National Theater in Breckenridge on December 7, 1941. When we came out after the movie my cousin Ernest Kirkland came up and said, "The Japs have bombed Pearl Harbor!" The next day we all listened to President Roosevelt's speech on the radio and pretty soon we were in World War II.

Not long after that, our community started gathering scrap metal as part of the war effort. We had the whole school yard full of wrecked-out Model Ts and As and other pieces of iron and steel. The drive organizers took the metal to the train station at Graham, filled the cars, and then sent it off to the smelters. Back before the war all the junk iron America collected was sold to the Japanese, but now we were scrapping for the good old USA. During this time all of America stood united. We had our backs up against the wall and patriotism was never higher. If our country could only be that way again America would be better for it.

I was only nine, so the war didn't preoccupy my mind as much as it did the grownups'. The most important thing to me was learning to ride a horse. I wanted to ride so badly, I started climbing up on calves. Finally, Mama paid $50 to get me a little paint called Cupid. She also bought me a Sears and Roebuck saddle for $19.95. I kept Cupid in a nice stall behind the house on Hill Street. Singing "Don't Fence Me In," I rode him every time I had a chance, all over town and out to the ranch. When I'd go to the drugstore, I'd tie him in back. I had Cupid before I had a bike.

CHAPTER 3
RIDING, ROPING, AND RUNNING

As much as I loved going to the picture show on Saturdays to see those black-and-white Westerns, sitting in the stands watching the dirt fly and the snot sling at a rodeo suited me even better. And growing up in northwest Texas, I had plenty of opportunity to see men and women show how well they could handle a horse, throw a loop, or stay on the back of a bull.

Some say rodeo was invented in Pecos, Texas, in the 1880s as an informal competition among cowboys. Others claim it happened in Canadian, up in the Panhandle. However the sport came about, by the time I was a kid, competitive rodeoing had become a big form of entertainment in Texas and across much of the rest of the country. I don't remember when I saw my first rodeo, but I must have been pretty young. Not only did I enjoy taking in all the action, but I had kinfolk who rodeoed.

My father and several of my uncles and cousins were all cowboys. Big John Hill, G. W.'s oldest son, had traveled for a while as a performer with one of the Wild West shows. Tom Hill, one of my great-uncles (he was my grandmother's brother), was a big guy who roped competitively. His son, my cousin C. T. Hill, became a real rodeo competitor in roping. Silas Hill, one of Sam Hill's sons, was also a great roper and a real showman. He had snow-white hair, even as a young man. One year he entered old man's roping and young man's roping and won both of them. Despite all the roping he had done, when he got up in his years he had a roping accident while working cattle on the ranch. That left him with a clubbed right hand except for one finger and pretty much put an end to his roping.

That Hill bunch could do just about anything and didn't let anybody run over them. I had a lot of strong role models. To me these men stood twenty feet tall. But God didn't make the Hills or the Smiths all perfect, that's for sure.

Dean, age ten, at the Fort Worth Fat Stock Show, c. 1942.

In 1938 and '39, Dad took me to Stamford to see C. T. and Silas perform in the famous Cowboy Reunion rodeo put on every summer by the Swenson family and their SMS Ranch. I was too young yet, but it wasn't long before I started dreaming about being more than a rodeo spectator. The more rodeos I went to, the more I wanted to ride and rope for money like others in my family.

Dad also carried me to Fort Worth for the Fat Stock Show and Rodeo, the biggest in Texas. He went on a big drunk while we were there, but that didn't keep me from enjoying the show. They had the rodeo in the old North Side Coliseum, a real wonder when it was built in 1907–08.

They called Fort Worth "Cowtown" for a reason. It was the livestock center of the Southwest. Mama would pick up her cattle sale checks from the livestock commission places there and then go buy me school clothes at Montgomery Ward. Of course, back then most Texans called it "Monkey Wards."

After Grandpa Pink had a stroke in 1942, Mama decided we should move to Graham so he'd be closer to Dr. Virgil Rosser. After giving the house on Hill Street in Eliasville to Uncle King, who had it relocated to his acreage at Ivan, Mama bought a place on Kentucky Street in Graham only about a block from the doctor's house. I was right around ten.

About the same time, Dr. Rosser told Mama I needed to have my tonsils removed. As he tried to give me ether I hit him and knocked his glasses off. Two or three nurses had to hold me down. Before I passed out I could hear someone saying over and over, "See what you get, see what you get." The good doctor and I never forgot my tonsillectomy.

Tonsils or no tonsils, not many men can say they have two good friends with the same name. I had a boyhood friend named Larry Mahan, and later became friends with Larry Mahan the rodeo star. The first Larry didn't know a horse from a cow back then. We met in Sunday school at First Methodist Church in Graham. His dad was in the oil business, and I loved his dear mother, Clara. When we were kids we had some good times together.

Larry had a bike and I had a bike. We took the front wheel of my bike and hooked it up to the back of Larry's bike, giving us a homemade bicycle built for two. We rode it all over Graham, it was something unique.

Charlie Hipp, a cable tool guy who moved to Young County in 1938, brought big-time rodeo to Graham. He made a lot of money operating an oil well service company based there. Charlie was a showman at heart, way ahead of his time. Not long after he settled in Graham, he helped form the Possum Kingdom Drillettes, a young ladies' horseback drill team. Within a few years he was taking the show all over the country, including performances in Chicago and New York. In June or July he would produce the big rodeo in Graham called the Possum Kingdom Roundup. Charlie later had a pet lioness named Blondie that went everywhere with him. She even made *Life* magazine.

Through Hipp, I got to meet Don K. "Little Brown Jug" Reynolds, a talented trick rider who later played Little Beaver in four Red Ryder mov-

Dean, age fifteen, on Crawdad at the old Graham Rodeo and Fair Grounds, c. 1947.

ies and went on to a long Hollywood career as an animal trainer. His father, Fess Reynolds, could train anything with legs. When I first knew them, they lived in Electra, where Fess put together a Liberty Bond act with horses. He also performed as a rodeo clown and bronc rider. Seeing Little Brown Jug do wonders in the saddle is how I became interested in trick horses.

I also became acquainted with William "Wild Bill" Elliott, a big, tall, handsome guy. Elliott had a ranch at Pierce College in Woodland Hills, California, and was partners with Buck Steiner and his son Tommy. The Steiners lived in Austin, and Buck had a ranch in Bastrop County. Hipp produced the rodeo, but Elliott and the Steiners furnished the stock. Buck had been a rodeo star and Tommy followed in his bootsteps. Elliott was a novelty for Steiner. He could ride well and he did well with the kids.

In 1944, Uncle Roy, my cousin Dennis Hill's dad, gave me a good quarter horse called Crawdad. We sold old Cupid to make room for Crawdad. He was a beautiful little sorrel with a stripe down his back.

Grandpa Pink lived for two and a half years after his stroke, dying January 14, 1945, the day before my thirteenth birthday. They had the services in the Methodist church on Gospel Hill in Eliasville, a church he had helped build. Going to his funeral at the Eliasville Cemetery was the coldest day I ever spent. Almost all my relatives are buried in that cemetery, just outside of town on the road to my ranch.

When school was out that May after Grandpa died, Mama sold our house in Graham and we moved back to Ivan. We hadn't been there long before Mama changed her mind. We could have stayed at Ivan without Pa, but Mama didn't think an older woman and a young boy needed to be on a place in the country by themselves. We only spent a couple of months there before Mama bought a house on East Walker—that's Highway 80, the main drag—in Breckenridge. It was a nice place on three acres with corrals out back where I could keep Crawdad.

That summer, my dad took me to Dublin, Texas, to see Gene Autry perform. We took Dad's black Ford pickup, a 1940 V-8 with wooden sideboards that was so big he could haul two horses in there. A small town in Erath County, Dublin is famous for the original-formula Dr. Pepper that used to be produced at the bottling plant there and nowhere else, but when I was growing up, we took Dr. Pepper for granted. Not nearly as well known today is that for more than twenty years, starting in the late 1930s, Dublin was home to the biggest rodeo company in the nation. Everett Colburn, a cowboy from Idaho, took control of a company that furnished rodeo stock for the big performances in New York and Chicago. He leased 14,000 acres southeast of Dublin, named the ranch the Lightning C, and started raising rodeo stock.

In 1940 Colburn started putting on an annual rodeo at an arena he had built in Dublin. The Dublin rodeo kicked off each rodeo season. When the last performance ended, the company and stock left Dublin in a twenty-four-car train for the national rodeo circuit. Colburn's operation became so successful Autry tried to buy him out. Colburn declined to sell, but he took Autry on as a silent partner.

I'll never forget that performance. Autry, an army warrant officer at the time, rode out into the arena in his military uniform, singing the song that made him famous, "Back in the Saddle Again." He didn't have Champ that year, but that didn't bother me. Dad bought me a program for twenty-five cents, and after the rodeo I got Gene's autograph on it.

Dean and Gene Autry with the program Gene first signed for Dean in 1945 in Dublin, Texas, at the rodeo when Dean was thirteen. Gene signed it again in 1988. Courtesy of Jackie Autry of the Gene Autry Museum.

Looking back, I guess I'm lucky I survived that trip to Dublin. Dad had been drinking when we left, drank while we were there, and kept drinking on the drive home. Still, seeing Gene Autry was one of the highlights of my life up until then.

Next year, Mama and one of her sisters, Aunt Mollie, took me and Larry Mahan to Fort Worth to see Autry perform at Will Rogers Coliseum. They had canceled the livestock show during World War II, using the old coliseum to store airplane engine parts. Despite the war, they had built the Will Rogers Coliseum in 1944 and started the stock show back up in 1946.

It started sleeting and snowing before we even left Breckenridge, so Mama and Aunt Mollie cut a bunch of onions in half and rubbed them on the windshield of Mama's car, a 1940 blue Roadmaster Buick, to keep the glass from icing over. We drove through snow all the way to Fort Worth, but it was an indoor rodeo. The cop on the gate was Jim Smith, one of my uncles. He let us in for free. This time Autry did have Champ and Champ Jr., his second horse. After the grand entry, they brought a piano out in the arena. Autry jumped Champ Jr. up on top of that baby grand piano, a microphone dropped down, and Autry started in with "Back in the Saddle Again." Backed up by the three Cass County Boys, who played on WBAP, he also did "I'm an Old Cowhand" and "That Silver-Haired Daddy of Mine." Even though my father caused our family a lot of problems because of his drinking, I always thought of him when I heard that song. Nobody's ever paid me to sing, but I can sing it pretty well, if I do say so myself. I also got to see Toots Mansfield and Louis Brooks, two cowboys who were idolized back then the way sports heroes are today. Toots, who was from Big Spring, was a world champion roper. Louis was out of Sweetwater.

One thing I remember about living in Breckenridge was walking along Highway 80 when news hit town that Japan had surrendered on August 14, 1945—V-J Day. Everybody started honking their car horns and celebrating that the war was over.

That year I was supposed to go into eighth grade, but somehow I entered ninth grade. It was a struggle from the start. I didn't give a damn about grades. Mama insisted I stay in school, but at that point in my life, keeping my mind on school was harder than staying on the back of the meanest bronc in the rodeo.

Larry Mahan visited from Graham as much as he could, but I made some other friends in Breckenridge, including a boy a couple of years my senior named Robert William Nixon, Jr. Of course, nobody knew him by that name. I never learned how he came by his nickname, but everybody called him "Booger Red." He had a reddish complexion and freckles, so maybe that's why. When I met Booger he was only fifteen, but he had already been riding bulls for two years and won the state schoolboy roping championship at Hallettsville.

One day after school, Booger took me to meet Byrel Hittson, a rodeo cowboy and part-time butcher who worked for Phillips 66. Byrel was

Booger's mentor and he kind of took a liking to me, too. Maybe that's because he didn't have a son of his own, just daughters. Teaching us what he knew about rodeo must have filled a need for him. Whatever was behind it, I learned a lot from him. He knew I came from cowboy stock, being acquainted with all my kinfolk at Eliasville. Byrel lived across the street from the Breckenridge rodeo arena, which is where he gave us lessons.

Four other rodeo cowboys who influenced me were Fat Boy Wright, his brother, Nig Wright, and my cousins C. T. Hill and Pete Reid. They were older than me and I really looked up to them, four really handy guys with horses and ropes. I spent as much time as I could soaking in all they knew. My drawback as a potential rodeo cowboy was being left-handed, though that turned out to be an asset later on. There are some good left-handed ropers, but being a lefty was a detriment to me when it came to roping. Team roping left-handed is really awkward. Still, Byrel taught me how to rope. He was about fifty at the time, and he sure knew how to throw a loop. Before long, Larry Mahan started coming down from Graham and Byrel taught him, too. Larry was also left-handed, so he and I were in the same fix when it came to roping.

One of the things I learned from Byrel is that if you want to be a good roper, you have to have a good horse. He used to say, "It's just as easy to feed a good horse as bad one." Every horse is different, and you've got to know their temperament before you ask a lot of them. The next thing I learned was practice, practice, practice. Byrel would get a bale of hay and put some horns on it so I could condition my horse and myself at the same time. If you're team roping, you don't get off your horse. If you're calf roping, you do get off your horse. I learned all that from Byrel.

I already knew how to ride, but Byrel taught me a lot about what makes horses tick. One thing he used to tell me was, "By God, always sit a horse that makes a good appearance." Well, I'm proud to say I've never ridden a horse that didn't look the part. Most of my horses were nines or tens. They had good color and nice manes and tails. It's just as easy to ride a pretty horse as an ugly one.

Byrel was a neat dresser and that taught me something, too. He always had a nice crease in his hat and wore his boots well. He taught me how to dress western and look nice. That's paid off for me over the years.

As I learned from Byrel, I've always looked for horses that had a good disposition. Once you know a horse has a bad trait, try to figure out that horse and make it get over that. Let horses know when you're walking up to them. You have to be kind, but make your horse mind what it's supposed to. Let that horse know who the boss is.

I had entered my first rodeo as a barrel rider when I was ten. The way that works is that you have to ride a figure 8 around three barrels as fast as you can without hitting any of the barrels. The fastest rider wins, usually inside ten seconds. Charlie Hipp and his wife, Grace, had a daughter my age named Juanita. She was also a barrel rider. Most of the time Juanita beat me like a rented mule, mainly because she had a slightly better horse, a beautiful palomino. But I could handle the horse I had pretty well.

I made my first rodeo money in 1946 at age fourteen. I had a bareback rig and a pair of spurs. In bareback riding, you have to stay on a horse for eight seconds. I was a pretty good rider and I rode more than I got bucked off. That's because getting thrown gives you a lot of inspiration to stay on the horse the next time. Faced with eating dirt, I'd ride that SOB till the hair wore off. I'd keep my mind in the middle and let both ends flop. I probably rode a hundred broncs a summer as a kid. Despite Byrel's roping lessons, being left-handed I won more money on bucking horses than in calf roping.

I rode three nights. On the second night, the horse I drew, Crazy Lou, jumped out from under me and put me on the ground. Thank God, the ground was soft. I had been putting a pretty wild ride on her until she jerked my hand out of the rigging.

In bareback riding you don't use a bridle, just a strap around the withers—the ridge between the shoulder bones of a horse—with a handhold. You get on the horse in the chute. Meanwhile, it's moving around, slamming your legs into the boards or pipes, depending on the setup. The horse can do anything it wants to. You put your boots up around its shoulders and start spurring it to make it jump. You have to spur a bronc at least three times in the shoulder or get a goose egg. But you don't want to spur too much. We'd stuff horsehair in the rowels of our spurs so they wouldn't roll too quickly, which can cause you to overspur your horse and loose control. The result of overspurring is usually a trip up into the sky without an airplane with enough time coming down for a bird to build a nest in your hip pocket.

Being able to drive a car made rodeoing a whole lot easier, since I could go town to town. Like many Texas kids back then, I got my driver's license early. I had a 1941 blue Chevy pickup with a 1946 front end on it that I bought from J. B. Stoker, a good roper. That old truck had black fenders, two chrome spotlights, and a double bumper.

That summer, Larry Mahan and I drove to Stamford for the July 2–4, 1946, Texas Cowboy Reunion rodeo. That was my first big rodeo performance. I had gone to small-jackpot rodeos in Breckenridge and Seymour, but the Stamford rodeo was the largest ranch rodeo in the nation. Will Rogers did trick roping there in 1934, only a year before he and Wiley Post died in a plane crash in Alaska.

When we got to Stamford, we set up camp on the side of the hill right behind the big tank and arena. We pulled cots out of my pickup and slept under the stars on that red, gravelly dirt. While we were there, a guy drove up in an old yellow Jeep pulling a stock trailer with two or three horses. The trailer also had a room to sleep in. After he had the trailer positioned like he wanted, the driver got out and introduced himself as Bob Crosby, one of the great cowboys of all time. Originally from Midland, Crosby lived in New Mexico. When it came time for the grand entry that night, I got to ride behind him. I couldn't believe it. I was only fourteen and had met Bob Crosby, a fifty-year-old rancher turned rodeo star who had won many championships at Madison Square Garden. Not long after that, in the fall of 1947, he had a wreck in that Jeep of his. He went off the road into an arroyo and it turned over and killed him. That happened long before they started putting seat belts in cars and trucks, but a seat belt wouldn't have done him any good in that open Jeep.

Not only was I riding bareback, but I also competed in the wild cow milking. That's a rodeo event that originated at the Stamford rodeo, and it's a lot harder than it sounds, particularly for a still-green fourteen-year-old cowboy. Like the old rodeo saying goes, all you need is a rope, a bottle, and guts.

Back then, wild cow milking was a two-person event, the object being to milk a big old Hereford cow weighing 1,200 to 1,300 pounds. They used wild ranch cows straight from the pasture, with their calves in a pen nearby to get them a little irritated. One rider ropes the cow and backs his horse to keep the rope tight while another rider, called a mugger, jumps off his horse and wrestles that snot-slinging cow down for milking. The idea is to stick a finger or two in her nose and hold her tight around the neck. Somehow, a cow doesn't like that. Eldon Hibbert did the roping, while I was the mugger. After I mugged the cow, Eldon got off his horse. He pulled a Coke bottle from his hip pocket and started trying to get milk into an opening that's a lot smaller than a bucket. When the bottle's full, you run to the judge and give him the bottle. All this is supposed to get done inside sixty seconds, a little longer if you have an extra snuffy cow. We took too long and didn't win, but doing this rough stuff in a rodeo arena toughened me up. By trial and error, I was learning how to keep from getting hurt while at the same time putting on a good show.

Mama came to Stamford to see me perform. When Eldon roped this old cow, I was trying hard to hold her. Back then I didn't weigh 120 pounds soaking wet and that cow stepped on me. I wasn't hurt, but to Mama sitting up there in the stands, it didn't look good. After the rodeo, she came to see me and said, "I'll never come to another rodeo and see you get torn to hell. You're trying to kill yourself." I don't think she ever did go to another rodeo, at least not one I was in. Mama thought I was gambling on my life. But from the bottom half of my thirteenth year until I was sixteen, I was sure getting an education in rodeo.

Truth to tell, I was learning more from Byrel Hittson than I was in school, where I wasn't doing very well. I'd skip class and go to the sale barn and buy orphan calves for $5 to take out to the ranch. I really wanted to quit school, and while I didn't drop out, I may as well have. I flunked the ninth grade, even though I was technically only an eighth grader. That's when Mama made a decision that changed my life.

"You know what we're gonna do?" she asked. "We're gonna sell this house and go back to Graham."

Mama thought the schools in Graham were better, and I'm sure she wanted to distance me from Byrel and my other rodeo friends in Breckenridge. After our house sold in the summer of 1947, we moved to Graham again. There was no place for old Crawdad in Graham, so we kept him on the ranch at Ivan.

At Graham, Mama enrolled me in ninth grade again. We lived on Cherry Street right across from Shawnee Park next door to Pat Clifford, the basketball coach. I wasn't really interested in basketball, so Coach Clifford suggested that I go out for football. Larry Mahan and I both started

Dean's Graham High School football photo, c. 1949.

on the B-squad. I was a running back and pretty soon they found out one thing: I could really run fast. Nobody could catch me. It wasn't long before they started calling me "Jackrabbit" Smith.

I competed at the Stamford rodeo again in the summer of 1947. This time I just did bareback riding. Some of the more experienced hands told me to put on some weight before I tried double-mugging a cow again. I didn't do anything too outstanding that year at Stamford, but I won in bronc riding in 1948 in Breckenridge.

Larry Mahan and I never were bad kids, but we were teenagers. At a rodeo in Weatherford, we met a couple of girls. The parents of one of those girls owned a grocery store and she gave us several pies. Somehow

Possum Kingdom Relays All-American 100-yard Dash, 1949.

Larry and I ended up having a pie fight in our motel room. On the way home the next day, we soon realized we'd left behind the western shirts we'd been wearing at the rodeo. When we went back for them the motel owner made us clean the room before she gave us back our shirts. Earlier that same weekend, with Larry driving and his girl next to him, I sat in the back with the other girl. I reached up to the front seat and pinched Larry's girl on the rear and she slapped the fool out of him. Despite that and a lot of other things, after all these years Larry and I remain the best of friends. My childhood friend has been mistaken for the other Larry Mahan, and he always tells people he is the bull shatter and the other is the bull rider.

After football ended, Coach Clifford recommended that I go out for track in the spring of 1948. My first track meet was the Possum Kingdom Relays in Graham that March. I beat everybody by fifteen yards in every race in the preliminaries earlier in the day. But then I ran into trouble.

Graham High School coach John E. Little congratulating Dean on making *Look* magazine's All-America track team, 1949.

That night, 10 yards into the 100-yard dash, I tore the lifter muscle on my left leg. My muscle popped like a shot and I went to the ground in excruciating pain. H. A. Hefner, the school principal, drove his car out on the track and took me to the hospital in Graham. From Graham they sent me by ambulance to Harris Hospital in Fort Worth. They kept me there four or five days. You'd think they would have operated, but they didn't. The doctors didn't know whether I would ever be able to run again. But slowly, I started getting better. I was used to moving fast, but I took my time and let my body heal itself. That's the wonderful thing about being young. Your body's pretty forgiving.

I laid off from football in the fall of 1948, but by spring, I was able to

Dean made the only touchdown for Graham versus Wichita Falls at the state high school championship, 1949.

run full speed again. That spring of 1949 I won district, regional, and state in the 100-yard dash, never losing a single race. The state track meet was in Austin, where we stayed in an old hotel off Congress Avenue called the State. The hotel wasn't much, but Memorial Stadium at the University of Texas was a great place to have a track meet. There wasn't a bad seat in the place. I made *Look* magazine's All-America team in the 100-yard dash that summer. When the magazine hit the newsstands, the *Graham Leader* published a picture of me and a story.

In the fall of 1949, my senior year, Graham got a new coach named John E. Little. He believed in me, which made me try ten times harder. I had the ability, but you have to have confidence on top of that to win. Coach Little was my rabbit's foot. I played right halfback for the Graham Steers and made the All-State football squad, though the team only went 5–5. When we played Wichita Falls, which went on to be the state champions, we lost 39–7, but at least I scored that one touchdown for Graham.

At the end of the fall semester, Coach Little left Graham and went to Belton to be high school principal. The new coach was Bruce Wilson, who carried the team to track meets in a station wagon the school owned.

Between football and track, in the winter of 1949, the assistant coach,

Glen Johnson, asked if I'd like to go with the boxing team to a match in Mineral Wells. I made the trip, basically just for the heck of it. When we got there, someone asked if I wanted to get in the ring to help the team out. I thought they were just pranking me, but I went ahead and put on a pair of shorts and the next thing I knew someone was tying gloves on me. The bell rang and this guy came at me and threw a punch. I blocked it with my right and hit him with a left and was shocked when he went down like a bag of potatoes thrown off a wagon. After that knockout, they told me I'd have to fight three two-minute rounds the next night. I didn't know if I was in good enough shape to do that, and probably I wasn't, but I outpointed each guy. When the next issue of the *Graham Leader* came out, there was a story about the Mineral Wells boxing match and Mama read it. When Mama found out about it, she said, "If I ever catch you do-ing that again, I'll disinherit you." I didn't like hearing that, but she must have known I wasn't cut out to be a boxer, though down the road I'd have plenty of fake fistfights. She just had good sense, better sense than I had for a good while.

Back then, the first track meet of the year was the Border Olympics at Shirley Field in Laredo. It was an open track meet for both high school and college. In early March 1949, the coach drove us to Laredo, which took all day. We went through San Antonio and had our pictures made in front of the Alamo. When we left Graham that morning, it was freezing cold. When we got to the border, it was nearly 100 degrees. We stayed in the gym at Martin High School, sleeping on cots. I had never run in a big track meet and this would be my first 100-yard dash since I had injured my leg. I ended up winning the 220-yard dash but I got disqualified in the 100-yard dash for jumping the gun twice. I was nervous and not comfort-able with the starter. He kept saying things like, "I want you boys to go to the mark and freeze like a bunch of bird dogs." Anyway, in my opinion he shouldn't have been talking so much.

Besides being my first big track meet, the Border Olympics is where I met University of Texas coach Clyde Littlefield, a sixteen-time letterman in football, track, and basketball as a student there from 1912 to 1916. Af-ter four years as head coach of Greenville High School in East Texas, he had gone to UT as track coach in 1920. Five years later he cofounded the Texas Relays. By the time I first shook hands with him, he was one of the best-known and most-respected track coaches in the country. He saw me run and I guess he liked what he saw. I'm sure he was looking for another Charlie Parker, a high school champ from San Antonio's Thomas Jefferson who had become a star runner at UT.

One week later, our Graham team went to a track meet at Farrington Field in Fort Worth. I won the 100-yard and 220-yard dashes. Then I ran in the Big Spring relays and won. My senior year, I won the Possum Kingdom Relays, district, regional, and state. I was on my way as a runner.

I had really hated it when Coach Little left Graham. He was the first coach who helped build my confidence. He taught me the importance of stretching before you run and helped instill the self-discipline that's lasted all my life. I think he saw that I had the makings of a track star. He took boys, all brute strength and awkwardness, and turned them into competitors.

On top of that, riding in rodeos hadn't hurt my development as an athlete. I had gotten pretty handy at staying right side up on a bucking horse, which toughened me up. Some mighty good horses had tried to beat me and failed, not that I didn't eat some rodeo arena dirt along the way. Rodeoing also helped develop my reflexes, which were fast.

Back then or even now, you don't see many athletes who are riding bucking horses also running track. It's usually one or the other. I had to be careful, though. I didn't want to get hurt so badly that I couldn't run, and I had to keep a low profile with my rodeoing. I'd compete in University Interscholastic League (UIL) events during the school year and then slip off to rodeos in the summer. But the UIL frowned on anybody winning money, which is why I had to be quiet about what I did. In 1949 we were to play Breckenridge and the word got out that if we beat them they were going to turn me in to the UIL for competing in bareback riding and winning money. I had won a couple hundred bucks in Breckenridge the previous summer. I was worried about it, but Breckenridge ended up winning anyway and no one ratted on me.

During track season in the spring of 1950, I finished undefeated in the 100-yard dash, most of the time running around ten seconds. In May of that year we went to the state high school track meet in Austin, my second trip there. I ran the hundred in 9.7 seconds at Memorial Stadium, but they gave the race to a kid from Odessa High School, Joe Childress.

But even he thought I had won. He was shaking my hand when they awarded the race to him. That's the only time I got a bad decision in high school. I knew I really won that race, and so did Joe.

I graduated from Graham High School in 1950. About that time, thanks to having my picture in *Look* magazine the summer before, every college in the United States started offering me scholarships. I really got courted by Texas colleges, especially Southern Methodist University in Dallas and Texas Christian University in Fort Worth. Dutch Meyer and Sammy Baugh called and wanted me to go to TCU, but I told them no thanks. SMU sent Doak Walker and Kyle Rote to try to talk me into playing football for them. Walker had been signed on to play with Bobby Layne on the Detroit Lions and Rote had gone to the New York Giants. The fall before they had sent me fifty-yard-line tickets to SMU home games. I told them if they would still be playing for the Ponies, I might go to SMU, but that wasn't going to happen. I didn't mind being asked by two guys like Walker and Rote, but I had already decided that I liked running track more than playing football. I really respected Coach Littlefield at UT and wanted to run for him. I had never been that good a student, but I was smart enough to know that if I was going to do any good as an athlete, I had to have a good coach. I probably would have played more football at other colleges than Texas, but I wanted to be a Longhorn. I announced I was going to UT.

CHAPTER 4

HILL HALL

I got a full scholarship to UT plus $10 a month from the UT athletic department to cover my laundry. That was a good thing, because my dad sure didn't have any money to help pay for my education. His drinking had gotten him into financial trouble. To bail him out, Mama sold a section of her land, but she didn't get near what the land was worth. In fact, she practically gave it away to my cousin C. T. Hill, the roper.

When I got to Austin in the middle of August 1950, coming from Graham it seemed like a big city to me, but at the time it had only about 145,000 people. The state government and the university—with around 13,000 students plus faculty and staff—kept the city going economically. Most of the UT athletes lived at Hill Hall at 204 West Twenty-first Street, but I got put in the Hill Hall annex, an old World War II barrack. I had three roommates—Chester Bradley, C. A. Rundell, and Charlie Thomas. They were three of the greatest guys a fellow could ever hope to be hooked up with. Chester and C. A. were distance runners. They were also a little more refined than Charlie and I. We were sprinters and both of us were as country as a gourd dipper. We took our meals next door at Hill Hall, which Mrs. J. M. Griffith ran. The food was good, but when I could afford it I also loved eating at the Night Hawk restaurant, a twenty-four-hour joint on the drag. It had the best peach pie with whipped cream, and I sure did eat my share of it.

Not long after I got to town in 1950, I went over to Buck Steiner's saddle shop on Lavaca and got reacquainted with Buck and his son, Tommy, whom I'd first met at the rodeo in Graham. By this time, Tommy and his wife, Beverly, had started producing their own rodeo. When I could, I would go riding with Tommy. Buck had some land near Camp Swift in

Bastrop County, but he lived in that old saddle shop just a few blocks south of the UT campus. He always carried a gun in the top of his boot. A big, tall guy, he was quite a character, a page out of the Old West.

I was a cowboy at a university not known for its cowboys. Except when I was on the football field or running track, I always wore Levis, hand-made boots, and a cowboy hat. I'd been wearing boots since I was a kid. I got my first handmade pair in 1941 or 1942, from Sam Caldwell, a boot maker in Graham. They were black with green tops. Mama paid $15 for them. I was mighty proud of them, but the first damn day I had them, I jumped a four-foot fence and ripped the top of one of them. I got it repaired, of course. In Austin, I bought boots from Buck Steiner's store.

The Korean War had broken out earlier that summer. I was eighteen with a 1-A draft classification, so I joined the Air Force ROTC. As for my major, I probably should have signed up for the school of drama. But at that time, if you went into drama, people thought you were a sissy. So I was in the school of education.

Coach Littlefield didn't want me to, but I went out for football and made the freshman team. I weighed only 160 pounds and stood five feet, eleven inches, but I figured my speed could make up for that. The UT freshmen played five games that year: SMU, Baylor, Rice, TCU, and A&M. I played halfback and scored a couple of touchdowns against A&M.

That year the Texas varsity team under Coach Blair Cherry was doing pretty well and drawing good crowds, though Memorial Stadium was a lot smaller than it is now. UT students received two free tickets and could purchase four more. I made a little money on the side scalping tickets and also sold programs at the home games. The biggest game of the year was November 4, 1950, when Texas beat SMU, the number one team in the nation. They played in Austin and UT won, 23–20. I sold all six of my tickets for $100 each, which was a lot of money in 1950. Being an athlete I still got into the stadium and saw the game with $600 in my pocket. The only regular game the Horns lost that season was a heartbreaker to Oklahoma, who beat UT 14–13 at their annual showdown in Dallas. The Texas team didn't lose another game until it got to the Cotton Bowl on New Year's Day 1951, when they were defeated 20–14 by Tennessee.

When I started at UT, seniors tormenting freshmen was part of the school's tradition. This was back before colleges started cracking down on hazing. The upperclassmen had all gone through hell as freshmen, so they didn't feel bad about passing it along to the next crop of fish. The seniors lived on the fourth floor of Hill Hall, and occasionally they ordered us up there so they could whip our butts with wet towels or coat hangers. I mean, they would draw blood. But it wasn't all violent. Sometimes all we had to do was stand up and sing "The Eyes of Texas." I liked that a lot better, and got pretty good at it.

Two senior football players who rarely missed a chance to torment the younger fellows were Lewis "Bud" McFadin, a big old boy from Iraan in West Texas, and Don Cunningham, whom I knew from Graham. They were best friends. McFadin had come from the oil patch to UT in 1948 and played offensive guard and defensive tackle, back when it was not that unusual for a good athlete to play both ways. Bud was an All-American and headed toward the pros. Like me, he had done some riding and roping.

Now, the annual Texas-Oklahoma game at the Cotton Bowl in Dallas during the State Fair in early October, the Red River Rivalry, is a big deal, but back then it didn't compare to the Thanksgiving UT–A&M game. Only 100 miles apart, the two schools had been playing each other since 1894 and every year the not-always-friendly rivalry continued to grow. My freshman year, the Aggies came to Austin to play in Memorial Stadium on November 30. Sometime the week before that game, McFadin and Cunningham sent for us freshmen and gave us an assignment. I don't remember what they told the other freshmen football players to do, but I sure remember my instructions: "When the Aggies hit town, we want you to bring us back one of those Aggie hats."

Not only was I supposed to swipe one of those pointy-topped campaign hats the members of the famous Corps of Cadets wear, it had to be an officer's hat. Well, I wanted to get along, and I figured I could outrun an Aggie in his high-top officer's boots. I don't remember if they told me what the result would be if I didn't come back with an Aggie campaign hat, but I got the picture.

I went to the Greyhound bus station at Fourth and Congress Avenue, where the Aggies were arriving from College Station. They looked all spit and polish in their olive drab uniforms, with their girlfriends in fur coats hugging their arms. The first corps officer I saw step off the bus, I ran up, grabbed his hat, and took off running northbound on Congress Avenue, heading toward the Capitol.

I was too busy trying to get the hell out of Dodge to look back, but it sounded like the whole corps was chasing me. I could hear their sabers rattling as all those Aggies took out after me. It must have looked like World War II had started up again. Those swords the officers carried were supposed to be for ceremonial use only, but I didn't want to find out if they kept them sharp or not.

Holding on to that hat as hard as I could, I outran those Aggies all the way to the Capitol, seven blocks from where the chase started. Back then, you could drive all the way around the Capitol. I was headed north, figuring on losing the Aggies once I got to campus, when a pickup truck drove up and stopped. I saw a decal on the back window that I thought was from UT, so I jumped in the back. That's when I noticed it was an A&M decal I'd seen.

About the time I realized that, there must have been twenty Aggies with sabers charging in my direction between all the statues on the grounds. They circled the pickup and one of them yelled, "We think somebody got in the pickup." It didn't take them long to discover who in the truck wasn't an Aggie. One guy grabbed me and slung me down to the pavement and I took a $500 fall. Then they started talking about what to do with me. Somebody said they should haul me off to the country, take off all my clothes, and let me get back to town the best way I could. I told them I was just a freshman doing what I had been ordered to do, and I guess they started feeling sorry for me. Anyway, they turned me loose and I still had all my clothes on. Of course, I didn't have a hat to bring back to McFadin and Cunningham.

I figured I was in for a whipping when I showed up at the athletic dorm without an officer's hat, but when I told them the story they just laughed and said I'd done enough. I had learned a good lesson—I wasn't going to do that ever again.

When I wasn't in class or working out, I spent a lot of time going to movies, especially Westerns. Two theaters, the Varsity and the Texas, were right across Guadalupe Street from the UT campus. Downtown, on Congress Avenue, were the Paramount and the State. On Sixth Street were the Queen and the Ritz. Charlie Root managed the Interstate Theaters in Austin and he always gave free passes to UT athletes. I'd take off right after lunch and see a movie and then go practice track.

Movies were my escape, one way I kept my mind off of being love-lorn. Most of the football players dated sorority girls or cheerleaders, but I was in love with a girl from Graham who was going to school in Virginia.

The wife of our family physician back home, Dr. Rosser, had a brother who was also a doctor there in Graham, Robert E. Lee Gowen. The doctor and his wife had a daughter named Abigail Lee Gowen. She had been born in Yeadon, Pennsylvania, the same year I was, but grew up in Texas. I met Gail in 1947 when we were sophomores at Graham High School, and we'd been dating ever since. That was fine as long as we were living in Graham, but her folks had sent her off to Mary Baldwin College, a private liberal arts school in Staunton, Virginia, when I left for UT.

So while my teammates were taking their girls to movies and dances, I spent a lot of my time running up a big telephone bill each month. I also wrote a lot of letters, probably the most letters I ever wrote to anyone. When classes let out for Thanksgiving, I drove to Virginia to see her. It was true love, because I had to drive through a hell of a snowstorm to see her. Riding along with me was Joe Don Dixon from Baylor. His girlfriend was Gail's roommate. We stayed two or three days, then we came back to Austin and finished out the semester.

At Christmastime, Gail took the train home and I met her at the station in Dallas. She wanted to transfer to UT, and that's sure what I wanted. We drove from Dallas to Breckenridge and got a marriage license. Then we went back to Dallas for the Cotton Bowl, where Texas would be playing Tennessee. The day before the game, New Year's Eve, we got married by a Dallas justice of the peace at his house. It was nothing too flamboyant and we intended to keep it secret. We didn't even have a honeymoon night. Gail spent our first night as husband and wife with some of her girlfriends at the Adolphus Hotel and I stayed with my friends at the Baker Hotel. Being married made me 3-A in the draft, but that's not the reason we did it.

After the game, I went back to Austin and Gail took the train back to Virginia to finish up at Mary Baldwin. Then she would be moving to Austin. The following week the cat was out of the bag when our marriage was listed in the public records column in the Breckenridge newspaper. Needless to say, Gail's parents were not happy to hear the big news. After the word got out, I drove to Virginia in my convertible and pretty much broke her out of school. Again, this was not something that her parents approved of.

When we got to Vicksburg, Mississippi, we ran into the damnedest snow and ice storm I'd ever seen. We had to stay at the Vicksburg Hotel until it was possible to drive again.

Back in Austin, I moved out of Hill Hall and Gail and I rented an apartment on Enfield Drive in West Austin that Byron "San Tone" Townsend, a great football player from Odessa, had told me about. That $10-a-month laundry money I was getting from UT was not going that far, but I was still able to eat a lot of my lunches at Hill Hall.

Early that spring of 1951, we found out that Gail was pregnant. She developed an ovarian cyst and we thought she might lose the baby, but thankfully it turned out fine. On top of having a wife who was expecting, however, I was taking a full course load and competing on the UT track team. I hadn't planned on all those things, but that's life.

That May, Coach Littlefield took Charlie Thomas and me to Los Angeles for the Coliseum Relays, one of the nation's most prestigious track meets. The 1932 Olympics had been played there, and the Coliseum Relays had been held there every year since 1941. I had a hard time believing that as a nineteen-year-old freshman I was running on the same track that Jesse Owens burned up in 1935. Running before so many people in such a famous place, it almost felt like I was in the Olympics.

We flew out to L.A. and stayed downtown at the Biltmore Hotel. We got to see Pershing Square and some of the other sights. That was my first trip to the land of fruits and nuts.

But some of the spectators weren't as excited about two members of the UT track team being there in the Coliseum as we were. When we walked out on the field wearing our orange and white warm-ups and the announcer introduced us as the University of Texas team, hell, they started booing. I couldn't figure what in the world we'd done.

Of course, we went ahead and ran the race, the invitational 100-yard dash. I don't know if it was the booing or what, but when the starter shot the gun it must have looked like we were just standing around swatting flies. In other words, we got off to a slow start and didn't win.

I never did figure out why Charlie and I got booed in the Coliseum. One guess is the Herman Sweatt case. Sweatt was a black postal worker who had tried to get into the UT law school in 1946 but was turned down because of his color. He sued and the case went all the way to the US Supreme Court, which in June 1950 had upheld his right to attend UT. But that had been eleven months before we'd gone to California. On top of that, UT had admitted two black students at the same time I had registered. Earlier than many southern schools, UT was slowly beginning to integrate.

While we were out there, J. W. Mashburn, a track star from Oklahoma State University, whom I had met at the Sugar Bowl New Year's Eve 1950, introduced me to Bev Barnett, Gene Autry's business manager. Bev gave me a ticket to sit in the audience during Autry's *Melody Ranch* radio show. Being in California was like being in a world that I never knew existed. I thought, *This is where they make Western movies.* I was already beginning to think I'd like to play cowboys and Indians for a living.

In June 1951 a bunch of us from numerous Texas colleges and universities who had qualified went back to California, traveling in three cars to Berkeley for the Amateur Athletic Union (AAU) junior track meet. The *San Antonio Light* sponsored the trip. In addition to those of us from UT, we had several black trackmen from Prairie View A&M and Texas Southern. When we got to Alpine, way out in West Texas, we stopped for supper at a small café on US Highway 90. I could hardly believe it when they wouldn't let the black athletes in the front door. They had to go around to the side. Only whites could go in the front door. Well, we had as many blacks on the team as whites. That was the first time I had ever noticed anything about segregation. I didn't like it, but there wasn't anything I could do about it. We spent the night in Alpine and the next morning drove to Flagstaff, Arizona, and on in to Sacramento and then Berkeley. I placed second in the 100-meter at that meet.

That summer Gail and I went back to Graham and stayed with Dr. Gowen and his wife, who since they would soon have a grandkid to play with had forgiven us a little bit and seemed to be warming up to the idea of us being married. I got a job working for Stephens and Stephens Trucking Company making $1.10 an hour. I was working in the oil fields, swamping on oil field trucks. A swamper was a truck driver's best friend, doing anything the driver or foreman asked, from picking up pipe or two-by-fours to hauling pumping units and opening gates. It didn't take me long to realize that I did not want to work in the oil field as a swamper for the rest of my life, so, come fall, I was thrilled to be heading back to Austin and school.

Before school started up again, Mama sold a few cows, drove to Austin, and made a down payment on a little house east of campus for me and Gail to live in. It was a nice little stucco house at 3503 Banton Road, right off Manor Road by the Austin airport, and it cost $2,500. Mama made the payments on it, because I didn't have any money. It was a real hard time for me. Gail's parents thought she deserved better, but that house was more than good enough for us. We were fortunate to have someone like my grandmother to help us out.

Little Charles Thomas Smith, whom I named after my best friend at UT, was born on November 19, 1951, at St. David's Hospital in Austin. I was proud but, not having much of a role model to learn from, nervous about being a father.

CHAPTER 5

HELSINKI

I'd had a good freshman year at UT, going undefeated in five track meets. As a sophomore in the fall of 1951, I played on the varsity football team, and I made varsity track that spring. Although I enjoyed football, track remained my first love.

On the last day of 1951, my first wedding anniversary, I won the Sugar Bowl track meet in New Orleans. I ran the 100-meter dash in 10.3 seconds, beating Georgia Tech sprinter Buddy Folkes, a real big win. On that particular track, that was really fast. Coach Littlefield and his wife, Henrietta, had driven Charlie Thomas and me down there. We stayed near Lake Pontchartrain, but because of the cost, I hadn't been able to bring Gail along and we spent our first anniversary apart. But that was my first major win and a thrilling time. Coach took us to the New Orleans Athletic Club. We also went to see Johnny Ray play at one of the clubs on Bourbon Street. He sang "Little White Cloud," his biggest hit.

In the spring of my sophomore year, now twenty years old, I was once again winning in every track meet I competed in. The Longhorns came in third at the Twenty-fifth Texas Relays that spring, but I won the 100-yard dash in a flat 10 seconds. Here's some of what the 1952 *Cactus*, the UT yearbook, had to say about the event:

> One of the greatest groups of trackmen ever to appear in the Texas Relays turned in performances to match their talents as the Memorial Stadium cinder carnival wheeled through its Silver Anniversary Friday and Saturday, April 4–5. . . . As expected the host Longhorns were in a class by themselves in the sprints and sprint relays. Led by Charles Thomas, Texas dash men figured in three of the nine record performances. Dean

Dean at track practice, 1952.

Smith, Carl Mayes, Jim Brownhill, and Thomas sped to a 41.2 record in the 440-relay and tied the 880-relay mark with a 1:25.6 clocking. Both were the fastest times in the nation to that date.

That May, we went back to California to compete in the Coliseum Relays again. This time I got beat by E. McDonald Bailey from Great Britain, but I came in second in the 100-yard dash. We stayed at the Ambassador Hotel, where word got around that the famous actresses Rhonda Fleming and Abby Lane were going to be out by the pool. Charlie and I headed for the pool and hung around a long time waiting to get a glimpse of those women in their swimsuits. We got horrible sunburns, but when they finally showed up we figured it had been well worth the wait.

While we were at the Ambassador we also ran into Frank Sinatra and Ava Gardner on one of the elevators. We were carrying our trophies and

National AAU championships, c. 1952.

Sinatra took one and looked it over. He congratulated us and was very nice to us. I thought Ava Gardner was one of the most beautiful women I had ever seen.

As I kept winning track meets that spring, I got to thinking, *As fast as I'm running, I might just be able to make the Olympic team.* I guess Coach Littlefield was thinking the same thing, because early that summer, he said that he wanted Charlie Thomas and me to try out for the upcoming Olympic Games in Helsinki, Finland. I think Coach knew I had the right stuff. He knew I was a competitor, that I'd always be willing to stick my head in there and give it a try. I think he thought I had a chance and I started thinking the same thing. If you think you can do it, more than likely you can do it.

So off we went with the coach and his wife. We traveled to Berkeley for the National Collegiate Athletic Association championship track meet, which started on June 13. The first four US citizens in each event, along with the top four winners from the Amateur Athletic Union competition and the first-place winners from the military's All-Service track meets, would qualify to compete in the Olympic trials set for June 27–28 at the Coliseum in Los Angeles. At Berkeley, I did pretty well and qualified for the Olympic trials. I also ran in the AAU meet at Long Beach, winning the national championship in the 100-meter dash.

After the AAU meet, we went back to Southern California, where we stayed at the Moroccan-style Figueroa Hotel in downtown Los Angeles. At the Olympic trials I won a couple of heats and qualified. Charlie Thomas, my running buddy, got the measles and came in fourth in the 200-meter trials, missing making the team. That was almost as much of a disappointment for me as it was for Charlie, because up to this time we had been inseparable competitors.

Not only would I be going to the summer Olympics, but Coach Littlefield would be the men's track coach under men's athletic coach Brutus Hamilton. Hamilton was the athletic director as well as the track coach at the University of California.

On June 29, the day after I made the team, Hamilton told reporters he thought the American track team would win a "smashing victory" in the Olympics. That win would come because America had its best Olympic track team ever, he said. He based that on the fact that the team had set four new American records and tied a fifth record at the just-completed trials. The team had also broken thirteen American Olympic trial records.

"Who could ask for more?" Hamilton said in an interview distributed by United Press on June 30. "We'll have more winners this time than ever before."

Hamilton went on to name a lot of names in that story, but there was no mention of anyone named Dean Smith. That didn't bother me because I'd made the team. I figured I'd get a chance to get my name in the papers down the road, but I cared more about winning than publicity.

After I made it through the trials, a lot of exciting things happened. Gail had come out to California with her uncle, Dr. Rosser, and her mother, to see me run in the Olympic trials. I got to take her to the Ambassador Hotel and show her around Hollywood. We went dancing at the famous Coconut Grove.

After Gail and her family flew back to Texas, they held a big telethon at the El Capitan Theater on Hollywood and Vine to raise money for the Olympic team. Hollywood's finest turned out and I was very impressed. I got to meet Bob Hope, Bing Crosby, Zsa Zsa Gabor, Jane Russell, Jesse Owens, Jim Thorpe, Jerry Lewis, and Dean Martin, to name a few. Olympic president Avery Brundage was also there. Seeing all those stars was just another experience that made me itch to be part of the movie industry.

This was only the second time the TV industry had tried a telethon and it turned out to be tremendously successful. When the show began at 8:00 p.m. on June 21, 1952, bars, restaurants, and movie theaters all across the country reported up to a 15 percent drop in business. An estimated fifty million Americans had parked in front of their TV sets to see Hope and his cohost, Bing Crosby. By the time the show ended fifteen hours later, they had collected more than a million dollars in pledges. Unfortunately, since the organizers had announced their goal as half of that, a lot of people never sent their money in. The final total actually raised came to $353,000, which after expenses left $310,000 for the Olympics. But with all the other contributions, there was still enough money to get us to Helsinki.

They gave us big dinners at the Helms Athletic Hall in L.A. It was mind-boggling. Here I was, a twenty-year-old kid from Texas, and I had made the Olympic team. For me, it was a dream come true.

Of the six Texans on the team, only two were from UT, me and Skippy Browning. A&M had two athletes going to Finland: shot-putter Darrow Hooper, who would earn a silver medal, and Walt "Buddy" Davis, who would win a gold medal setting a new high jump record of 6 feet, 8.32 inches. Skippy ended up winning a gold medal in swimming. (He later became a navy pilot and died in a jet crash in Kansas in 1956.) Jim Gerhardt, a hot-stepping jumper, represented Rice, and Javier Montez from Texas Western in El Paso (now the University of Texas at El Paso) competed in the 1,500-meter run.

On June 30, they loaded the track team on one of those triple-tailed, humpbacked Trans World Airlines Constellations in L.A. and flew to New York, where we'd be fitted for our uniforms. That was back when Howard Hughes owned the airline. The plane had four big engines, which is a good thing, because as we flew over New Mexico, one of them caught fire.

That wasn't my first airplane flight but it scared the fool out of me. I thought, *Here I've made the Olympic team and I'm gonna die.*

The pilot started circling our plane, looking for a good place to land down there in the desert. Somehow, they got the fire extinguished and we went on to St. Louis where we landed and changed planes. One of the boys on the team slept through the whole thing, but I paid pretty close attention.

When we got to New York City, we were met in buses and taken to Princeton University over in New Jersey. We trained there for a few days, staying in various private clubs. Then we were taken to the Waldorf-Astoria in Manhattan for a big dinner. From there, the team went to Sam Wanamaker's tailor shop for our uniforms. Everyone got a navy-blue flannel blazer with an American flag on it, gray flannel pants, a red-white-and-blue tie with a white shirt, white buck shoes, and a canvas hat.

We paraded down Broadway in our new uniforms. Those white buck shoes raised a damn blister on my foot, but we looked pretty spiffy. While we were in New York, we were taken to different places, including Leoni's, a famous Italian restaurant that had excellent food with eight or nine courses—something I sure wasn't used to back in Texas.

Finally it came time to go to Finland. We boarded a Pan American prop plane at Idlewild Airport on July 7, but there was some kind of mechanical problem with it. I was beginning to wonder whether we were jinxed, considering our close call over New Mexico on the way to New York. We were herded onto another plane and we took off with no problems. It took five planes to get all the American athletes to Europe.

Our first stop was Gander, Newfoundland, where they checked our passports. From Newfoundland we flew across the North Atlantic to London, and then on to Finland. We got there around two or three o'clock in the morning, but it was still light outside. In the sky we could see the great northern lights. Finland was a real poor country at the time, but it was beautiful with very friendly people.

Finally we arrived at our dorms at the Olympic village at Käpylä.

They put me in with two guys I already knew—J. W. Mashburn, from Oklahoma A&M, and Wes Santee, from Kansas University, the athlete who would end up breaking the four-minute mile. When you are in a foreign country halfway around the world, Texas, Oklahoma, and Kansas don't seem that different. Both of my roommates were good ol' boys and we got along fine. I can't say the same about me and my bed, however. Our "beds" were cots filled with straw, which made sleeping a challenge. Since the sun shined all day that far north at that time of the year, we slept with black goggles on to make us think it was dark. But that didn't make the straw mattress feel any better.

We had more than 100 guys just on the men's athletics team. In all, 286 Americans competed in the games. Sixty-seven nations took part, sending a total of 4,955 athletes.

We started training right away, but the weather wasn't cooperating. It was rainy and cool, the running tracks covered with pools of water. On July 14, Hamilton put the track team on a midnight curfew. Some on the team complained, but as he put it, "We're adults. We know how to behave."

This was the first time that the Soviet Union had ever taken part in the games and, with the Cold War going on, that made Helsinki an even bigger deal. The Russians would be competing against us, but they did not live with us. They had their own village at Otaniemi on the other side of town, adjacent to the Russian-controlled Porkkala naval base. Barbed wire surrounded their compound, and at first no one but the Russians could go inside.

While we couldn't go see them, the Russians were sure watching us. When we practiced, they would be there taking pictures, scrutinizing us like you wouldn't believe. I guess they wanted to see what we could do and look for any weaknesses they could take advantage of. They wanted to get as good as we were and kick our butts in the Olympics to prove the might of the Soviet state. There's no question they had some fine athletes. They were tough and durable and came from damn strong stock. Russian Premier Joseph Stalin was a communist, not a fascist, but the Russian notion of superiority was almost Nazi-like.

The Russians later eased up their security and allowed some visitors, but we had been told by our coaches not to go there. Even though we weren't supposed to go to the Russian village, we did. Fred Wilt, a distance runner who was later an FBI agent, Jim Fukes, a champion shot putter who went to Yale, and I went over there and walked through it. We were just curious, not looking for a fight or anything. They treated us all right and nothing came of it.

I didn't have any use for communism; I was more worried about the track we would be running on. The brick-colored cinder track had been rebuilt only a few weeks earlier, but the word was that it was way too soft. On top of that, all the rain had made it even softer. Everyone was saying that the track was too spongy for any records to be made on it.

Not too long after we got to Finland, a pretty blond Finnish girl who worked in the Olympics office asked me if I'd like to meet her parents and have dinner at their house, followed by a sauna bath. Home cooking sounded pretty good, so I accepted her invitation. I was country and very naive, so when I went back to where we were staying I asked somebody what the heck a sauna was and they said that's when you take all your clothes off and go into a steam bath. I didn't think Gail would like that idea, so I passed on the home cooking.

The opening ceremonies would be July 19. In choosing a day for the big event, the Finnish organizing committee had studied a century's worth of weather records to come up with the one day that month that statistically had the least chance of seeing any precipitation. Naturally, it rained that day.

The rain had no affect on how exciting it was for me to march in that stadium with all those people sitting there. The stadium held 80,000 and it was full. I was so proud of my country and I think everyone else on the team was, too. The Greeks entered first, since their country started the Games. The other nations followed in alphabetical order, with the host nation entering last. The United States team would be next to last.

When the Russians walked in wearing their white suits and symbolically red ties, they got only polite applause. The spectators gave us a much warmer welcome. We walked in looking like a paramilitary unit. All the other nations had dipped their flags, but we did not lower the Stars and Stripes. We came in and centered up for the lighting of the torch as Finland's president Juho K. Paasikivi pronounced a traditional sentence: "I proclaim open the Olympic Games of Helsinki, celebrating the fifteenth Olympiad of the modern era."

The Finnish military fired a twenty-one-gun salute and thousands of caged pigeons were released to soar over the assembled teams. Well, when they turned those damn pigeons loose, I was sure glad we had hats on. Those birds must have been from the United States, because they pooped all over those Russians. Finally, Finnish Olympic hero Paavo Nurmi entered the stadium with the Olympic torch to light the flame. Who would have that honor had been kept secret, so the mostly Finnish crowd went berserk.

The track-and-field competition started the next day, Sunday, July 20. I knew I was capable of running just as fast in Helsinki as I could back on the track at Memorial Stadium in Austin, but I sure didn't feel as comfortable as I felt in Texas. I had no security blanket. Gail and Mama were half a world away, keeping up with the Games by listening to radio, reading the newspapers, and watching the newsreels in the movies. Back then, Dallas and Fort Worth had television stations, but you couldn't pick them up in Graham, where Gail was staying with her parents while I was overseas. Even if they could have watched the Games on TV, there was no live coverage. They filmed the events and then flew the footage back to New York for broadcast.

I was a long way from home and the opening ceremony had been almost overwhelming. I was uncomfortable physically, as well, and I knew that could affect my speed. After I had made the team, I had started having trouble with my right sacrum, a part of the backbone connected to the pelvis, and by now it was really bothering me. For one thing, we were sleeping on those sorry straw-filled cots. Also, it was damp, and even though it was summer, the climate was not warm. Sometimes it was just plain cold. On top of that, Adidas had given each of us a pair shoes with four spikes in the toes. For some reason, they thought they were better than six-spike shoes. Anyway, when I ran in those new shoes, I jammed a toenail and got a bad blood blister. I ended up doctoring it myself, sticking my pocketknife in my toe to drain the blood. Needless to say, I was not in the prime physical condition I was hoping to be in.

We started doing heats for the 100-meter competition. But I was still having that trouble with my sacrum. If I could have taken Motrin or strong aspirin, I would have done fine, but they didn't have that back then. Despite my aching back, I got through round one, the quarter finals, and the semifinals to reach the finals, my times ranging from 10.4 to 10.6 seconds.

In the finals for the 100-meter dash, I'd be running against John Treloar from Australia; E. McDonald Bailey from Great Britain (I'd already run against him at the Coliseum Relays); Lindy Remigino, a relay runner from Manhattan College; Herb McKenley from Jamaica, the world record holder; and Vladimir Sukharev from Russian. I was the youngest person in the race. Bailey was the old man at thirty-one, followed by McKenley at thirty. The Russian was twenty-eight, Treloar was twenty-four, and Lindy was just a little older than me at twenty-one.

The run for the medals came on July 21. Each race was started by someone from Finland, and in the Finnish language. When our starter held the pistol up, a near-capacity crowd sat in the stadium waiting to see us run. As we stood in front of our blocks, he said a Finnish word that meant "Go to your marks." Then, instead of saying "Get set," he said another word in Finnish. When we heard that, we got set, and then he shot the gun.

I think I was ahead for about sixty-five or seventy yards, though just a little, but then Remigino, McKenley, and Bailey caught up with me. Bailey got in my lane a little and crowded me. After that, it seemed like the four of us crossed the finish line at the same time. We were so close together no one knew how we had finished, though I later heard that most of the spectators thought McKenley had won. Remigino even went over and congratulated him.

It was a photo finish, but the photo timer they had was not as accurate as they are today. Nobody really seemed to know just what that thing was about. It took them a couple of hours to figure out who won the race. Meanwhile, we just stood around on the track until the judges made up their minds.

When they finally made the announcement over the public-address system, I ended up fourth, behind Remigino, McKenley, and Bailey, in that order, all with the same time—10.4. But I felt I should have been at least third, which would have earned me the bronze medal. It was the closest finish in Olympic history, with the margin between Remigino and Treloar (who came in last) being only 0.12 of a second.

Before I ran, I realized I was the youngest sprinter and that I would be running against the fastest men in the world. Just being on the Olympic team was the biggest accomplishment of my career to that point. Making the final competition was the icing on the cake. Still, losing out on a bronze medal by such a tiny margin was devastating because I honestly believed I was the best sprinter. Had I run as well in that race as I had run all that year, I'm convinced I would have won. I had beaten McKenley in Long Beach earlier that year, so I knew I could do it again. Only problem was, I didn't.

I knew I was a better runner than fourth place, but I'd just had an off run. I think Coach Littlefield thought the photo timer had not been working properly. But no matter how it came out, I knew he was proud of me. One of his boys was running in the Olympics. I think if I had had a good bed and some Motrin, I would have won the thing. At least we had defeated the Russians. That was a great achievement.

As soon as the news got back to Texas that I had not won a medal in the 100 meters, the mayor of Graham sent a telegram to the Olympic committee asking that the race be run again. That wasn't going to happen, but I was touched that my hometown stood behind me like that.

My next competition would be against the Russians and Hungarians in the 400-meter relay. I would be the lead-off man, the biggest responsibility on the team. That's critical, because if you don't get a good start off the blocks, you ain't gonna have a good finish. The others on the team were Harrison Dillard, from Baldwin at Ohio, the 1948 Olympic champ; Remigino; and Andy Stanfield.

The United States had the fastest sprinters, but the Russian team had won in the 1950 European games and had a reputation for working well together and being very sharp in the handoffs. The Hungarians had done pretty well in the heats, but we figured the Russians as the ones to beat.

When we came to the finals on July 27, I got a good start, ran my 100 meters, and handed off to Dillard, who just sprayed me with cinders as he kicked into gear. Dillard handed off to Lindy and then Lindy handed to Stanfield. Andy got a kink in his arm when he reached back for the baton but came around on the final turn ahead of the Russian and Hungarian runners and crossed the finish line a clear first, at least two meters ahead of Sukharev.

All four of us got the gold medal, which came in a nice blue case. Finland's president, Juho Kusti Paasikivi, presented one to each of us. I've still got mine in a bank vault. The gold is worth a lot more per ounce than it was back then, but to me, the value of that medal has nothing to do with money.

The gold medal Dean won in the 400-meter relay in Helsinki, Finland, 1952.

The Olympic athletes got to be tourists when we weren't competing. I remember seeing *Gone with the Wind*, which I had first seen with Mama back in Graham, but this time it was all in Finnish with English subtitles. They took us by ship to a restaurant on an island off Helsinki for lunch, which was smoked reindeer. It tasted like raw meat to me. In the downtown square, they had urinals all over the place. Men stood and peed in public just as casually as I might take a leak behind the barn back in Texas.

When you're thousands of miles from home, it's pretty easy to make friends, especially with people from your part of the world. One of the many people I got close to was Bob Mathias, a great athlete. He was a couple of years older, but we got along great. At seventeen he had won a gold medal in the decathlon at the 1948 games in London, and he also won the gold in the same event at Helsinki. I first met him at a track meet in California and made a point of stopping by to see him at the Olympic village. Bob's dad, originally from Oklahoma, was a doctor in Tulare, a suburb of Fresno, California.

I had won a gold medal and so had thirty-nine other Americans. The

USA Olympic relay team gold medal winners, 1952.

US team also earned nineteen silver and seventeen bronze medals, for a total of seventy-six, making us the top winners, followed by the Russians, who earned seventy-one medals, including twenty-two gold.

When the news that I'd won a gold medal hit Texas, everybody who knew me or my family started calling Mama to offer their congratulations. I think she knew what she had put into me, that she had done the right thing. Without her, things wouldn't have been nearly as good for me.

After the Games ended on August 3, they sent the American teams on tours across Europe. Our first two stops after we left Helsinki were Ebaskula and Turkcoo, both just little villages in Finland. We were being used as goodwill ambassadors for the United States, which was fine by me.

While we were still in Finland, Coach Littlefield got sick. I think he had a bleeding ulcer. Anyway, he had to have emergency surgery and they were going to have to leave him behind while he recovered. I went to see him as soon as I could. I told him I felt a little insecure about having to leave him, since he was the one who had shaped me into who I was. He told me I'd do fine and gave me some money—not for me to spend on me, but on him. He said, "Dean, when you get to London, buy a cashmere sweater for my wife. When you're in Germany, buy me a cuckoo clock and some crystal." I assured him that I would do as he asked, but it was very hard for me to leave him. He pulled through and was my coach for the rest of my career.

From Finland, we went to Germany, Belgium, and England. In Cologne, Germany, we ran in a couple of track meets and got to visit the Cologne Cathedral. We ran on a track where bombs had fallen during the war. You could tell where they had exploded because they had replaced the cinders and the colors were different. We also went on a cruise along the Rhine River, where I got to drink a little of that famous Rhine wine. You could still see the ruins of all those beautiful bridges the Allies had bombed only eight or nine years earlier. In most cases, all that was left of them were majestic statues. Like I promised, I bought a cuckoo clock and crystal for Coach Littlefield. At Dartmouth, Germany, we took a ride on the Autobahn, which had no speed limit. It was fast and narrow.

After that, we went to England to take part in the British Empire Games in London. I got to go to Buckingham Palace and saw the changing of the guard. Being from Texas, one thing that really interested me was the mounted officers. Their horses were eighteen hands tall. They were trying to move back a bunch of tourists and one old gal didn't listen. One of the cops bumped her with his horse. That knocked her down and her dress flipped over her head—a pretty shocking scene for all of us. It was amazing the way they worked the crowd with their horses.

We also got to see the Tower of London, Windsor Castle, and Westminster Abbey. While we were in London, someone stole the Stone of Scone, but it wasn't anyone connected with the Olympics.

Then we took a ride on the Thames River, passing under the famous bridges, and went to see Gary Cooper in his classic movie *High Noon*. At a London museum, I tried to buy a chocolate bar. Even though the war had been over since 1945, England was still having a hard time. You had to have a ration stamp to buy chocolate. An English woman heard me getting turned down and gave me one of hers. It wasn't an American-made Hershey bar, but it sure beat having nothing.

When we went to Piccadilly Circus, I saw another reminder of the war: all the prostitutes who didn't have as many customers as they used to now that most of the American airmen and soldiers were gone. To my surprise, they started propositioning all the young, clean-cut Olympic athletes. While I was watching them try to drum up some business, damned if didn't see Randy Moore from Omaha, Texas, a little town near Sherman. Randy was in the Silver Spurs at UT and we were friends. (His dad played for the New York Yankees.) Randy and his mother were there on vacation.

At Simpson's of Piccadilly I bought some expensive cashmere for Coach Littlefield's wife.

We ran at White City Stadium, Americans against the British Empire's Olympic track team, and did pretty well. Our handlers were always giving us Ovaltine or Horlick's Malted Milk Tablets to put in our milk. They thought it would perk us up, sort of like athletes today drink Gatorade all the time.

Our time abroad finally came to an end. Seeing Europe had been wonderful, but by the time our plane took off for the States, I was happy to be on it. I think most of us had begun to get homesick. I know for sure that I was.

Coach Littlefield had enough money to give me to buy souvenirs for him, but I didn't have two nickels to rub together. Things were horrible financially when I went off to the university and they hadn't gotten much better. Oil royalties were minute and cattle prices had slumped. Coming off a gold medal win at the Olympics I'd done everything a guy twenty years old could possibly do, but I was sort of down in the dumps. Sometimes when you're right in front of something, you can't enjoy it until you remember where you've been.

On the way back to the United States, our plane stopped in Shannon, Ireland. We were overweight, but it wasn't because of me. About all I brought back from Europe were my gold medal, my clothes, and the stuff I had bought for Coach Littlefield. Once that issue was settled, we flew from Ireland across the Atlantic to Gander, where we had to show proof of vaccinations before the last leg of the flight to New York's LaGuardia airport. All the team members dispersed from there.

I flew on to Grand Lake, Colorado, where Gail and her folks met me. I was ready to get home, but we stayed there for a couple of days with B. F. and Louise Allison, formerly of Graham. B. F. was a wealthy oilman and his wife, Louise, was a good friend of Gail's mother. Up in the mountains, it got cold at night, but when we finally got home to Texas, it was still summertime.

I'd been to the Olympics, but like I said, I didn't have a quarter to my name. Being an amateur athlete at that time meant you could not take any money for endorsements the way they do today. I had won a gold medal but I couldn't capitalize on it. So, not being able to appear on a Wheaties box or promote tennis shoes, I went back to work for Stephens and Stephens Trucking in Graham, hauling pipe to the oil fields as I had the summer before.

CHAPTER 6

BACK TO THE REAL WORLD

had won gold at the Olympics, the ultimate goal in track and field. While that medal in its fancy case gave me a lot of confidence, I was back in the real world again—going to school, competing on the UT track team, and of course I had the additional responsibilities of being a husband and father. On top of all that, we didn't have much money. I was feeling a lot of pressure.

One way I handled the stress was by going to movies with that free pass all UT athletes got. I know now that I should have concentrated more on my classes and my family, but when you're that young, you don't understand things like that. Gail liked movies, too, but a lot of times I went to the show by myself in the afternoons. In the cool darkness of the Paramount, I could escape to the days of the Old West, at least for a couple of hours.

Gail had a part-time job at the Ex-Students' Association office on Guadalupe Street across from campus. She also worked at the Capitol for one of the legislators there. Her folks didn't care much for the whole situation. Despite my gold medal, Gail's parents thought I wasn't going to amount to anything and that she should be going to school instead of working and taking care of our son. Looking back, I probably should have gotten a part-time job, too, to make things easier on Gail. But I also had a responsibility to the university since I was on full scholarship, so I didn't have much free time. It took me a long time to finally understand that you can't judge a guy at twenty. Gail's parents wanted me to be something at that age I couldn't have been until I was forty.

One thing I was proud of was my God-given ability to run. Even though I was more of a track man because of my sprinting abilities, in the fall of 1952, my junior year, I played another season of football for the

Longhorn varsity team. We won the Southwest Conference that year under Coach Ed Price, who had replaced Coach Cherry the year before. Our
only defeats were back-to-back losses to Notre Dame and Oklahoma.

We were staying at the Melrose Hotel in Dallas, fixing to play OU,
when my dad showed up—drunk. The team was about to get on the bus
to go to the Cotton Bowl. It embarrassed me for my teammates to see that
my father was a drunk, but I wasn't going to let it ruin my game. The
Oklahoma team did a good enough job of that, beating us 19–14.

On Thanksgiving Day that year, Austin's first TV station, KTBC, went
on the air. It carried a live broadcast of our game with Texas A&M, the first
time that rivalry had ever been televised. That was our last regular game,
though we beat Tennessee 16–0 in the Cotton Bowl on January 1, 1953.

When the Longhorns enjoyed a good season, the sugar daddies and
others were always happy to buy the good tickets the players received, especially for the big games, like when we played SMU. Since I had a family,
the money I made selling tickets really came in handy. I might get $100 a
ticket, sometimes $200 if it was a real important game.

The sweetest of the Longhorns' sugar daddies was Colonel D. Harold
Byrd, a relative of the famous polar explorer, Admiral Richard Byrd. An oil
man, the colonel was one of the wealthiest men in Dallas and he loved UT.
Among other things, he bought Big Bertha, the giant drum UT still uses
at every football game.

In 1953, before the Cotton Bowl game, the Cotton Bowl Association
treated both teams, Texas and Tennessee, to see Danny Kaye at the State
Fair Music Hall. Colonel Byrd threw a big party for both teams at his
ranch, which was where Highland Park is today, right off the expressway.
He was one heck of a Texas host and did everything first class. After the
game both teams were treated to a banquet at one of the hotels downtown.
On top of that, the Cotton Bowl Association gave all the players a watch
and Cotton Bowl blanket. I was in awe of the wonderful treatment and
quite honored.

One day the colonel called me and said, "Dean, I want you to go over
to Sy Devore's on the drag. They're going to fit you for a suit." I did as he
said and got myself a gray flannel suit. I guess he had gotten tired of seeing me in Levis.

Even though I was married, I still hung out a lot with my fellow athletes at UT. In the winter of 1952 I saw Hank Williams in Austin a few weeks before he died on New Year's Day in 1953. We football players loved country-western music. Our favorite spot was Dessau Dance Hall, way out in the northeast part of Travis County. That's where I saw Williams play. Several big-name country-western stars also came to Austin and performed at Gregory Gym on the UT campus.

In the spring of 1953, I was having trouble with my back again and didn't compete in track. I did get invited to run the 100 meters at the Coliseum Relays in L.A. that spring and I went, but it was more or less just for the trip. I ran the 100 but didn't do very well. But looking at it another way, I won big. My Olympic roommate, J. W. Mashburn, had also been invited to compete in the relays. We stayed at the Roosevelt Hotel, and while we were there, J. W. brought a young man to the hotel to meet me. He was a good-looking big guy with dark hair. J. W. thought I'd enjoy being around him since he was from Norman, Oklahoma.

His name was Jim Bumgarner. He had spent some time in the Merchant Marines and had later served for fourteen months as an infantryman in Korea. He got wounded and ended up with two Purple Hearts. After he got out of the army in 1952, he'd gone back to California, helping his dad with his floor covering business. He was four years older than me, but we hit it off, a real nice fellow. He had an old beat-up Plymouth coupe, and the three of us—J. W., Jim, and me—went out to Compton for a barbecue they threw for the track athletes. All of us sat in the front seat and we had a lot of fun. Jim was a very personable guy you couldn't help but like. Truth is, there's not that much difference between an Okie and a Texan except which side of the Red River you're on.

During my junior year, in the spring of 1954, I started running again and won all the major track meets. At a dual meet with A&M at Kyle Field I ran my fastest 100-yard dash ever. Some of the officials timed me at 9 seconds flat but I received a 9.2 on an oiled track that was a quick son of a gun. I also ran the straightaway 220 there, clocking 20.3, my best time ever.

I went back to the Coliseum Relays again in May 1954 with Charlie Thomas, Alvin Frieden, and Jerry Prewit. I was coming off a leg injury, but this time I was free of back pain and ready to run. When the starter said, "Get set," and shot his gun, I was out of there like my butt was on

Dean winning in Los Angeles at the Coliseum Relays, 1954.

fire. I won the 100-yard dash in 9.6. One of the people I ran against was Andy Stanfield, my fellow gold medal winner. But some of the spectators thought I'd jumped the gun with a rolling start, and after I won they booed me. When I went to get my medal and everyone shook my hand and congratulated me, I got bowed up about having been booed. When I got on the stand, as soon as it looked like everybody in the stadium was looking in my direction, I just flung them the bird. I hadn't done a thing to piss them off, but they sure did piss me off by showing me bad manners. Coach Littlefield never said a word to me about it.

After winning again in the Coliseum, I assumed that two years later I'd be running in the 1956 Olympics.

In the summer of 1954, when *The High and the Mighty* opened in Austin, John Wayne came to town for the first showing. At that point I wasn't a huge fan of the Duke, but Gail sure was. Since we didn't live very far from the airport, she and I went to see Duke get off the DC-6 he came in on, a large, four-motored plane. There was a big crowd there waiting for Wayne to arrive. When he appeared at the door of the airliner, he was wearing a tweed jacket and an Irish-style hat. He just waved, walked down the metal steps, and got in a car to be driven to the Paramount Theater. After he left, we drove downtown to see the movie. Before the show began, Wayne went up on the stage to say a few words. Gail and I enjoyed the movie but didn't get to meet Duke.

By this time, I had definitely decided to try for a career in Hollywood. Whenever anybody asked me what I planned to do after college, I told them I wanted to go to California and get into the movies. Everyone thought I was crazy, but I was young, photographed pretty well, and had a lot of confidence. I didn't really want to be a coach or a teacher. I wanted to be in the movies.

Not having much money, Gail and I didn't get out that often. But that fall, we did go to Gregory Gym on campus to see a performance of *The Caine Mutiny Court-Martial*, which had opened in New York on Broadway earlier that year. The cast included Henry Fonda, Lloyd Nolan, John Hodiak, and Eddie Firestone. I'd seen Fonda in movies, but during the play, I noticed another actor who looked familiar. I thought, *That guy looks like Jim Bumgarner.* I checked the program, and sure enough, it was him. He was playing one of the judges, but he didn't have a speaking part. When the play ended, we went backstage to see Jim. We ended up joining him and most of the rest of the cast for a late supper at Hill's Steak House on South Congress. We took up two big tables, and I picked up the tab. I don't know how I happened to have enough money to do that, but a steak didn't cost as much in 1954 as it does now. Only thing I regret is not getting a picture of it.

Instead of going out for football, in the fall of 1954 I joined the Silver Spurs, the honorary student service organization that takes care of Bevo, the UT mascot, and gets him to the football games. The Spurs had seventy-five members, but I was one of the few who had ever been around a horse or a cow. I think that had a lot to do with why they let me in. I was just about the only person able to handle that longhorn without getting hurt.

They had picked this particular steer—he was the fifth Bevo—when he was too old and already set in his ways. He was mean, and I don't know that I blamed him. The only way to get a rope around his neck was to look in his eyes and show him you weren't afraid.

The Bevo we handled was white with beige markings that could pass for orange. He had a ring in his nose, and that's how we controlled him. When we led him on the field, we'd have two long ropes attached to each side of that ring. I would usually have one of those ropes, with another Spur handling the other. We had to really watch the tips of his horns. Part of our job was keeping away any goofy spectators who wanted to pet him. In addition to the Spurs holding the ropes, two Spurs had to walk on his backside so no one would get kicked. I'm proud to say that no one ever got injured by Bevo during my time in the Spurs. That's a good thing, because a longhorn steer weighs 1,600 to 1,700 pounds.

The biggest adventure I had in the Silver Spurs was driving Bevo to South Bend, Indiana, for the September 25, 1954, Texas–Notre Dame game. Willie Morris, who was a reporter for the *Daily Texan*, went with me along with Dan Burke, who lived in Dallas.

A smart Mississippi boy, Morris was quite a character. He spoke with that smooth, sweet Mississippi accent. We got to be good friends. He was like me in some ways, kind of adventuresome.

We left Austin on Thursday, two days before the game, in an orange and white Pontiac on loan from Jack Stableford, the local Pontiac dealer. We had a trailer hitch put on it to handle the state trailer we carried Bevo in. It was full of hay, covered with a canvas tarp, and had a bunch of orange and white streamers attached to it.

Well, we drove and drove and drove, and that old steer kept poking his head up into that damned canvas, ripping it with his horns. By the time we got to Springfield, Illinois, our trailer cover looked like streamers on a goal post.

We stopped at some motel on the edge of town and unloaded Bevo, tying him on the side of the trailer. We weren't too worried about him running off, but that was just our opinion. I went up to the lady at the motel and told her we needed a couple of rooms.

"Son," she said, "what are you going to do with that steer?" I looked outside at Bevo and then back at her. "He'll be all right. We just need a little rest, then we'll be taking him the rest of the way to South Bend for the Notre Dame game." She looked at him again. "No," she said, "he'll run off all our business. People up here have never seen an animal like that."

The woman flat refused to rent us rooms, so we walked out, loaded Bevo back up, and drove all the way to Chicago. I hope he left a big pile of cow patties in her parking lot, but I don't remember whether he really did. He sure should have.

We got to Chicago Friday evening and drove straight to Soldier Field. We were just a bunch of ol' country boys and figured that would be a good place to leave Bevo for the night. We were fixing to untie him when here came the cops.

"What're you going to do with that steer?" one of them asked.

"We're gonna tie him here," I said.

"Son, you can't leave that steer here," he said. "These people will either eat him or run him off."

So once again, we loaded Bevo back into his trailer and drove downtown looking for a place to leave that steer while we got some sleep. By this time, it was ten or eleven o'clock at night and we were so tired we couldn't see straight. Believe it or not, we actually found a livery stable in downtown Chicago. They'd put up Bevo for $40, about ten times what a good hotel room cost.

"By God," Willie said, "I think our problem is solved."

We put Bevo in a show ring, but before we could leave, it seemed like every kid in Chicago turned up at that stable. Those kids—all different nationalities—filled that whole place. Like the woman at the motel back in Springfield, none of them had ever seen a Texas longhorn. We were proud to show him off, but like I said, we were dead tired. We'd driven roughly 1,200 miles from Austin with just a few catnaps between turns driving. Black coffee was what kept us going.

We found us a highfalutin' hotel, a big brick Hilton, and got rooms. We took a bath and shaved and got four or five hours of sleep. When we got back to the stable in the morning, a lot of kids were still there, gawking at ol' Bevo.

We hooked the trailer back up to our car, cajoled Bevo inside, and headed for South Bend, which was only a hundred miles away. We finally got there just in time for the game, which was that Saturday afternoon. When we pulled up to that big brick stadium, the first thing I remember seeing was the Notre Dame band with their big bearskin helmets on. We led Bevo in that stadium and those people just went nuts.

The school had built a place to keep him, a pipe corral about the size of small living room, and the Notre Dame fans and students were for the most part very respectful. No one tried to do anything to Bevo, which is more than can be said for some of the students at Texas A&M or Baylor, who had a history of trying to rustle him.

If having Bevo there on the sidelines did anything to boost the spirit of the Longhorn football team, it didn't show. Notre Dame, which went on to a 9–1 season that year, beat us 21–0 in front of a tremendous crowd. But Bevo seemed to take it in stride. I guess he was like me, tired from the trip.

Right after the game, we loaded him back in the trailer and headed for Austin, the tattered trailer cover still flopping in the wind. The three of us alternated driving so two of us could get some sleep, and we went straight back without a bit of trouble.

We hit Austin late Sunday night or early Monday morning. When we got to the state farm off Highway 183 northwest of Austin, we opened the end gate of that trailer and Bevo was so tired he just stumbled out and went to his knees. I don't know if he was kissing the ground because he was so happy to be back in Texas or what. But he was a tired son of a buck, I tell you that.

I grew up learning how to handle cattle, but my time with the Silver Spurs was the first opportunity I'd ever had to be around a longhorn. I learned one thing about longhorns when I was with the Silver Spurs. They are durable. They can look after themselves.

UT had one week off after the Notre Dame game before they played Oklahoma, the number-one-ranked team in the nation. Texas was fifteenth-ranked, but it's always a big game, however the teams stack up.

I was driving Bevo to Dallas, and I had Gail and little Charlie with me in that orange and white Pontiac. Before going to Dallas, we had to drive to Lampasas to meet Gail's parents, who were going to keep the baby for us while we were in Dallas. I stopped on the side of the road where we were supposed to meet her parents, and a brown Chrysler that I didn't

Dean winning the Sugar Bowl 100-yard dash for the third time, 1955.

recognized drove up. Turned out it was Senator Lyndon B. Johnson. He said he and Lady Bird were on their way to the game and that he'd seen the trailer and just wanted to stop and say hello. That might have been the truth, because when he stopped, he had no way of knowing the UT student driving Bevo would be twenty-one and old enough to vote.

Gail and I had our happy moments, but being married was hard. I was trying to stay in school, I was trying to excel in track and support my family, but her parents wanted more for her and probably she wanted that, too. In late December 1954, Gail and I went home to Graham with little Charles. After Christmas, I came back to Austin for a few days to train and then went with Coach Littlefield and his wife to the Sugar Bowl track meet in New Orleans for the third time. After I ran, I called Gail to see how she was doing, and she said, "I'm staying home in Graham." Her mother had made her think that I was not going to amount to a damned thing. Of course, you can't always judge a book by its cover. I was not cut out to be a doctor, lawyer, or Indian chief, but I could ride, jump, and run like hell. In the end, those things didn't matter. Gail and I divorced, and she stayed in Graham with her parents and Charles. It was a sad time for me, but when you have a disappointment like that you can't let it ruin you. I think it made me a stronger man. I went on to pursue my dreams.

In the spring of 1955, I went to Mexico City to run in the second Pan

University of Texas relay team Bobby Whilden, Jerry Prewit, Alvin Frieden, Dean, and Coach Clyde Littlefield, c. 1955.

American Games, which started March 12. We competed in front of 100,000 people at the stadium there, but I didn't get any medals even though the US gold medal winner in the 100-meter dash won at 10.3 seconds, a time I had beaten many times. The main thing I remember about being down there was trying to get used to the high altitude and the heat.

Back in Texas, I did better. The UT track team won the Southwest Conference championship that year. But that summer, I decided to give up on college, still needing nine hours of English.

Gail leaving had really affected me. I thought, *How much more bad luck can I have?* Besides losing my wife and child, getting a divorce also meant I would be I-A in the draft, which was still going on even though the Korean War was coming to an end. I didn't want to get drafted, so I joined the army at Breckenridge and reported to Abilene for my physical on October 31, 1955.

That night, which was Halloween, I was visiting with a pretty girl from Stanford who was going to Hardin-Simmons. We were walking outside the dorms around the campus when I heard a truck coming up and a bunch of boys yelling. Next thing I knew, something hit me in the back. When I reached around with my hand I felt the goo of a broken egg. I was wearing my red Pan American corduroy jacket, and I had egg all over me. The young lady took me to her dorm, and I had to stay in the parlor while she and her friends cleaned that jacket. They managed to get all the yolk off and I still have that jacket today.

Not long after that, the army shipped me to Fort Ord, California, for infantry training. I marched all over that fort, which overlooked Monterey Bay and was considered one of the most attractive posts in the country. Officers are not supposed to fraternize with enlisted men, but one of the lieutenants I ran into turned out to be a fellow Texan named Marvin Leach. He may have outranked me in the army, but he and I had played football together at UT. Marvin—I mean, the lieutenant—managed to get me some weekend passes and showed me around. I didn't mind at all helping to protect Monterey and Pebble Beach while I was there.

The army taught me how to fight and shoot, but I still got a chance to compete in track. In the summer of 1956, at the All-Army Track and Field Meet at Fort Ord, I was Sixth Army champ in the 100 and 200 meters. After my basic training on the beautiful Pacific coast, I was moved downstate to Fort MacArthur at San Pedro near Los Angeles. The army was willing to give me a chance as an athlete, and I like to think I would have run well in the 1956 Olympics. I did try out but I just didn't have my heart in it and didn't do well enough to make the team. I was stuck worse than a truck up to its hubcaps in sand.

I got a furlough and came home for Christmas in 1956 to see Mama and Uncle King, Aunt Teena, and their son Don, my cousin. A few days before Christmas, I borrowed Mama's Pontiac sedan to go to Weatherford to see a young lady who had moved there from Breckenridge. Before I got there, a darned old cow stepped out onto the highway about where it crosses Ioni Creek near Brad. I was driving about sixty-five miles an hour when I hit the cow and knocked her down on her side. She scooted from one end of the bridge to the other, but got up when I stopped the car. I got out of the car and managed to keep her from getting back on the highway.

The collision hadn't hurt me, but it knocked in the front of Mama's Pontiac and it had to be towed. Uncle King came and picked me up and took me back to Breckenridge.

Hitting that cow turned out to be only my first piece of bad luck on that trip. One cold morning in early January 1957 before I went back to California to finish my military service, Don and I went over to the old Lyden place to feed some cattle for Uncle King. Don had a one-and-a-half-ton International pickup truck with an oversized bed that had sideboards on it. For some reason that must have seemed like a good idea at the time, I had gotten out of the truck and was running in front of it, down one of the winding two-rut ranch roads where it crossed a rolling hill, while Don drove the truck. We both were acting like kids. I jumped over a mesquite bush and, somehow, one of those sideboards hit me. That spun me around and I went smack under that truck. A set of those dual wheels ran right over my back. I thought, *Son of a bitch, is this my time?* After figuring out that I was still breathing, Don put a couple of small bales of hay on either side of me and covered me with some tow sacks to make me as comfortable as he could. Then he left to get help. Cattle had gathered around to check out the hay, and I was lying there looking up at the clouds rolling by, wondering if I was going to die.

Don drove to Eliasville to find a telephone to call for the Morrison Funeral Home ambulance out of Graham. The ambulance, back then just a station wagon with a red light on top and a gurney inside, came out there to get me. By that time, I was so stiff I could hardly move. One of the funeral home attendants got me loaded in that ambulance, and with sirens blaring, we went through Eliasville and South Bend to Graham.

When they got me to the hospital, the doctor pretty quickly figured out that I was a real mess. Those tires had torn my belt and Levis—even my old orange and white University of Texas boots. I remember hearing somebody say, "Oh my God, he's bleeding to death." They cut my clothes off and found that my right lung and a kidney had been bruised, which is why I had started passing blood. I also had a separated shoulder.

I stayed in the Graham hospital five or six days. Finally my family got me on a plane to California. When we arrived in Los Angeles, an army ambulance picked me up and took me to Fort MacArthur where I spent another two or three days in the hospital. When I got out of the hospital, I started working out at the YMCA in San Pedro and got myself back together. Since I was in such good shape before the accident it didn't take me long to be back to my old self.

Around that time, Jerry Lewis, David Wayne, and Gene Evans came to Fort MacArthur to do a movie called *Sad Sack*, based on the comic book character. They started shooting in mid-March and had it wrapped up by the end of May. So far as I know, I didn't show up on any of the stock footage showing the real soldiers at the fort, but that was the first time I had been around during the making of a movie.

That June, courtesy of the US Army, I got a free trip back to Texas to compete in the All-Army Track and Field Meet at Fort Hood from June 13 to June 15, 1957. I ran the 100 meters in 9.3, tying Willie Williams, the former Big 10 track champion representing the Second Army. There at Fort Hood, I saw my old coach from Graham, John Little, who had come to see me compete. He had become a school principal there at the post.

While in the army, any time I could I'd go see the Los Angeles Rams when they played at home. I like football, but the main reason I went to the games was to see Bud McFadin, who had signed on with the team. Since we were friends, he connected me with his agent to see if he could get me a pro contract. I was only twenty-four, but I had sure learned one thing: it never hurts to have a lot of friends, and most of the time it is all in who you know and who they know that helps you get to that next step.

CHAPTER 7

GOING PRO

Bud McFadin was sure one friend I'm glad I had. He introduced me to Eddie Kotal, a guy originally from Lawrence, Kansas, who had played halfback for the Green Bay Packers back in the 1920s. Eddie became the first full-time college scout in the NFL when he joined the Rams in 1945, and by the time I met him he was working as their personnel director. He knew about my college career and that I was a gold medalist and offered me a $4,200 contract to play for L.A. even before I got out of the army. That doesn't sound like a lot of money now, but it sure seemed like a lot back then. When I signed with the Rams, it made the front page of the *Los Angeles Times*.

I was really excited about playing for the Rams, but I still had to serve my enlistment. In June 1957, not too long after competing at Fort Hood, I received an honorable discharge from the army. About a month later, I reported to the Rams' training camp.

The team did its preseason training at Redlands, a college town near San Bernardino just up the road from Palm Springs. I traded in my old Pontiac and headed for camp in a brand-new white Oldsmobile V-8 convertible with a red interior that I'd bought on credit thinking I was about to become a big-time professional football star. That car looked like it was a block long, but it sure could run down the road. It was a pretty day and I was driving with the top down at only fifty-five miles an hour when a cop pulled me over. I wasn't speeding but he gave me a ticket for driving in the inside lane. The officer said I was going too slow and needed to keep up with the traffic. That was the first and last time I ever got a ticket for going too darn slow.

When I got to Redlands it was hot and I soon found that we would be staying in Melrose Hall, a un-air-conditioned dorm at the University of

Redlands, where the team used the university's football field. George Allen was end coach and Sid Gilman, who had made a name for himself as head coach at the University of Cincinnati, was beginning his third year as the Rams' head coach. The team, which had begun in Cleveland, would soon be starting its twelfth season in California. The 1955 Rams had done well, but they'd had a losing season in 1956 and were looking for a much better year in 1957.

Kotal and Gilman figured my Olympic speed could help out in their rebuilding effort. In fact, I would be the fastest man in the NFL. Linebacker Les Richter, who had been on the team since 1954, nicknamed me "Beep Beep" because I was small and fast, just like a roadrunner.

I met a lot of great people that summer at the Rams camp. Norm Van Brocklin was quarterback. I got to know "ponderous, plunging" (as the sportswriters liked to call him) Tank Younger, the team's outstanding running back, and all the other guys. Standout receiver Elroy "Crazy Legs" Hirsch (who got the nickname because a Chicago sportswriter once wrote that he ran like a woman) had been with the Rams as long as they had been in L.A., and he taught me more about catching balls and pass patterns than I ever learned playing in high school or at UT. Pete Rozelle, later commissioner of the NFL, was the PR guy for the Rams.

Being a rookie free agent was like being a freshman at UT, where the upper classmen made me sing "The Eyes of Texas" every time we ate lunch. Another rookie that season was Dale Schofner, who had been a track star at Baylor when I ran for Texas. He played wide receiver and was pretty fast, but he had never outrun me on the track.

I had showed up for camp, but not my friend and security blanket Bud McFadin. Turned out he had gotten into a scuffle with a guy at a Pitch and Putt Golf Course in Houston and gotten shot. He wasn't in danger of dying, but he sure wasn't going to be able to play football for a while.

The Rams' other go-to receiver was Bob Boyd, whom the sports reporters liked to refer to as "Swift Bob Boyd . . . the fastest man in a football uniform." Bob had played college ball at Marymount University in Los Angeles and was in his seventh year as a pro, but as the *Redlands Daily Facts* put it, "he will be getting plenty of competition in the speed department from rookie Dean Smith." The newspaper added this about me: "The mercurial Mr. Smith from the University of Texas has run the 100 in

9.4 and has taken second [*sic*] in the 1952 Olympics. He will be out for an end slot." That was inaccurate: at the University of Texas I ran the 100 in 9.2, 9.3, and 9.4, and I had taken fourth in the 100-meter dash in the Olympics in the closest finish in Olympic history. The newspapers don't always get it right.

Forty-three hundred Rams fans watched the offense scrimmage with the defense at the Redlands stadium on August 3. The defense won the game 50–27, but that score is misleading. They used a special point system for scrimmages. The offense got one point for every first down and three points for every touchdown. On the defensive side, they got three points for holding on downs, four points for recovered fumbles, and five points for an interception.

Playing in the second half, I caught two of six completed passes by backup quarterback Billy Wade and managed to outrun my defenders. On August 5, the Monday after the scrimmage, the Redlands' afternoon daily published my official team mug shot and this short write-up:

> Dean Smith, No. 41, the scooting Texan with the big smile, is undoubtedly one of the fastest ends in a football uniform.
>
> According to the weight listings, Smith qualifies as the lightest man on the Ram squad, tipping the scales at a light 170 pounds.
>
> Smith, who has had the displeasure of being run over by a truck and the pleasure of running the 100-yard dash in 9.3 is 25 years old and stands 5-11.
>
> Ram fans got a look at the boy's blazing speed Saturday when they saw him continually out-distancing defensive backs as he caught two passes during the annual scrimmage at the university.
>
> Along with another speedy end, Bob Boyd, Smith is expected to give fits to defensive NFL backs this season.
>
> The ex-Olympic sprinter may challenge Boyd's title as fastest man in a football uniform.

Our first real game would be August 10 at Veterans Memorial Stadium against the Southern California All-Stars, a semipro team. Gilman intended to see what I could do in that game. I didn't have a whole lot of experience, but I was fast. As the *Long Beach Independent* put it on August 7:

"Ram coaches feel that if Smith can stick with the club this year and get a season's experience, he will go on to become one of the most feared pass receivers in the league." In referring to me as the Rams' "leading 1957 experiment," the writer concluded: "There's no doubt Smith can run with the ball. The only question is can he catch it with a couple of halfbacks draped over him."

After summer camp, I played in a couple of exhibition games, earning $50 a week. I sure wasn't getting rich. I still only weighed 160 pounds (the team claimed I weighed 170 and in my full uniform I might have), and they were concerned about my size. Sid called me in and said, "Dean, your size is against you. We want to trade you to Pittsburgh." I said I wanted to stay in California, since I also wanted to break into the Westerns. Had it been the era of Terry Bradshaw and Lynn Swann I would have probably jumped on the train and gone to Pennsylvania. But those two stars were not there yet and Pittsburgh was too cold for this Texas boy.

Sid placed me on waivers on August 29 just before the Rams left for Portland to play their final preseason game with the Chicago Cardinals (they later moved to St. Louis and then to Phoenix). The Associated Press ran a story with that news, saying that Sid had released me so I'd have time to find a new club.

But I had no interest in playing for the Steelers. Who knows if I could have made a difference for either team that year? The Rams went on to a 6–6 season that year, finishing fourth in the league's Western Division. The Steelers also lost as many as they won that fall. Los Angeles wouldn't have a winning year until 1966.

If I had stayed in professional football, I imagine I would have taken a lot of hits and maybe gotten badly hurt or crippled. And I would have done all that for very little money. But even when things don't go your way, in the long run, it usually works out.

CHAPTER 8

MAVERICK WAS HIS NAME

Bud McFadin had gotten me in a jam back when I was a UT freshman when he told me to steal an Aggie's hat, but then he had used his influence to help me get into pro football, so I guess we were about even. I think Coach Gilman would have listened if Bud had told him he should keep me on the Rams and not trade me to the Steelers. Unfortunately, he wasn't around to help me.

I had wanted to play pro football and still dreamed about working in Western movies, but I was beginning to wonder if I'd ever amount to anything. When it came to figuring out where to go from here, I was like a penned-up bull looking at a heifer grazing in the pasture: I had some interesting ideas, but I couldn't do anything about them. At least I had a nice new car, but I also still had thirty-four payments to make on it. I didn't know where I was going or what I was going to do other than that I was through with football.

The only other person in California I knew was Jim Bumgarner, whose old stomping grounds in Oklahoma weren't far from where I'd grown up in northwestern Texas. I had run into Jim a couple of times since getting out of the army and we had associated a little bit. I'd heard he'd done some work on a few television shows, so I decided to go see him and ask if he had any idea how I could get in the movie business. This would have been early September in 1957, before the NFL regular season started.

I drove that aircraft carrier–size Oldsmobile of mine to the Warner Bros. studio in downtown Burbank and parked in front. I walked up to the security guard, gave him a big smile, and said, "I'm Dean Smith and I'd like to see Jim Bumgarner. He's a good friend of mine."

The guard, probably an off-duty L.A. cop working a second job, said he'd check. When he came back, he told me they didn't have anybody there by that name. I said I'd heard Bumgarner had been doing some work on some of the shows being filmed there, and he said, "He's not here." The way he said that told me the matter was closed. I left the studio not knowing what to think. I couldn't believe that Jim would have gotten so uppity since the last time I saw him.

At this point, I was pretty much out of ideas. The only thing I could think to do was drive home to Breckenridge. I made the trip back to Texas around the first of October and stayed with Mama. I had a gold medal from the Olympics and an honorable discharge from the army, but no job. For a while I had thought I was going to be a professional football player, but the season had started without me. I felt like my career was fading away even though I was only twenty-five. I told Mama I guessed I'd go to the bank, borrow a little money, and buy some cattle. Of course, I knew better than to think I could make a living as a rancher. To pay the bills, I'd have to find a coaching job at some high school.

I hadn't been home long when one Sunday morning I picked up a copy of the *Dallas Morning News*. The newspaper included the latest issue of *Parade* magazine, and on the front page of that weekly insert I saw a picture of Jim Bumgarner wearing a black hat and black western suit with a string tie. Inside I read an article about James Garner, a promising young actor at Warner Bros. who had just done a pilot for a TV series called *Maverick*. Now I knew why that security guard in Burbank had said the studio didn't have anybody by the name of "Bumgarner" on the lot. Jim hadn't given me the brush-off after all. He had changed his name for show business, and not that many people knew there used to be a "Bum" before "garner."

After I finished reading the story, I showed the magazine to Mama.

"This is James Bumgarner and he's a friend of mine," I said.

The *Morning News* had a separate article saying Jim would be featured at the State Fair of Texas, which started that week. I told Mama I was going to drive to Dallas and see if Jim could help me get in the movies.

I'll never forget what Mama said: "Dean, if that's really what you want to do, I want you to try it. If you wait a few years and don't try, I think you'll regret it."

So I jumped in my Oldsmobile and headed to Dallas. When I hit town, I drove straight to the fairgrounds. This time, I didn't have any trouble finding Jim. He was all decked out in western clothes and making an appearance at a calf scramble. When we shook hands, he said, "I've been reading about you. Saw where the Rams wanted to trade you to Pittsburgh."

After I told him I had turned down the chance to play for the Steelers, I got right to the point.

"Hell, I need a job. I've got to do something," I said. "I can ride, run, and jump. You think you could help me get in this business?"

I guess maybe Jim felt sorry for me, but there was more to it than that. When he was going to Hollywood High School and pumping gas at a service station, Jim had met and become friends with a guy named Paul Gregory who worked at a soda fountain across the street. Gregory said he wanted to become a talent agent. He also said he thought Jim could become an actor. Well, not long after I first met Jim, he was driving along La Brea Avenue and saw a sign that said "Paul Gregory and Associates." He stopped and went in and found that his friend had accomplished what he had said he would. Gregory got Jim the part in *The Caine Mutiny Court-Martial.*

"Dean," he told me, "I really don't know if I should get you into this business. I don't know if you can make a living. It's a hard business."

In Dallas with Jim were William T. "Bill" Orr, Jack Warner's son-in-law, and Hugh Benson. Bill was head of TV at Warner's, and Benson was one of the producers. After I'd made my pitch, Jim looked over at Bill and Hugh. He was silent, but his look said, *Well, what do you guys think?* Finally, one of them said, "You'll have to get him in the union." By that he meant the Screen Actors Guild. Without that membership card, you were locked out and couldn't work in the business. They were all nice men and all of them seemed to like me. Jim said when I got back to California to call Hoyt Bowers, head of casting at Warner Bros.

I drove back to Breckenridge, told Mama I thought I might have my foot in the door as a Hollywood stuntman, packed all my clothes, and turned my convertible to the west once again. Back in California, as soon as I could, I got in touch with Orr and he got me in to see Hoyt. On November 7, 1957, thanks to Jim and Bill, I got my SAG union card.

I had begun to realize that who you know is real important in life. You can be talented and good-looking and still not get anywhere if you don't know the right people. That may not be fair, but that's the way it is. Anyway, that was the beginning of my Hollywood career—a lucky break that came just because I happened to read a newspaper Sunday supplement. Of course, you still have to be willing to work hard and go with the breaks, good and bad.

When I went to Warner Bros. for the first time after joining the Screen Actors Guild, I showed up in slacks, loafers, and a short-sleeved shirt. I met Roydon Clark, who doubled for Garner, and Ted White, another Okie who had just started in the stunt business. Both of them had western clothes on. I walked straight back to my car and changed into my cowboy hat, shirt, jeans, and boots. I went back to the studio, dressed like a Texan.

About that time, plans were being made for a world's fair in Brussels. Rodeo legend Casey Tibbs was organizing a rodeo to perform there. Since I'd had a taste of Europe, going to Brussels sounded like a possibility for me. It didn't work out, but I was beginning to get acquainted with Hollywood's real cowboys—the guys who provided the four-footed stock for the studios and the guys who got paid to do the rough stuff the name actors couldn't do.

For $80 a month, I rented an apartment in North Hollywood near the Victory Shopping Center a couple of blocks from the Palomino, a famous western honky-tonk. I started learning how to get around L.A. and to the various studios. Now that I was in the union, I had to call the studios to see about getting jobs.

I got hired to do my first stunt around the first of December 1957. Warner Bros. was doing *Cheyenne* with Clint Walker on a back lot at the studio. That was the first Western they did for television. The script for the episode I would be in called for an actor named Will Wright to be shot off his horse, and I got the job. That stunt's called a saddle fall. Under the Screen Actors Guild pay scale, I made $90 for that one stunt. Back then, that was a good week's pay in most places.

To do a saddle fall, you need a saddle rigged with what they call a step, which is a round leather ring hooked to a metal bar that hangs from one of the front D-rings on the saddle. When you fall off the saddle, you keep your foot on that step and not the stirrup, because that could hang you up and get you killed. If you tie the step just right, the part you put your foot on will be hidden by the stirrup. I had practiced these kinds of falls before, but this would be the first time I'd be doing it on camera.

When I showed up for the shoot, they brought me a horse that looked seven feet tall. I don't know if they did that to test me or not, but by golly, I was going to fall off that horse. I later found out that most stuntmen would have had them dig the ground up where they would be falling and pack it with something soft, but I didn't know any better back then.

I soon learned there are two kinds of saddle falls when your character gets shot. They either kill you by the shot, meaning you fall when you hear the gun go off, or the director cues you to fall and they add the sound later. Sometimes the director would fire the shot himself, which is the way William Hale handled this scene.

When Hale hollered "Action!" I rode until I heard a shot and took that fall. I must have bounced eight feet in the air when I hit the ground. It was a hard-ass fall, but I got up and dusted myself off. And then they had to shoot the scene again. After taking a fall for the second time, as far as I was concerned, that proved that I was there to stay and there was nothing they could do about it.

Each studio had a casting person. At Warner Bros., Dorothy Shaw sent out the casting calls. I'd call Dorothy every few days. If she had something available, she'd say, "We have a job," and give me a time to report at the studio. I'd show up at makeup, check a wardrobe out, and then go to the set.

Most of the time I either got what was called a walking check, which was about $17, or a riding check that was usually $24. If a stunt came up they would adjust my check up to $90. We also got overtime and meals.

The first movie I was in, filmed late in 1957, was *Quantrill's Raiders*. Directed by Edward Bernds, it starred Steve Cochran as a Confederate officer and Leo Gordon as Quantrill, the famous Kansas guerrilla. This movie was produced for Allied Artists Pictures, which shot at the old Republic Pictures lot, where Gene Autry and Roy Rogers had made so many of their movies.

In one scene, forty of us extras and stuntmen were riding down the street and shooting up the town, which was supposed to be Lawrence, Kansas. Before we galloped out of the frame, I rode up where somebody had parked a tractor and my horse jumped it. I sure liked riding a horse with that much sense, but I thought, *Geez, I don't know if they'll even let me finish this movie after pulling a stunt like that.*

Quantrill's Raiders premiered the following spring. I'm sure I went to see it, though I don't remember any details. I couldn't pick myself out from all the other riders, but I knew I was in the scene and sure thought I was a star. Back in Texas, Mama would be proud.

My next gig, toward the end of 1957, was a job on *Born Reckless*, with Mamie Van Doren, Jeff Richards, and Arthur Hunnicutt, the actor who had played Davy Crockett in *The Last Command*. In 1952 he'd gotten an Oscar nomination for best supporting actor in *The Big Sky*, but he had his demons too. When we were working on *Born Reckless*, a black-and-white movie about the rodeo world, Hunnicutt would be drunk by noon every day. He'd take a sack of oranges and inject them with vodka. Anyone who didn't know better might think he just liked sucking oranges for his health, but what he really liked was the booze. I had my first speaking part in this picture, the start of my acting career, though it was just one line: "Did you draw that old spook?" My character was asking someone if they would be riding a bull with a bad reputation. I got paid $100 for being in that movie and thought I was rich.

I did some riding, nothing big, in an MGM movie starring Robert Taylor and Richard Widmark called *The Law and Jake Wade*. Other than getting some "horse checks," I got to see some pretty country when they filmed outside Lone Pine, up in the Owens Valley near the Alabama Hills on the edge of the Sierra Nevada north of L.A. A lot of movies have been shot there over the years, including the classic *High Sierra* with Humphrey Bogart in 1941.

I had a brief appearance putting Rosalind Russell up on a horse in *Auntie Mame*. It was a comedic scene where she was dressed up for a fox hunt and I had to really struggle to get her up in that saddle, but we got it done. The rumor mill back home in Graham later had it that Louise Allison (who had just moved to Denver from Graham) was eating dinner with Rosalind Russell when she told her that the guy putting her up on the saddle in her latest movie was a boy from Graham by the name of Dean Smith. "I thought that skinny boy was gonna drop me," she supposedly told her.

I also got a bit part in *Darby O'Gill and the Little People*. I doubled a long-nosed Irishman in that film, riding a white horse around an oversized throne. Whitey Hughes, another stuntman who was quite small, doubled the king of the little people. They shot the scene in the Disney studio on stage, and everything went fine until the horses started relieving themselves on the floor. Several horses slipped in the manure and went down, but I managed to keep my horse upright. Walt Disney did this film, which was for the most part shot on the Disney ranch at Burbank.

After a lot of hard work, my career was getting off the ground, and things were looking up in my personal life as well. I had met a girl while I was in the army, Pamela Markarian. She was from San Pedro, where her dad was a commercial fisherman. Her aunt and uncle owned the Tides, where Alfred Hitchcock later shot *The Birds*. Five years younger than me, she was good-looking and a real nice person. We got married in 1958 at the Dunes Hotel in Las Vegas. Pam had a little girl by her first marriage, Christine Henkles, whom I helped raise.

That year I got to work on a Gary Cooper movie, *They Came to Cordura*, a film based on a novel by Glendon Swarthout about General "Black Jack" Pershing's punitive expedition into Mexico after Pancho Villa's men attacked Columbus, New Mexico, in 1916. Also starring in the movie were Rita Hayworth and Van Heflin.

When they started shooting the movie, I met stuntman Jack Conners, which turned out to be quite an experience. He was a character, and he also had great jumping horses. His favorite line when someone asked him how high his horses could jump was, "How high do my jumping horses jump? We have to feed those horses in the trees at night, they jump so high!"

Some other great stuntmen I got to meet during the filming were Tony Epper, Fred Learner, Doug Gunther, Rita Hayworth's stuntwoman May Boss, who was an accomplished trick rider, and Walt LaRue, a fine western artist and best friend of Richard Farnsworth. Walt and I ended up becoming good friends.

Early one Saturday evening, stuntmen Slim Talbot, John Cason, Fred Learner, and I decided we would drive from L.A. to Las Vegas. Slim was Cooper's stunt double and John was Heflin's stunt double. Not only did they have more show business experience than Learner and me, but those two stuntmen could throw down whiskey just as quick as they could make a horse fall. Though we did have a little to drink, you could say Fred and I were the designated drivers. By the time we got to Vegas, Slim had gotten sick and thrown up on his shirt, and John was loud and boisterous.

Slim said that Cooper was at the Sands Hotel visiting Frank Sinatra
(Frank sang the lyrics for the movie's theme song) and that he wanted to
see Gary. As we walked in the Sands, Slim and John led the way, though
not too steadily. People started staring and gasping, saying, "Look, there's
Gary Cooper and he has thrown up all over himself." I was so embarrassed I wanted to crawl under a table. At the front desk, they told us that
Cooper and Sinatra were about a mile down the road at a Japanese restaurant.

By the time we got to the restaurant Slim and John had decided they
needed another drink. Fred joined them, but I've never been too keen on
being around a bunch of drunks, no matter how likeable they were when
sober. So I decided to wait outside. Before he walked in, Slim told me that
if I saw Cooper and he offered me any money to take it. As I was standing
there out walked Cooper and Sinatra. Gary came up and asked how I was
doing and introduced me to Frank. He told Frank I was working on the
picture with him and that I was an Olympic gold medal winner. I told
Frank that he might not remember me but that I had met him and Ava
Gardner in an elevator at the Ambassador Hotel when I ran in the relays
at the Coliseum. He said he remembered and that it had looked to him
like I had an armful of trophies that day. Gary asked me where the others
were, and then, sure enough, he asked if I needed anything or any money.
I told him Slim and John had gone inside the restaurant and that we were
doing fine and didn't need a thing. We said our good-byes and off they
went. Two minutes later out came Slim and the others. I told them that I
had seen Cooper and Sinatra, but that they were in a hurry to see a show.
Slim wanted to know if I had asked for any money and I said I hadn't.
"You damn fool," he said, "they would've given you a sock full of money!"
That didn't mean much to me. I sure wasn't used to asking for any money
or taking any.

When I got back from working on *They Came to Cordura*, I got a call
from the Disney Studios. They wanted me to double Zorro at an event at
the Hollywood Bowl. The reason they needed me was that Guy Williams's
stunt double Buddy Van Horn couldn't be in two places at one time.

The scene consisted of Buddy, as Zorro, climbing down the shell of
the Bowl and doing a saber fight with some other stuntmen. Suddenly the
stage went dark and a spotlight found Zorro (me) at the top of the hill rearing his horse. I enjoyed the bit, but the greatest pleasure of the night was

getting to spend some time with a man I had met before but didn't know well—Ben Johnson. His father-in-law owned Fat Jones's stable.

Ben brought me the horse I would be riding. As we stood there talking they brought my costume. Everything was a fit but I couldn't get my feet in the boots. My calves were too big and I didn't know what I was going to do. That's when Ben took out his pocketknife and cut both boots from the top to the ankle. Then he took black tape and taped those boots around my calves. Off I went and reared that horse all over the Hollywood hill that night.

I had made it to Hollywood, but I still needed a big break.

CHAPTER 9

TALES OF WELLS FARGO

I was kicking around Hollywood, doing odd jobs for this studio or that, but nothing to set the world on fire. L.A. is a big city, but by word of mouth, I began to get acquainted with people there who knew horses. I liked to hang around the Hudkins Brothers Stables in North Hollywood, the L. C. Goss Stables, the Myers and Wills Stables, or Fat Jones' Stables on Sherman Way. Ralph McCutcheon, who had furnished Black Beauty for *Fury*, also had great horses at his ranch in the San Fernando Valley. Those guys would let me ride some of their stock, and by watching and spending time with other Western stuntmen, I started learning how to do fancy mounts and trick riding.

One friend I made was an old Hollywood horse wrangler named Johnny Hawk, who'd been handling stock for the movie industry since the silent film days. Bob Burroughs, a rodeo cowboy I'd met when working on *Quantrill's Raiders*, had introduced me to Hawk, who lived near Bob close to Hudkins Brothers Stables. Hawk told me he wrangled on a television show called *Tales of Wells Fargo*, which NBC had begun airing in March 1957. Starring Dale Robertson, another guy from Oklahoma, the show enjoyed good ratings moving into its second season.

Dale's good looks had gotten him his first acting job. He had served in the army during World War II, and while stationed in California, he went to Hollywood to have a professional photographer take a picture of him for his mother, Varvel. The photographer put a big blowup of that picture in his studio window, and Dale started getting letters from talent scouts who had seen his picture. After the war he returned to California. In 1949 he played Jesse James in *Fighting Man of the Plains*, a movie produced by Nat Holt for 20th Century Fox, and his career took off.

In 1956 western writer Frank Gruber wrote a script for a show about a troubleshooter working for the Wells Fargo stagecoach line, and he and Nat Holt got Dale signed on to play the lead character, Jim Hardie. Dale later told me they promised him things he never got, and his relationship with Holt and Gruber was never that good.

I asked Hawk if he knew Dale and he said, "Sure. Would you like to meet him?" I told Johnny that I sure would. I thought I could double Dale, and we set a date for Hawk to walk me on the set so I could talk to him. I didn't know if I had much of a chance, since Hawk said Dale was quite a cowboy, but I wanted to give it a try. Anyway, Hawk set up a meeting for me in August 1958.

They were shooting the series at the old Republic Pictures lot, then owned by Revue Studios. When Hawk and I got there, they were in the middle of a scene. As we stood on the edge of the Western town set, here came Dale riding up the street on Jubilee. He did a running dismount like a calf roper tying a calf and the director hollered, "Cut and print!" I'm thinking, *I don't know if he needs a double or not. That was pretty good.*

Like me, Dale was an athlete. He had won sixteen letters at the Oklahoma Military Institute, was a good boxer, and knew horses as well as or better than I did. In other words, he was a good rider and certainly able to do his own stunts, though he had a bad knee from a World War II jeep wreck. In fact, he did do some of his own stuff, especially for establishing shots where he had to be in the picture. But when you're starring in a series and have a grueling production schedule, if you get hurt, that shuts the company down and everybody's out of a job. Time is money in that business. That's why Hollywood uses stuntmen—for insurance purposes.

I'd had a lot of people say that Dale and I resembled each other. I was tall, dark-haired, and left-handed. Dale was an inch and a half taller, dark-haired, and also used his left hand. Of course, that was just a gimmick. He was really right-handed, but he always shot with his left hand in the show.

When Dale came over to where Hawk and I had been watching the scene, Hawk introduced us and I got down to business.

"I know you've already got a stuntman, but if you ever decide you need another one, I'd sure like a chance to double you."

Dale looked me over from under his black hat and said, "OK, I'll keep that in mind," and then he went back to work.

Two weeks later, I was working as an audience extra on the *Desi Arnaz Show*. They were paying me just to fill a seat. When I got a chance, I called my answering service and they said, "Paul Donnelly's trying to get a hold of you." I called Donnelly, who was head of production at Revue Studios, and he said, "Dale Robertson says he wants you to double him, nobody else."

That "nobody else" part sounded strange, but I later found out that Jack Corrick, an assistant director who worked under Donnelly, did not want me doubling Dale. All the producers had their own stunt friends, and I was still an unknown. They also didn't like giving up control of anything, but Dale wanted his own control. I got over there as fast as I could and got the job.

Next thing I knew, I was on a plane to Sonora, California, where they were going to shoot a train scene on the famous narrow gauge railroad there. Sonora's an old gold rush and lumber town with a railroad roundhouse. The locomotive they used had rolled out of the factory in 1891 and had already been in a lot of famous movies by the time I saw it puffing down the track for the first time.

Turns out Dale had come down with blood poisoning in one of his feet. The dye from his boot had soaked through his sock and gotten into a blister and things got worse from there. Laid up in the Sonora hospital, he couldn't shoot any scenes.

I filled in for him there in Sonora, and pretty soon I was doing all of Dale's riding. Dale seemed to like me, even though I was still greener than a fresh cow pattie. After we wrapped every scene we needed to shoot in Sonora, we went back to the studio. To save money, television producers tried to avoid shooting on location as much as they could. They had a saying, "A rock's a rock, a tree's a tree, and that's why we stay on the back lot."

Back then, there was no stuntman school to attend. You learned the business from other stuntmen, from seeing stunts being filmed, and from doing them yourself. My athletic abilities and rodeo experience gave me a leg up, but I had to educate myself by watching and listening.

We did one shot where Dale had been tied up in a barn by a bad guy. When the director hollered "Action!" I (as Dale) was supposed to rush out the barn door, jump over a rock fence, and run out of the scene. When

Bud Thackery started the camera rolling, I ran out so fast he didn't have time to pan. I'd been running like it was the last leg of a relay. We had to redo the shot, this time with me running a lot slower. I guess that's when I learned that in the movies, you don't always have to move fast to look fast. They could always speed up the film. I was making mistakes, but that's how you learn.

Another shot I remember from *Tales of Wells Fargo* is a scene where Dale had to fight some heavies, including Bob Morgan. (Morgan, by the way, was married to Yvonne De Carlo, known today for her role as Lily on *The Munsters*.) This would be my first stunt fight. We were just about to begin the scene when Corrick came walking up.

"Does he know how to do a fight?" he yelled, pointing at me.

"I'm sure he does," Dale said.

Morgan helped me choreograph the fight and we did it in one take. After that, the guys in production kind of backed off and left me and Dale alone.

Dale had bought Jubilee at the Hollywood Race Track, and he used him a lot. Jubilee was over sixteen hands high, but just as Dale had me as a double, Jubilee also had a backup. It was always up to the wrangler to decide which horse to use, and that depended on what kind of scene they would be shooting. Jubilee might not be able to jump over a wagon, for example, so they'd use the double. Jubilee's double horse was a small sorrel, a little over fifteen hands high. He was a stocking-legged horse named Goldie, owned by Hudkins Brothers Stable. I rode him all the time and he was always dependable.

Pall Mall cigarettes and Buick sponsored the show. They'd shoot a commercial where Dale came riding up on Jubilee and said, "This is my cigarette . . . Pall Mall . . . Good-tasting, good-looking, and this here's my horse Jubilee." Then Old Jube would perk his ears up a little.

Earl Bellamy, already a TV old-timer, and Sidney Salkow codirected the series. They did alternating episodes to keep up with the pace of a weekly show. We did two shows a week, spending only two and a half days per episode, and always tried to stay five or six shows ahead. Each day, the cast and crew worked from 6:30 a.m. until they finished. We did interiors and exteriors, but they used a lot of stock footage for train scenes.

On Wednesday we'd start talking about the next episode, which we would begin shooting the following Monday. This would be done in a meeting with the director, the assistant directors, the production managers, and the wrangler. They'd go over the script and decide which stunts needed to be done, and I'd start planning those. On a typical Monday, they'd shoot exteriors on the Western street at the lot with nondescript (they just used the letters ND, which could also be applied to an extra) horses tied to the hitching post, and ND wagons on a street. In a typical week, I might do a couple of fights, jump a horse over a fence, transfer from a running horse to a train, ride my horse down a street and stop just long enough to save a damsel in distress by grabbing her as I rode by—anything that was risky or took a lot of athletic ability.

TV stuntmen made a living, but they didn't give stuntmen screen credits. Everyone who watched the show saw us in action, but nobody except our friends and family knew who we were. Most viewers thought Dale did everything on the show.

One of the funniest things I remember was a scene where I was up on the second story of one of those western-looking buildings on the old Republic set. Doubling Dale, I was supposed to climb off the balcony with a jewel box, and then run and jump on Jubilee and ride off. Well, I climbed down that SOB and put that box over the saddle horn all right, but then a nail came out of the box and scattered jewelry all over. They had to collect all that fake jewelry, fix the box, and shoot the scene again.

We had broken for lunch and Dale was taking a nap, which he liked to do. While he was asleep, they wanted me to do a shot where he chased a guy running down a railroad track in a handcar. The scene had Dale roping him from his horse and jerking the bad guy off the handcar. Dale was somewhat ambidextrous and used his left hand for his pistol work in the show but was right-handed with everything else. Me being a lefty usually played to my advantage. I did most of the scene, but they had to film Dale on Jubilee throwing the loop. When he got ready he naturally put his rope in his right hand. The director said, "Whoa, you can't do that, we shot Dean throwing it left-handed." It was humorous to see Dale throw that loop with his left hand. That rope was all wadded up, but he finally got it to look believable.

We shot thirty-nine episodes a year, way more than they do today. In the summer they'd rerun the better ones. Then we'd start the routine again.

Knowing how to take a fall is a big part of being a stunt double. If you didn't fall just right, you'd end up crippled. In Westerns, a lot of falls were from a saddle. When you're going to be coming off a horse that's four and a half or five feet tall, you'd better know a little about how to land on the ground. I also learned how to do slump shots, where you get shot and fall over, but keep riding the horse.

In stuntman talk, a "jerk off" is when a guy gets shot off a horse. He'll be wearing a special vest under his costume shirt with a strong but thin wire attached to what's called a dead man, usually an old Model A axle stuck in the ground. When he's riding, at a certain point, he gets jerked off his horse. Later they started using a shock cord at the end of the wire, which made the sudden stop a little easier on us stuntmen. They'd have a sand pit for the rider to fall into.

You've got to give people their money's worth and make a stunt look believable. It's called "selling the shot." But by God, you've got to be able to walk away from it. A producer couldn't hire a guy who didn't know how to ride a horse and take a fall. It's an art form.

After a while, in addition to doubling Dale, I got to be stunt coordinator. I'd get the script, read it, and see what actors I had to find a double for. I'd work with casting to pick the right folks for a particular episode. A lot of the time, I'd call them and say we had a job for them on the show. I'd also work with the boss wrangler in getting horse doubles. For instance, if I had to do a stunt for Dale where his character jumps from Jubilee to another horse, I'd need that other horse to be just the right horse.

Dale was eight years older than I was, but we got to be friends and, finally, like family. I respected him and I think it was mutual. If he was not doing anything, sometimes he'd come over to my house and visit, or Pam and I would go see him.

Through Dale I met some amazing and well-known people with all different backgrounds. I would go to rodeos with Dale, where he was the main attraction, and to many of his Hollywood events. We shared the love of horses and the western way of life. I met Ernest Borgnine, Jane Wyman, Lucille Ball, Robert Stack, and a list that goes on.

Pretty soon I met Nudie Cohn, his wife, Bobbie, and their daughter, Barbara. Nudie, who had a western store on Victory near where I lived, was known as the rodeo tailor. He made a lot of Dale Evans's and Roy Rogers's costumes, as well as that gold single-breasted suit Elvis Presley made famous. I became good friends with Nudie and his family. I loved to go to his shop, where I'd always end up meeting some well-known person. Nudie had me model some of his clothes—ornate jackets and pants with lots of detail work.

Nudie later moved to Lankershim Boulevard in Universal City. One time he asked me if I'd mind driving him in his car to his bank in North Hollywood. I didn't mind that at all, because he had an automobile that was one of a kind, as fancy as the clothes he made for Hollywood stars. It had a set of longhorns on its hood and several different types of western guns mounted on it. As we sat at a red light at Lankershim and North Magnolia, two women crossed in front of us. Nudie pushed a button and out from the speakers came the sound of an old bull bawling as loud as he could. Those two gals jumped as high as the hood of the car, their dresses went over their heads, and they ran out of there. I was so embarrassed I wanted to crawl under the seat, but that's the way Nudie was.

He liked a good prank, but he also was a very generous man. One time I needed a left-handed holster but couldn't afford one. Nudie told me to go to a certain leather shop where they would make one for me. All he asked was that when I was through with it to bring it back so he could sell it in his shop for the man. Nudie and Bobbie were great people.

Dale worked hard, played hard, and was always on the go. He was single in 1958 and the gals thought Dale was the cat's meow. I remember going to his house and meeting Rhonda Fleming, whom he was seeing. This was the second time I'd seen her, and once again she was in a swimsuit, which sure wasn't disappointing. But that relationship didn't last but two or three weeks. He'd been married for a short while to Mary Murphy, an actress, but they'd gotten a divorce.

Sometimes Dale's mother, Varvel, would come out to see him and I'd spend some time with them at his place on Rayen Street in North Ridge. He had a nice house on ten or twelve acres not far from Devonshire Downs, a racetrack in the north end of the San Fernando Valley. Dale knew more about horses than just about any man I ever knew. We spent a lot of time looking at horses together. Sometimes, when we had a break in the shooting, I'd take a horse to Oklahoma for him. When I was in Hollywood, I was always around good horses and interesting people.

When I was doubling Dale, we sometimes shot for two or three weeks, then we'd be off for a week or two. During the slack times, I'd do stunt work for other productions. Dale was connected with Tommy Steiner and his rodeo. He'd work all week, get on an airplane on Friday, and go do personal appearance somewhere. Dale had a high energy level, but with the schedule he kept, I sure understood why he took naps. I've seen him fall asleep in his chair during meetings.

I learned a lot about Westerns when I worked on *Tales of Wells Fargo*. The most important thing is action and plenty of it. But when you have a producer trying to save money, he'll start cutting stunts out of the script. When that happens, the series suffers. You want good words for the actors, but it's the fighting, shooting, and horse wrecks that make a Western. Unfortunately, some producers got so damn tight they were stepping over dollars trying to save nickels. After a while, they started taking all the action out of pictures and talking the SOBs to death.

Dale always wore a jacket and pants made out of ducking, but he didn't like how that fabric restricted his movement. He said it felt like he was wearing a corset. It was too stiff, and it made his pants too tight. He used to say, "My damn pants are so tight, I can hardly stand up in them." Dale was a cowboy at heart, but he was very inventive. He went to Nudie Cohn and told Nudie to get some of that stretchy material they make bathing suits out of. Nudie got it, made Dale a jacket and pants, lined them with silk, and dyed them the same color as Dale's ducking costume, which was purple. (Purple looked better on black-and-white film, so they used a lot of it.) Well, with that new costume, he was able to bounce all over the place. I inherited Dale's old duck jacket and pants, but pretty soon I split the crotch during a stunt. Finally Dale had Nudie make a couple more of those costumes and I got the first one he had. Both of us found them a whole lot easier to get around in.

Nudie had a boot maker he liked to use, and Dale got him to make him a pair of brown boots out of the same material. Coming off that blood poisoning, Dale said those boots from Nudie made his feet feel a lot better. I had a pair, but they were too spongy for me, so I just stuck with traditional cowboy boots.

We got around quite a bit for our location shots. On days we were shooting in Sonora, we would fly from the Van Nuys airport in two DC-3s and go to a landing strip there. They'd bring the equipment in trucks. Joe

Yrigoyen, a stagecoach stuntman, had a ranch near Chatsworth, and sometimes we'd shoot there. We also shot some on Iverson's Ranch, in Chatsworth. If we had to swim a horse, we'd do it in the Tuolumne River up at Yosemite National Park. The trick to that is that you've got to have a horse that has a natural instinct to swim. I've been on horses in the water when nothing but their nostrils were sticking up. You hold on to the saddle horn or grab the mane and let the horse's instinct take its course.

The *Tales of Wells Fargo* company always stayed at the Sonora Inn. The inn had a bar, and after we finished shooting for the day, most of us ended up there. I didn't drink much, but I liked socializing with my friends. One time, a bunch of the stuntmen had a little too much to drink and started a fight. At least that's what people who weren't part of the production thought. Actually, the stuntmen were just having a stunt fight. Even so, it almost got out of hand. They did such a good job of making it look like a real fight that somebody called the cops. Right quick, we had to explain we were just a bunch of stuntmen having a little fun.

As stunt coordinator, my job was to see what stunts in the script needed to get done and make sure no one got hurt when they did them. If the scene had what we called a "picture fight," where the leading man or woman gets into a bar fight, my job was to choreograph the fight among the principals. I had to be sure there weren't any misses and that the fight didn't look phony. If the actor was not a physical fellow, I had to pick a stuntman to double him.

A barroom fight usually starts with a master shot that gives the viewer an idea of what the whole thing is about. Then the cameraman moves in for a particular action scene. They'll do a close-up of the actor to establish who it is, then go wider for the action done by the stuntman. That's when I'd come in. A fake fight doesn't involve any real punches; it's all camera angles and reacting to a punch so it looks like you got hit. I'm not saying that a stuntman or ND extra wouldn't sometimes get carried away and miss, socking somebody on the jaw. But doing a fight scene is about making it look real, not being real. If you saw a guy going through a plate-glass window, for example, it was breakaway glass. But like most things, it's not as easy as it looks.

Since the show was about Wells Fargo, a lot of scenes involved stagecoaches. They had a Concord that was the main stagecoach they used, but there was a backup. You couldn't stick with just one. Everything had a backup, from people to props. Even cowboy hats had doubles in TV. Most stagecoaches were pulled by six horses, but viewers paying real close attention would notice that sometimes we used six horses, called a six-up, and sometimes only four horses, a four-up. Sometimes the number of horses would change in the same scene. That meant the editors had spliced in some stock footage. This was all about cutting corners to save money.

If the script called for a wagon wreck, I'd work with the wranglers and special effects folks to rig the wagon where it would turn over when we wanted it to. A wagon wreck looks pretty serious on film, and it takes some work to make it happen. The wagon's got to be rigged so you can break the horses loose. I remember one scene where I got on the tongue and stayed with the horses. I pulled a plug that disconnected the tongue from the wagon and jumped up on the tongue, which of course was still connected to the horses. When the tongue left the wagon, it tripped a crimp that made it overturn. It would usually break up the wagon, but they'd keep broken ones and figure a way to reuse them.

Another stunt is what we called a horse-to-horse bulldog. That's where a guy is riding after someone and jumps to another horse. One scene where I doubled Dale had me on a horse, chasing after a train. On film, it looked like the train was really whistling through Georgia, but as the camera rolled the train was actually moving slowly. When my horse got close enough to the train, I jumped on the caboose. Then I ran along the top of the train to the tender and climbed down to the cab of the locomotive, where I held a gun on the bad guy who had been trying to rob the train. We were cheating with the train speed, but I did jump from my horse onto a moving train.

Another common stunt was what we called a Pony Express shot. That's where somebody would be standing next to a saddled horse, holding the reins, and I would jump down from one horse, hit the ground feetfirst, bounce up into the empty saddle, and ride off.

I knew horses and what they could do. My philosophy was to hire the best damned horsemen I could get, men who didn't mind hitting the ground. You need horses as good as the stuntmen you've got. If you don't have that, you had damn sure better be lucky.

We had people get the air knocked out of them doing a stunt, and every once in a while, somebody would get an arm or shoulder broken. Despite all the action in that show, we never had anybody get badly hurt. But you had to be careful not to put somebody's eye out.

You couldn't have a Western without gunplay. For obvious safety reasons, we used blanks, but the rounds came in different strengths. We'd have quarter-load, half-load, three-quarter-load, and full-load blanks. If we were shooting up close, our guns would be loaded with quarter-loads. But even they could put your eye out. You had to be careful, just as if they were real guns. We'd use a full-load on the street when there was plenty of room. They made a lot of noise, so if we were going to be using full-load blanks, we'd put cotton in the horse's ears. People would have earplugs. The blanks we shot used regular smokeless powder, but the gunpowder they used in the Old West made plenty of smoke. To make it look like we were shooting black powder, they'd put some oil down the barrels of our guns.

As a stuntman, job number one is what we call selling the shot, making it look as realistic as possible without killing someone. If a script called for me to fall off a horse or a wagon, I had to make it look like that's exactly what I did. I knew if I didn't, it would look hokey on screen and I might end up out of work.

Several actors who later got to be real famous had minor parts in *Tales of Wells Fargo*. Jack Nicholson played a heavy, along with Steve McQueen. Both of them were always real personable. They liked sports and we'd talk about that.

Dale was an actor-cowboy, not a writer, but he had good judgment on scripts. The writers were always on the set, but as the star, he sometimes did a little writing-editing on the wing. One time he was having trouble with a line. Not that he couldn't say the line, he just didn't think it sounded right. It was something like, "When you get down there, cut his trail." Dale said, "What the hell do you mean? It sounds like somebody with a knife. That sounds like somebody from New York." He didn't dig that and changed the line.

For this and other business reasons, Universal and Dale were not getting along. It was a mutual un-admiration society. But they knew he was very popular with the viewers. Just about everybody loved Dale, but he did have his run-ins with studios and producers.

Back then Universal had the justified reputation of being tighter than a tick on a dog's behind. Still, I was happy to have consistent, paying work. Depending on what I did, I'd make $80 to $120 a day. That doesn't sound like much, but back then it was enough to get by on. I liked what I was doing and my wife and I were pretty comfortable.

I spent most of my time working for *Tales of Wells Fargo*, but I was moonlighting stunts anywhere I could. Producers liked my abilities and I was beginning to get a good reputation. I did some stunts on *Wagon Train*, where Ward Bond played the wagon master; *Laramie*; *Whispering Smith*, a series about a detective in Denver in the 1870s; and *Riverboat*, which starred Darren McGavin and a young Burt Reynolds. All of these Westerns were done at Universal Studios. In that business, you're likely to be working one day here, another day there. That's how I got so much experience.

I was in several Disney productions, including *Zorro*, *The Nine Lives of Elfego Baca*, *The Swamp Fox*, and *Texas John Slaughter*. Walt Disney was a great creative guy. I'd always see him around the sets observing what we were doing. One thing I liked about working for Disney was that the studio paid better. I also really liked Buddy Van Horn, who doubled Zorro. He was a terrific stuntman, very good with swords. He taught me some of the saber stuff, which stuntmen called click-clacking.

In 1959, I did an ND stunt scene in *Pork Chop Hill*, a movie about the Korean War. Directed by Lewis Milestone, the movie starred Gregory Peck. That's one movie where my military training had a practical civilian application, since I had to dress and act like an infantryman for my scene.

For *Wagon Train* I had to wear a suitcase-special cowboy hat that looked too much like a rodeo hat. I took a lot of kidding over that. Frank McGrath, an old-time stuntman who got his start on silent Westerns in 1921, played Charlie Wooster, the crusty cook. I remember one time they had a mountain lion on the set for an episode. That lion started going crazy. They kept trying to get it calmed down before somebody finally figured out that it was that time of the month for a script supervisor on the set. The lion was reacting to that, so the lady had to leave the set for the scene involving the big cat.

Delbert Combs worked as head wrangler on *Wagon Train*. He partnered with his son, Gary, whom I got to know pretty well. I'll never forget one time at Universal Studios when he pointed to Raymond Burr, who was doing the *Perry Mason* series. He said, "See that old boy over there? He'd rather hear a fat boy fart than a pretty girl sing." I had never heard anyone put it quite that way before. Delbert was a real piece of work.

I was just a freelance cowboy stuntman, going from the set of one Western series to another. I did lots of falls and fights, utility stuff. This was the golden era of TV Westerns and I didn't have to worry about work. Back home in Texas, Mama was happy to know I loved what I was doing. I was getting paid to play cowboys and Indians.

I'd go back to Texas at least twice a year, Christmas and summer. Mama came to see me in 1958 with my Uncle King and Aunt Teena. My cousin Don, their son, drove them out. Over by the Hudkins Brothers barn the railroad hoboes had a town where they slept out in the open on old mattresses. For some reason, Uncle King got the biggest kick out of seeing that. The next day I took them to Long Beach, where we went on the ferry to San Pedro. I also took them by the studio, but they were not too impressed. They only stayed in California for about seventy-two hours. Mama woke up on Monday morning and said, "Well, we'll be on our way home." I asked if she was sure she wanted to leave so soon, and she said, "Yes, son, I'm too far away from my burying grounds. I'd better get home." With them following me in their car, I escorted them as far as Palm Springs.

Also that year, I got a call from MGM Studios. Paul Newman was starring in the movie adaptation of Tennessee Williams's *Cat on a Hot Tin Roof.* They wanted me to go over there and give Paul some pointers on jumping over hurdles. It really thrilled me to meet Paul. Someone from the studio publicity office came up to me and said they were going to put a little blurb about me in *Daily Variety.* Sure enough, the next day there was an article on how MGM's promising new actor and Olympian, "Dean Jones," was giving Paul Newman instructions on jumping hurdles. The real Dean Jones was an actor under contract to MGM. I think someone was giving him a little tune-up at my expense. I figured out real quick you were better off doing your own publicity.

That same year, Hoyt Bowers sent me to do a silent bit in the John Wayne movie *Rio Bravo,* my first movie with Duke. I was in his movie, but I didn't meet Wayne at this time. The director was Howard Hawks, as good as anyone I have ever worked with. Hawks was a very kind man who treated me wonderfully, and I thought he was just great. Duke had turned fifty the year before and had been worrying about whether the rock-and-roll craze would cause teenagers to lose interest in his Westerns. To guard against that, they cast singer Ricky Nelson to play a young gunfighter in the film. I had dark hair and was about Ricky's size, so I asked about doubling him. But Nelson didn't have much to do in the movie that would require a stuntman. Besides that, I was still too new for anyone to pay much attention to me. Not only didn't I get to double him, I wasn't even in what looks like my one scene with him. In that scene, he took a shot at the bad guys and in the editing process they superimposed a shot where horses jumped over him. There was also an edited-in shot of me reacting to that scene but not saying anything. In another scene inside a saloon, I had a shot reacting to Dean Martin and Wayne. I also had a shot reacting to Claude Akins doing something with Wayne. For me it was a one-day deal, each reaction shot done indoors on the Warner Bros. stage.

Also that year, Paramount called and wanted to know if I could rear a horse on a stage. I said I could make a horse rear up anywhere I wanted to. Danny Kaye was doing the movie *Red Nichols and the Five Little Pennies*, and there was a scene where he was supposed to rear his horse and blow a trumpet. Dressed in a Royal Canadian Mountie uniform, I doubled Danny in that scene, rearing the horse and blowing a bugle. It was exciting meeting him and getting a chance to tell him that I had sure enjoyed him when I saw him at Fair Park in Dallas with my fellow UT teammates in 1952. He was very nice to me and said he thought I had done a good job on the horse stunt.

I went to a lot of part interviews and learned pretty quickly that you have to have a lot of gall if you're going to work in Hollywood. You'd better be prepared to brag on yourself. You've got to hustle, because that business is just as competitive as the 100-yard dash. You're up against someone else who's probably just as good as you are, though you've got to make that director think you're the best at what you do. You go see a director and at first they just look at you, studying what you look like to make up their mind if they think you'll look good standing thirty feet tall on a movie screen. Then they start asking questions like, "Can you ride a horse?" I'd always say, "Yes, sir, I sure can. I've been riding all my life." You had to sell yourself and I did.

I was still working on *Tales of Wells Fargo* when I heard that Wayne would be doing *The Alamo* in 1959. I wanted very badly to be in that movie, which was going to be shot in Texas, but I didn't know how I'd be able to meet and get acquainted with someone as famous as Duke. What I did know was that my Olympic teammate Bob Mathias of Tulare, California, was under contract with Batjac Productions, Wayne's company. Being an Olympian is like belonging to a brotherhood, so I asked Bob if he could help me get connected.

Bob picked me up and took me to the Batjac offices on Sunset Boulevard, where he introduced me to Bob Morrison, Wayne's brother. I also met Duke's son, Michael Wayne, and Cliff Lyons, a cowboy stuntman who'd been around Hollywood since the silent movie days. Lyons did all second unit and stunt coordinating for Wayne's pictures. If you worked for Lyons, automatically you'd be able to work for Wayne.

"I'm from Texas and I've been doubling Dale Robertson," I said. "I'd give anything to work on *The Alamo*. I think I've got ability."

Pretty soon Wayne walked in wearing one of those embroidered Mexican wedding shirts. He was as much a man in person as he was on the big screen, but for a big guy, he had a flow to his movement, light on his feet. Bob Mathias introduced us.

"Duke," he said, "this here's Dean Smith. He was on the '52 Olympic team with me. He's from Texas."

Wayne grinned, shook my hand, and said, "Well, I can't hold that against you."

I didn't wait long to play my cards.

"Duke," I said, "I sure want to go back to Texas and be in that Alamo movie you're doing."

He looked at Lyons.

"You think this boy can hold up?"

"He's faster than a turpentined cat," Lyons said. "He can ride a horse, too."

"Sounds to me like he'd be kind of an asset for us," Duke said.

"Yeah, I think so; he's a good kid," Lyons replied.

All I could think to say was, "I sure do thank you. I won't let you down."

That day I also met two other stuntmen who worked for Wayne,

Chuck Roberson and Chuck Hayward. Roberson, the more flamboyant of the two, was known as "Bad Chuck." They called Hayward "Good Chuck." Good or bad, Duke liked both men. Bad Chuck doubled Wayne, while Good Chuck handled Wayne's horses and did stunt work. Both of them seemed to take a liking to me, which I knew had also helped me get the job.

I was a happy young man. I thought, *I'm going home to Texas to be in a movie about the Alamo*. My dream had really begun to come true.

Plate 1. Dean, without helmet, in football game, Graham versus Cisco, 1949.
Plate 2. Doug McClure and Dean on the set of *Overland Trail*, 1960.

Plate 3. Headshot of Dean in 1962. Plate 4. Publicity photo of Dean as a working cowboy in 1962. Plate 5. Stunt in the documentary *Dean Smith, Hollywood Stuntman*, 1964. Courtesy of Bob Hinkle.

Plate 6. Dean on Sox preparing to do a horse fall for the documentary *Dean Smith, Hollywood Stuntman*, 1964. Courtesy of Bob Hinkle.

Plate 7. Photo shot for the documentary *Dean Smith, Hollywood Stuntman* of Bob Hinkle, Darrell Royal, Dean Smith, and Coach Clyde Littlefield at the University of Texas Longhorn Hall of Honor, 1964. Courtesy of Bob Hinkle.

Plate 8. Dean, Jorge Rivero, Mike Henry, and director Howard Hawks while working on *Rio Lobo*, 1970. Plate 9. Dean jumping over stuntman Gary Davis as Evel Knievel in *Evel Knievel*, 1971.

Plate 10. Dean as Trooper Horowitz in *Ulzana's Raid*, 1972. Plate 11. Director Earl Bellamy, James Griffith, and Dean on the set of *Seven Alone*, 1974.

Plate 12. Dean on his trick horse Sunday, rearing just like Roy and Gene, 1990.

Plate 13. Dean on his trick horse Sunday, "End of the Trail" at Vasquez Rocks National Monument, Southern California, 1983. Plate 14. Dale Robertson on Hollywood with Dean at Lazy E Arena, Oklahoma, 1997.

Plate 15. Dean's boyhood friend Larry Mahan, Dean, and world champion cowboy Larry Mahan, 1997. Plate 16. Trick horse Hollywood and Dean, 2004. Courtesy of Mark Engebretson. Plate 17. Ernie Taylor, Dean, Wilford Brimley, and Mike Baily at the 2004 Dean Smith Celebrity Rodeo. Courtesy of Mark Engebretson.

Plate 18. Dean cutting at the 2006 Dean Smith Celebrity Rodeo. Courtesy of Mark Engebretson.

Plate 19. Debby Smith, Finis Smith, Dean, Nancy Reagan, and Patrick Wayne at the John Wayne Cancer Institute Odyssey Ball, 2006. Courtesy of JWCIA.

Plate 20. Dean and Debby's ten-year anniversary at Alamo Village, Brackettville, Texas, October 2006. Courtesy of Mark Engebretson. Plate 21. Dean at Alamo Village, Brackettville, Texas, October 2006. Courtesy of Mark Engebretson.

Plate 22. Dean and oldest son Charles at the 2007 Western Heritage Awards, Oklahoma. Courtesy of Joe Ownbey Photo, www.ownbeyphotography.com.

Plate 23. Finis Smith and Dean at Nebraska's Big Rodeo, 2011.

Plate 24. Bob Lilly, Dean, and Walt Garrison at the Texas Sports Hall of Fame Golf Tournament, 2011. Plate 25. At the 2006 Jimmy Rane Foundation Golf Tournament; back row: Jimmy Rane, Terry Bradshaw; front row: Dale Robertson, Tony Rane, Dean. Courtesy of Jimmy Rane.

CHAPTER 10

JOHN WAYNE AT THE ALAMO

John Wayne and Dean on the set of *The Alamo*, 1959.

The Alamo was going to be shot in South Texas near Brackettville in the late summer and fall of 1959. I left California for Texas toward the end of August, driving to Ruidoso, New Mexico, where I spent the night with Dale Robertson, who kept an apartment there because he raced quarter horses at the track nearby. From the high country I drove home to Breckenridge, where I stayed for a few days with Mama.

Not only was I going to be in the movie, but I had also gotten my cousin, Don Smith, a job with the Alamo production company working as an extra. He was living on the old home place near Ivan that belonged to Uncle King. When we left Stephens County, Don followed me in his car, but he only stayed about a month because his parents, who were getting up in years, needed his help on their ranch.

Most everyone involved in the movie, 340-plus people, would be staying at old Fort Clark, a longtime cavalry post across Las Moras Creek from Brackettville 140 miles southwest of San Antonio. The army abandoned the fort after World War II, and the government sold the property for a song to a subsidiary of Brown and Root, which turned it into a first-class guest ranch. The same group that operated the Driskill Hotel in Austin ran Fort Clark.

When Don and I got to Brackettville we turned off US Highway 90 and crossed the creek onto the fort to check in. Wayne's production company had set up its office in the old headquarters building in the middle of the parade ground, a two-story frame and limestone building. The stone first floor was more than a hundred years old.

Al Ybarra, Wayne's art director and set builder, had been working in Texas for more than a year before the cast and crew started showing up. Starting in the fall of 1957, he had supervised the building of a three-quarter-scale replica of the Alamo along with the town of San Antonio de Bexar out at James T. "Happy" Shahan's 22,000-acre ranch, located about eight miles north of Brackettville. Some of the fancy-looking features were carved from Styrofoam and painted to look authentic, but Al also used a million or so adobe bricks they made there on the ranch. Happy got a lot of people from Mexico, Del Rio, and Eagle Pass to work on the set, which for Hollywood was an amazingly accurate representation of what the Alamo and early-day San Antonio had looked like at the time of the battle. One thing they did differently, for reasons of visual appeal, was build the movie Alamo facing east. The real Alamo faces west.

I was one of thirty-one stuntmen hired to work on the film. The men I had the most dealings with were Bad Chuck Roberson (in addition to doubling Duke he played one of Davy Crockett's Tennesseans), Good Chuck Hayward, Billy Shannon, LeRoy Johnson, Bill Williams (he doubled Richard Widmark), John "Bear" Hudkins, brothers Joe and Tapedero "Tap" Canutt (their dad Yakima had doubled Wayne early in his career; Tap doubled Laurence Harvey in *The Alamo*), Ted White, Jackie Williams, Ed Juaregui, Jim Burk, Boyd "Red" Morgan, Tom Hennesey, Wally Rose, Gil Perkins, and Rudy Robbins.

My boss was Cliff Lyons. We called him "Mother" Lyons, but he was a hard-boiled man in his late fifties who'd been in the business for a long time. One thing I learned about him: he really liked drinking margaritas and eating the Portuguese tortillas they served at one of the restaurants at the fort.

Bill Jones was head wrangler. He had overall responsibility for 600 head they kept in a corral on the side of the hill above where the mission replica stood. They had acquired some damn good horses for us to use. For all my horseback scenes, I rode a buckskin gelding that belonged to Chuck Roberson. It had a black stripe on its back and was a fine animal.

Besides all the horses, Jones had to tend a herd of longhorns on loan from Bill Daniel. Bill's brother, Price Daniel, was governor at the time, and Bill was then governor of Guam. Both of them grew up in Liberty, Texas, which is where the longhorns came from. Seeing all those longhorns got me thinking that when the time was right I would like to own my own herd.

I had a room in one of the former barracks at the fort, but I only stayed there a few days before a couple of other stuntmen and I decided to rent our own house over in Brackettville in what they called Tortilla Flats. My housemates were Bad Chuck and Jackie Williams, one of the greatest falling horse stuntmen in the business. They invited me to bunk with them because they said they enjoyed my company, but I think cutting their rent from one-half to one-third was what really made me popular with them. They were funny guys and we had a million laughs during the filming of the movie.

Finding a house hadn't been hard. When the army pulled out of Fort Clark in the mid-1940s, about the only thing that kept Brackettville going was being a county seat. They said the population had dropped from nearly 5,000 in World War II to about 1,200 before we got there and temporarily swelled the head count. Those who still lived there were open to making a little money any way they could, including renting rooms or one of the many empty houses. Our place was a little frame house across from Luna's Grocery Store and just a little down the street from the old movie theater that hadn't seen a packed house since the soldiers left. The house had a picket fence around it, which I used to jump rather than go through the gate to keep my legs in shape. I lived in the front room, with Roberson and Jackie sharing the back room. We had a kitchen, but we ate most of our meals at the company commissary or at Ma Crosby's, the famous

Bill Williams doubling Richard Widmark and Dean
doubling Frankie Avalon in *The Alamo*, 1959.

restaurant in Ciudad Acuña, Mexico, across from Del Rio. Sometimes when we had the night off we also went to El Moderno, a well-known eating place in Piedras Negras, across from Eagle Pass.

Rolly Harper was the production company's caterer. He had come to Texas from Hollywood. His crew furnished breakfast and lunch on the set, with supper back at the commissary at the fort. If we worked late, Rolly put the food in trucks and sent it out to the set.

The script, which we all had copies of, called for lots of horse work and a lot of hand-to-hand action. The master shooting schedule listed 566 scenes, and I would be in darn near every action shot.

Second unit preproduction started September 4 with the opening shots of the Mexican army on the march to San Antonio. We actually did the scene where the caissons are splashing across what the movie audience thinks is the Rio Grande on the Nueces River near Garner State Park in the Uvalde area. Later, they did the love scene with Wayne as Davy

Crockett and Flaca (played by the Argentinean actress Linda Cristal) at the same location.

After a prayer led by the local Catholic priest, Wayne yelled "Action!" for the first time on September 9, directing a couple of early scenes in Bexar, including the arrival of Sam Houston, who was played by Richard Boone, star of the TV Western *Paladin*. After lunch, Wayne borrowed actor Laurence Harvey's sword to cut a giant Alamo cake Harper had baked to celebrate the initial day of production. They did some minor scenes for the rest of the week, including half of Saturday, and then took off for the rest of the weekend.

A lot of the company headed to Acuña, which offered everything from good food to cheap booze and cheaper women. That night, two production crew members on their way back from Mexico swerved out of their lane and crashed head-on into a car with several Brackettville teenagers in it, including Happy Shahan's daughter Tulisha. She suffered critical injuries and three people were killed. The next day, Duke went to San Antonio to visit Tulisha at the hospital. The accident was a downer, but the show had to go on. It cost $60,000 a day to keep that operation going.

Since it was still pretty hot in South Texas, for the first three to four weeks we worked mostly at night at the Alamo set. Back then a lot of producers adjusted their cameras and shot their "night" scenes during the day, but Duke wanted this movie to look as realistic as possible, so we shot at night. Head photographer Bill Clothier did a great job on that and every other aspect of the filming.

By this point in my career, I had only two and a half years' experience, but I was learning fast. A lot of what we did for *The Alamo* was extremely dangerous, from falling off running horses to reacting to exploding charges designed to look like artillery fire. I figured out pretty quickly that if I didn't listen and pay close attention, I could get myself killed. Doing stunt work is tricky. Directors are always looking for a wild stunt that's bigger than life, and my job was to try to do that. But you better be damn sure you know what you're doing, or you'll be short-lived. I couldn't take anything for granted.

(Over the years, I've known and worked with at least four stuntmen who died doing their job: Fred Kennedy, Bill Williams, Jimmy Sheppard, and Jack Tyree. Kennedy was killed in 1958 when his horse fell when they

John Ford, sitting, with Dean standing in the
background on the set of *The Alamo*, 1959.

shot the final scene for Duke's *The Horse Soldiers*; Williams, whom I
worked with on *The Alamo*, was killed in 1964 during the filming of *Hal-
lelujah Trail*; Sheppard died in 1977 during the making of *Comes a Horseman*; and Tyree died in 1982 doing a high fall in *The Sword and the Sor-
cerer.*)

At various times during the filming, I wore fourteen different types of
Mexican costumes. I was a dragoon, a lancer, and a foot soldier. The Mexican army in that movie was the prettiest army I ever saw. Frank C. Beet-
son, Jr., coordinated the men's wardrobe, and Ann Peck oversaw the ladies' wardrobe. Fae Smith, the hairstylist, was wonderful to work with.
The wardrobe department was inside one of the sets on Happy's ranch.
There was also a room for the stuntmen.

We'd been working for about two weeks when legendary director

Dean hurdling a horse and taking off its rider,
stuntman Bear Hudkins, in *The Alamo*, 1959.

John Ford showed up on the set. Wayne had gone to him for advice while putting the project together, but he had always made it clear that he intended to direct the film, not have Ford do it. But Ford was the man who had made John Wayne, and I think he thought that once he was there, Duke would let him take over the Alamo movie. Duke had no intention of doing that, but he didn't want to hurt the old man's feelings either, so he let him do some of the second unit stuff. It was a delicate situation for Wayne, but it turned out to be a pretty good break for me.

One of the scenes Ford handled was the skirmish early in the film where some of the Alamo defenders ride out to gather and drive cattle back into the old mission. I was in two out of the four stunt bits, including a shot where I played one of Davy Crockett's men and jumped horse-high from off-camera to take down a mounted Mexican herdsman. Wearing a coonskin cap, I did what I was supposed to do with no problems and apparently a little flair. In other words, I must have sold the shot. After he yelled cut, Ford walked up to me. He was wearing a blue blazer, cream-colored trousers, white buck shoes, and a slouch hat, and he was chewing on the bandana he was holding. He pulled up his eye patch and said, "I've never seen anybody do that and you didn't even use a trampoline. My name is John Ford. If you ever hear of me doing any pictures, you've got a job."

In another one of the scenes Ford supervised, Bad Chuck and I were playing Mexican dragoons charging Patrick Wayne's character, who was pointing two pistols at us. When Patrick fired one pistol, Bad Chuck's horse went down. Then I got jerked off my horse by a wire tied to the back of my uniform coat. There was no shock cord and I came down hard, my helmet skinning my nose when I hit the ground. Trouble was, one of Patrick's pistols had misfired and they had to shoot the scene again. I went ahead and did it, but about a week later when they had a shot where I'd get jerked by one of those wires, I let Billy Shannon take it. That turned out to have been a good idea for me, because it knocked him out cold.

Being young and new to the business, I didn't have a whole lot of dealings with the big stars. Of course, hardly anyone seemed close to Richard Widmark, who played Jim Bowie. He could be sort of irritable. I know for sure he and Duke didn't have much in common. Their politics were a hundred miles apart. Duke and most of his friends were real conservative guys, but Widmark was a liberal Democrat. They could get into some pretty heated discussions. He and Wayne might have had a little rumble about a scene, but fortunately it was never any big deal. One time when I was riding in a car with Widmark, I found out he didn't hear very well out of his right ear. I think part of his aloofness was because he couldn't hear you.

Laurence Harvey played the character of Texas commander William Travis pretty darn well, really capturing his cocky, arrogant style. Harvey was from Britain and while we were working on the movie, his wife, actress Margaret Leighton, wrapped up her role in the Broadway play *Much Ado about Nothing* and came to see him. The crew built a big sign welcoming her to the set and Duke threw a party in her honor.

For Wayne, *The Alamo* was a family movie in two ways: first, it was a film he hoped families would want to see, and second, most of his own family was involved one way or another. Aissa, his young daughter by his second wife, Pilar, played the daughter of Lieutenant Dickerson and his wife, Susanna. Michael Wayne was assistant director. Patrick Wayne played James Butler Bonham, the messenger who left the Alamo with a letter from Travis asking for help. Daughter Toni, along with her one-year-old daughter Anita, was in the movie and Toni's husband, Don LaCava, worked on the production staff. The Waynes stayed in the biggest house at the fort, the two-story former commanding general's quarters. I got to know all the Wayne kids and after a while, I was sort of like their uncle.

One day I was told to go to wardrobe to pick up a costume for another scene I'd be in. When I reported to wardrobe they handed me this fancy black outfit that came with a little cap. It was a boy's costume and I looked pretty silly standing around in it. They didn't even end up calling me for a scene. The next day I was wearing that costume again, still waiting for someone to call me for a scene, when I began to realize something wasn't right. Too many crew members were laughing their heads off. I guess they thought they were initiating me since I was new to the business. I finally figured out they were just having a little fun with me and I got rid of that costume in a hurry.

When they filmed Santa Anna's troops riding and marching into San Antonio, I was one of the soldiers who jumped his horse over a fence. They brought busloads of Mexicans in from Del Rio and Eagle Pass to be extras in the Mexican army. They paid them $10–$15 a day and fed them a box lunch. I think they ended up hiring about 1,200 extras.

During the establishing shots, when the Mexicans were coming in and surrounding Bexar, Carlos Arruza, a matador from Mexico, played Lieutenant Reyes, the head of the lancers. That man may have been a bullfighter, but he sure knew how to ride a horse. In the movie, Carlos is the one who reads the proclamation from Santa Anna, demanding that the Alamo garrison surrender or be put to the sword. During that scene, I was standing on the wall with Wayne, Harvey, and Widmark. I was supposed to be an eager beaver and shoot Carlos, but that was cut out of the script and Harvey ended up using his cigar to touch off a cannon as his answer to Santa Anna.

Fairly early in the filming they had a shot where they were setting off what they call pots, buried explosive charges rigged by the special effects crew. These were supposed to be exploding cannonballs fired by the Texans. I was dressed as a Mexican lancer, riding along, when they blew up one of those pots a little closer to my horse than he liked. That horse jumped out from under me, and I went to the ground hard about the time the next pot blew up. It practically exploded in my face, covering me with dirt. That's about as hard a fall as I took in that movie. It must have looked like I'd been splattered all over the ground. It shook me up, but I was ready to go again in a few minutes and it made a great shot.

I wasn't the only one who took some hard falls during the filming. Guinn "Big Boy" Williams, originally from Decatur, had a ranch near Brackettville, and he and his wife, Toddy, would invite me out there every once in a while. Sometimes I'd go by and pick up Big Boy and we'd go to Ma Crosby's in Acuña. While we were in Mexico, he'd always buy a couple of bottles of Oso Negro. Given his nickname in 1919 by fellow cowboy Will Rogers, he had been one of Errol Flynn's good buddies and Wayne had given him a part in *The Alamo*. In a scene where he rides through the gate, his horse reared up and he slipped off. He'd been riding on a cavalry saddle with steel stirrups and his foot got hung. He hurt his knee, but he was a tough old boy and went on working.

I got picked to double one of the movie's stars, Frankie Avalon, a wonderful kid from Philly with a great singing voice. Wayne cast him in the movie to pull in younger viewers. Of course, the fact that he was married to Michael Wayne's sister-in-law hadn't hurt his chances any. I was twenty-seven and Avalon was only eighteen (he turned nineteen during the shoot), but my hair was dark and with a little help from makeup and the wardrobe department, I could pass for him in the wide shots.

I think I made him look pretty good at times. I doubled Avalon during the scene where some of the defenders ride out of the Alamo to blow up the big Mexican cannon early in the movie. In the process, Bowie gets hurt and I rescue him.

My other part was playing one of Jim Bowie's men. To do that, I had to grow a beard. But when it came time to double Avalon, makeup clipped my beard and left only the stubble. I went ahead and shaved. The next time I went in the commissary, I happened to sit down right across from Mother Lyons. When he noticed my clean face, he hit that table so hard all the dishes went six inches in the air.

"Goddammit," he said, "you didn't have to do that. Now they'll have to put glue and hair on you."

Lyons didn't like what I had done, but he got over it and in a couple of days my beard grew back. The reason I shaved was that my wife and step-daughter were on their way to spend some time with me there in Brack-ettville. That was a long time before it was considered cool to have a beard, especially in Texas.

Knowing my housemates, the last thing in the world I wanted was to have Pam and little Christine staying there. I had the whole front room, but I knew that wasn't enough space for my family. The night before Pam got to town, Jackie Williams and Bad Chuck brought over two girls from Mexico. They proceeded to have a hell of a party, all night long. I had al-ready decided to rent a room somewhere else in town, but that didn't do me any good that last night. I don't think I got any sleep at all.

The next morning I groggily backed my car up to the gate to start loading my stuff when Mrs. Peña, the lady who owned the house, came walking up. I could tell she was really mad about something. I was carry-ing my hatboxes out and putting them in my convertible when she said, "After last night you boys have to leave. I did not like all that noise . . . and I will not stand for it."

Looking all innocent and concerned, Bad Chuck pointed to me and told her that they were getting rid of the troublemaker now. He said that it was me who had made all that noise and they had kicked me out. She believed him and let them stay. Of course, Roberson knew I was moving out, so he wasn't really selling me down the river. Like all good stuntmen, he was just thinking on his feet. Later at dinner when they told Duke about it he had a good laugh. From that time on my nickname on that picture was "Troublemaker."

As we moved through the script, I did all kinds of action scenes. I did a double horse fall in a scene where I was playing one of the Texans run-ning from a Mexican patrol. I did some scissoring, which is when you run and jump on a horse over its rump. If I wasn't a Mexican bugler falling off a horse, I was getting dragged down a road or jumping a horse over an-other horse.

Not all my scenes involved horses or fighting, though. One of the most fun scenes I had was playing in the big fandango they had in the cantina to celebrate the arrival of Davy Crockett and his Tennesseans be-fore the Mexican army got to Bexar. Eighteen of us who played Bowie's men got to dance with a bunch of pretty Mexican girls. Wardrobe had me wearing a pair of Mexican pants, a fancy shirt and vest, a flat-brim hat with a tie down, and black boots. I had springs in my legs and was born to dance.

The biggest bit of action connected to *The Alamo* wasn't part of the script. It was the real-life murder of one of the cast members. Twenty-seven-year-old LaJean Ethridge and her boyfriend, Chester Smith, had been staying at Spofford, a wide spot in the road nine miles south of Brackettville on the mainline of the Southern Pacific. Both of them had come in from Hollywood with an acting troupe looking for bit roles, but Ethridge was the one who caught Wayne's eye. Calling her a young Mar-jorie Main, Wayne took it upon himself to give her a break. He got her a Screen Actor's card and built up her part as the wife of one of the defend-ers. In an emotional scene, which she handled really well, she left the Al-amo in a wagon with their kids knowing they'd probably never see her husband again. Unfortunately, not long after they did that scene, she and her boyfriend had some kind of beef and he stabbed her to death with a hunting knife early in the morning on Sunday, October 11. I think the guy resented her getting the opportunity that Wayne had given her. That mur-der took the breath out of everything there for a while. It shut the produc-tion down because Wayne had to give a deposition and later testify in the boyfriend's trial.

As we progressed with the filming, despite the pranks they'd pulled on me I had gotten to be pretty tight with the other stuntmen. They all knew I had won a gold medal in the Olympics and one of them came up with the bright idea of setting up a race for me. Not against another per-son, but a sorrel thoroughbred that really could run. Jesse Owens had done the same thing when he went on tour after winning in the 1936 Olympics.

I was to race a horse for forty yards down the main street of the Bexar set. Good Chuck would be riding the horse. Knowing I could still do the forty in 4.1 seconds, I said I'd do it and called Mama to put my starting blocks on the bus to Brackettville. Meanwhile, the guys began placing their bets, Duke included. Quite a bit of money went down, most of it on the horse.

Just about the whole crew lined up along the street to watch the race, which we did about midafternoon on a warm fall day. I had shucked my costume and put on shorts, a T-shirt, and my track shoes.

Inside an hour, I ran three races. Somebody started each race with a prop pistol. Good Chuck did everything he could to beat me, but I got out quicker and won the first two races. He finally won the last race, but that horse had four legs to my two and a dang bigger set of lungs. All the bets were one-on-one and several thousand dollars changed hands each time I ran.

I had outrun the horse two out of three times, but it's a good thing I didn't have to race him any farther than forty yards. I finally figured out that after that first forty or so, there's no way a man can outrun a good Texas quarter horse with somebody in the saddle who knows how to ride. He'll pass you like a train going by a white picket fence.

Another stuntman pastime was a race that was really just a prank. The stuntmen would pick a victim and talk him into taking part in a race where he'd be tied upside down on the back of another guy. The upside-down man's legs would be wrapped around the runner's shoulders and neck, which meant his face hit about at the runner's butt. The race was forty yards with the opposing runner spotting the guy with a man on his back by ten yards. This time the patsy was a nice gullible extra from the area named Ben Dorsey, who later worked as a roadie for Willie Nelson. Stuntman Ted White had Ben tied up on his back and would be running against another stuntman. As the race was fixing to start, Ted began telling Ben that he was feeling a little queasy and thought he might have an accident. He went on with the race still complaining of feeling ill. Maybe it was something he ate in Mexico, he said.

Of course, Ben started yelling for them to get him off of White. About that time White did some good acting. He started moaning and saying he didn't think he could hold it any longer. As Ted started pulling down his pants, Ben just about kicked his head off trying to get loose. The whole bunch of us who were watching busted up laughing.

Wayne wanted as much publicity for the movie as he could get, so he was generally willing to allow guests on the set. They came by the thousands—individuals, families, school groups, and VIPs. One day that fall, about the time we broke for lunch, a privately owned DC-3 landed just beyond the Alamo set. It was University of Texas head football coach Darrell K. Royal and several of my old coaches who had stopped by for a tour before going on a deer hunt. They didn't stay long, but it was good to see them and I enjoyed getting to meet Coach Royal, who had been at UT for only a couple of years.

They say bad things often come in threes, and that's the way it played out during the filming of *The Alamo*. Barely a month after the sordid murder of LaJean Ethridge, which had made page-one news all over the country, and two months after Tulisha Shahan was nearly killed in a car accident, the old Fort Clark headquarters building that Batjac used as its field office caught fire about one o'clock in the afternoon on Sunday, November 15. Eight Batjac employees lived on the second floor, but they all got out OK. A lot of the cast members helped the local volunteer fire department fight the fire, but the place was gutted. I think they lost some costumes, but they kept most of the wardrobe on the set at Happy's ranch. Only the limestone walls of the downstairs part of the building survived. After the fire, they moved the production office to the former officers' club, which also had one of the guest ranch's two restaurants. The rock portion of the onetime headquarters building dated back to 1857 and still stands as an empty shell in the middle of the former parade ground, now a nine-hole golf course.

Working with Wayne was a pleasure. He was always just one of us guys, not arrogant like some big stars. I was only a young stuntman, but we visited and talked. Sometimes we'd have lunch together. One thing that doesn't fit Wayne's macho image is that he liked to play chess. When things were slow, he'd play with Red Morgan, or his double, Bad Chuck.

During the workweek, if we didn't have a scene, we'd watch the filming. When everybody had time off, we'd play pool at the dude ranch's headquarters building or go swimming in the big spring-fed pool there. But we usually worked six days a week. If we got off early, we'd go to Mexico.

Every once in a while I'd go to San Antonio on Saturday night to eat at Big John Hamilton's steakhouse and unwind. They called him "Big John" because he was six-foot-six. He and Chill Wills, whom I knew from Hollywood, were good buddies. Chill, originally from the Dallas area, was playing one of Crockett's Tennesseans. Big John had a hand in getting Duke to do the movie in Texas. Duke had thought about doing the movie in Mexico, but nobody in Texas wanted that to happen.

One Saturday I drove to San Antonio after work to visit Big John and Chill. When I got back on Sunday, I found Brackettville and Fort Clark deserted. Then I remembered that Carlos Arruza was performing in a bullfight at Acuña and that most of the crew had gone over to see it. I headed for Del Rio and crossed over into Mexico. I drove to La Macarena, the big bullfighting ring, and started scanning the stands for my stunt friends. I located them at the top in the southwest corner. They were intermingled with gals that they had checked out from the bordello in Boy's Town. Those women had their hair dyed just about any color you can imagine: green, orange, yellow, red, pink, and blue. They were whooping and hollering and having a good old time. I thought, *Jesus Christ, I'm glad I am not up there with them.* I found some of the other cast and crew and sat with them. Carlos fought Portuguese style, on horseback. He put on a fine show and let the bull live that day.

After the bullfight, we went to a place called Garcia's Bar. Garcia had gone to Sul Ross College in Alpine and was a real nice guy and a good friend of Happy Shahan's. Bad Chuck Roberson said to me, "Since you've got your car, when you go back I want to ride with you to Fort Clark." I told Chuck that would be fine but that I was going to go buy me some of those Mexican wedding shirts like Cliff Lyons and Duke wore. I bought a couple of the shirts and then, about dark, I went back to Garcia's to get Roberson. Needless to say, he had had a few drinks. The truth is he'd had more than a few, but I was stone cold sober. Anyway, I went inside the bar, got Chuck, and said, "OK, let's go back to Fort Clark."

He agreed, and I held him by the arm as he walked down the gutter along the street. All of a sudden, two big Mexican cops showed up. One policeman grabbed me by the arm and one got Chuck by the arm.

"What the hell is this all about?" I asked.

"I don't know what it's about," Chuck said.

Whatever the problem was, I had an idea. Whispering, I told Chuck that I was going to shove the two cops into him and then run back to Garcia's to get his help.

"Oh, hell, no," Chuck said. "They'll shoot us."

They took us to an old Bastille-like office and the next thing I knew they were frisking us. They took my pocketknife, the new shirts, and all the money I had on me. Chuck and I were taken to a cell that looked like it had been made for midgets and locked in. I was furious and protested loudly while Roberson sat down and had a smoke. In frustration, I said, "Give me one those damn cigarettes," even though I didn't smoke. But I was so frustrated by the situation, I lit one up. About that time, something rolled out from under the bunk we were sitting on. It was a drunken Mexican. When that Mexican jumped up, Chuck and I jumped up in surprise and hit our heads on the ceiling of the cell. That Mexican must have thought we were the baddest SOBs he ever saw. But what I was thinking was, *What the hell did I do to deserve this?* The place smelled of urine and vomit and Lord knows what else.

We sat there for thirty or forty minutes and I was thinking about how I had to be at work in the morning, but there I was, sober as a judge, locked up in a filthy Mexican jail. Bad Chuck was too crocked to think. Then I noticed blood on Chuck's shirt and asked him again what happened. He said a bunch of airmen from the base in Del Rio had gotten in a fight and he and some of the other stuntmen had tried to break it up. Finally, here came one of the cops and he took me out of that tiny cell. By now, the moon had come up and it was pretty late. I could see that we were in a courtyard of a police station surrounded by walls lined on the top with jagged broken glass. I was taken to a fat man who was lying on a mattress supported by two saw horses and a board. It looked like a scene out of a movie. He was the officer in charge of the jail. I told him I wasn't drunk, which when you compared me to Chuck was pretty damn obvious. He said, "Would you be willing to pay a $12 fine?" By amazing coincidence, that's exactly how much money I'd had on me when they arrested me. I paid my fine and got out of there and made it back to Garcia's. I was one mad SOB. I told Garcia to come with me to get Chuck out of jail. The jailer knew Garcia had a little pull, so they let Chuck out too. I went to La Macarena and got my car and we got the hell across that damn border. On top of taking all my money, that jailer kept my new shirts.

Back on the set the next day, they kidded me and Roberson about getting thrown in the slammer in Mexico. To this day every time someone wants to go to Mexico my mind goes back to my one and only time in jail when I hadn't done a damn thing but try to help a buddy. Needless to say, I stay the hell out of Mexico.

Wearing our Mexican lancer outfits, fourteen of us stuntmen jumped our horses into the Alamo during the filming of the final attack. We were out there about forty yards, waiting for Duke's order for the cameras to start rolling, when the prop men started hanging canteens and bedrolls on us. We didn't like that a dang bit because we didn't want anything on us that might get hung up and get our horses in a wreck. As soon as they left, it looked like a prop shop out there. We threw all that extra stuff on the ground. We did the scene in just one take, so if anybody noticed what we had done, they didn't make a fuss about it. Of course, they seldom had to redo any of the big action scenes.

Once the Mexicans made it inside the Alamo, I was in another scene where I came in for a hard landing. A bunch of us playing Mexican soldiers were supposed to jump fifteen or twenty feet off the long barracks across from the old mission when the balcony got blown off. After exploding a charge for the visual effect, they used a wire attached to a Jeep to jerk the balcony away. I came down on a shed pretty hard but got up OK. I also played one of the soldiers who crashed through the front door of the chapel toward the end of the battle.

In that movie all the major characters had to have a death scene. Crockett sent Flaca off on a mule, which was the "death" of their romance. Ken Curtis, John Ford's son-in-law, played Lieutenant Dickinson, who fell off an artillery emplacement after getting shot. Harvey as Travis broke his sword and threw it before getting killed. Widmark playing Bowie died in an interior scene, and, of course, the Duke as Davy Crockett got the biggest death scene when he blew up the powder magazine inside the chapel.

I got a little more action than I'd bargained for when we shot Chill Wills's final scene. Playing one of Crockett's Tennesseans, during the final battle he gets killed defending the wall. The script called for two Mexican soldiers to run him through with their sabers. I was supposed to charge up the stairway with a bunch of the extras dressed as Mexican infantrymen, but I also had a stunt to do. I was wearing one of those tall infantry caps, and Chill was supposed to swing at me with his rifle and knock it off before he gets stuck by the swords. Chill had a real rifle for the scene, but it had a rubber handle. He was supposed to hit me with that rubber part. Wayne hollered "Action!" and I ran up there with a sword in my hand. Somehow Chill missed me with the rubber part of that gun and hit me with the trigger guard and knocked me about half silly. A lot of times in the movies, the actors get carried away doing an action scene and

Dean and Chill Wills on the set of *The Alamo*, 1959.

Dean in character as one of Jim Bowie's men in *The Alamo*, 1959.

you can get yourself hurt. That's what happened this time. Old Chill was acting all over the place and knocked the crap out of me, leaving me dizzy. He told me he was sorry, but that didn't make my head feel any better. Thank goodness they didn't need to redo that scene. The first take made a hell of a shot.

The final battle scene, just as had been the case in 1836, pretty much ended the story. Wayne had hoped to wrap up production by Thanksgiving, but unexpected events and the weather teamed up to delay things until December. Pam and Christine stayed with me until the end of the movie, watching the filming. But much of the time Pam was really sick with allergies and asthma.

When the filming ended just before Christmas, I went to Breckenridge to see Mama. I had been making $400 a week, real good money back then, and I used some of it to buy her a new bed and mattress. I had been sending my checks to the First State Bank there in Brackettville.

It had been a wonderful, fun time, almost four months. I don't think I ever worked on a picture more exciting or better done than *The Alamo*. I was going to be in a movie about one of the most important events in Texas history and I was happy as a bird dog. Wayne did a terrific job on that picture. This wasn't just a little Western. It was a big-time production, a bigger-than-life Texas epic. Being from Texas, I was even more proud to be in the film. I also figured it would earn me recognition as a professional stuntman, making the next job a little easier to get.

The Alamo premiered at the Carthay Circle Theater, off Wilshire Boulevard in Hollywood, in March 1960. Most of the cast showed up and all my stunt friends. They had a cocktail party at the theater for the people in the crew and distribution, which United Artists handled.

Wayne told me he wanted to do a sequel to *The Alamo*, a movie about the battle of San Jacinto. Richard Boone had played Sam Houston in the Alamo, and Wayne wanted him to reprise the role in the sequel. But either he didn't get the financing or he got preoccupied with doing other pictures, because he never did that sequel. That's too bad, because it would have been a great picture.

During the making of *The Alamo* I made some wonderful new friends, including Happy and Virginia Shahan and their children; rancher Bill Moody; Rudy Robbins, a Texan who later had the Spirit of Texas band; Governor Bill Daniel; former University of Texas football player William "Bud" Conoly, and many more. I fell in love with that part of Texas and many times throughout my life would go back and visit Fort Clark, Alamo Village, and the Shahan family.

Being in *The Alamo* was one of the highlights of my career. For me, the real Alamo always will be in Brackettville, not San Antonio. The only bad thing about *The Alamo* was something I didn't give much thought to at the time: I wouldn't be getting residuals on the film.

CHAPTER 11
IN THE MONEY

hen I started getting work in Hollywood I knew I needed to get an answering service. Someone suggested I go with the service Teddy O'Toole ran, telling me that a lot of the successful stuntmen, actors, and directors used it and liked it. Most of the advice I had gotten so far had been pretty useful, so I went with Teddy. She turned out to be a wonderful and kind woman who informed me immediately of any calls so I wouldn't miss the chance to work or at least get an interview. Always in my corner, she became a good friend.

I had started my stunt work just in time to meet some of the Hollywood old-timers. When we got back to California from the Alamo movie shoot, Big Boy Williams invited me to a party at his house where I got to meet Western star Johnny Mack Brown, comedic actor Jack Oakie, and Jim Davis, who went on to play Jock Ewing in the TV series *Dallas*. John Ford had a yearly party at his ranch in Reseda. Everyone would be there, from Duke Wayne and his son Michael to Ben Johnson and Harry "Dobe" Carey, Jr., who had been in *Red River* with Duke. The party was like a big family reunion for Western actors and stuntmen. I was the last young actor or stuntman to be included in that company. It was very impressive to be around all those folks, and I felt very fortunate to be a part of it.

In the summer of 1960 actor Woodrow Wilson "Woody" Strode, who had tried out for the 1936 Olympics and played college football at UCLA and professional football before he started acting in the 1950s, called and told me John Ford wanted to see me. He and Ford had become good friends. In fact, as Ford had gotten older and more cantankerous, some people said Woody was about Ford's only friend. Woody picked me up and drove me to Ford's house on Copa De Oro Drive. We walked into the house and Woody took me to Ford's bedroom, where the old man lay in

Monty Montana, Jimmy Stewart, and Dean on the set of *Two Rode Together*, Brackettville, Texas, 1960.

bed. He still had his eye patch on, but he didn't lift it like he did when we met during the filming of *The Alamo*.

With no small talk to speak of, he asked me if I wanted to go back to Brackettville and work on a picture he would be shooting called *Two Rode Together*. Naturally, I said I sure would.

In October, just a year after we'd finished making *The Alamo*, I was back at Fort Clark, doing scenes in Brackettville, at Alamo Village, and at Bill Moody's Rancho Rio Grande. I was working again with Richard Widmark and Linda Cristal, who had both been in *The Alamo*, along with Jimmy Stewart, Shirley Jones, and Woody.

When I first arrived I saw assistant director Wingate Smith (Ford's son-in-law) drive up with Ford in the car. I was so thrilled to see Ford again

Monty Montana (leaning against wall), Dean, Red Morgan, Andy Devine, and Chuck Roberson on the set of *Two Rode Together*, 1960. (Names of two men in background right are unknown.)

that I ran up to say hello. He looked at me and asked what I was doing there.

"I'm down here because you hired me," I said.

Icily, he told me someone had seen me giving out his private telephone number to opera star Josephine Ashley and he didn't appreciate it.

"I don't know who she is and I didn't give your number out to anyone," I said.

Then I realized he was just pranking me, which he did to people he liked. To those he didn't like, he was just plain mean.

I roomed at Fort Clark with Cliff Lyons, who snored. That kept me awake for half the picture. While we were working on Moody's ranch in early November 1960, Ken Curtis drove out to tell Ford that Ward Bond had passed away of a heart attack up in Dallas. Ford sent Dobe Carey and Ken to Dallas to escort Ward's body back to California and started making plans for the funeral. Ford and Bond had been friends for more than thirty years and his death seemed to kill any interest Ford had in *Two Rode Together*. It had been raining a lot down there, so Ford shut down production in Texas and we went back to Hollywood to finish shooting at Columbia Ranch. Ford's heart clearly wasn't in it, and the movie got lukewarm reviews at best.

Next year, Cliff Lyons asked me to double Stuart Whitman and Ina Balin on the movie *Comancheros*. We did that film in the summer of 1961 on the Scoffield Ranch near Moab, Utah, on the Colorado River. Some scenes were also shot at White's Ranch, also near Moab.

The director was Michael Curtiz. He was getting quite old at that time and Duke gave him that job to try to help him out. Duke and Georgie Sherman, who had been with Duke at Republic, really directed most of the movie. Bill Clothier, who had shot *The Alamo*, was the cinematographer.

In a scene where Duke and Patrick get shot at by Indians, as Whitman's double I scissor-jump on a horse, turn the horse around, and ride fast toward a fence, which I jump. Then I ride through an alfalfa field to ask a bunch of Texas Rangers, led by actor Bruce Cabot, for help. It doesn't take long to describe that action, but it took a day or two to shoot that scene. After we shot the scene for the last time, Curtiz said to Duke, "We have to shoot it again. The boy made it look too easy." Duke looked at him like he was crazy and said, "Hell, he did a good job, print it."

Wearing a wig and other feminine attire, I doubled Ina in a scene where a burning covered wagon driven by Good Chuck Hayward came flying out of a canyon after the Comancheros had attacked it. Wayne rode in the back of the wagon with me and a dummy made up to look like the girl's father. This was the first time I'd ever doubled a woman, but there weren't many stuntwomen back then.

After we did that shot, they put Bad Chuck Roberson in the wagon to double Wayne. I was still in there next to him, sweating under that wig. In this scene, Indians in war bonnets are chasing the wagon, which is about to turn over with Bad Chuck, me, and that dummy onboard. To keep the horses from getting hurt, after crimping the wagon to help it fall, Good

Dean as an Indian doing a stunt in the *Comancheros*, c. 1961.

Chuck was supposed to release the pin holding the team and then jump. What the audience doesn't see is that wires are connected to the tall brake handle and the wagon bows. Those wires are wrapped around the saddle horns of the off riders, wranglers off camera who then veer their horses to the right to pull over the wagon. When that happened, everyone was supposed to jump out. But because of the sand we were on, we weren't going fast enough for the wagon to topple. It just went about halfway over. Of course, I didn't know the wagon wasn't going to go all the way over, so I jumped. And when I jumped, Bad Chuck jumped.

Afterward, Cliff said to Bad Chuck, "I know why Dean jumped, but why did you jump when you realized the wagon wasn't going to fall?"

"I thought Dean knew something I didn't know," Bad Chuck said.

It took an hour to set up that scene again. The next time they shot it, when they turned that SOB over, it flung me out like a cannonball and the wagon fell right on top of the dummy, like it was supposed to.

We stayed in Moab about five weeks, and while we were there, I got to be pretty good friends with Whitman. I also enjoyed the time I got to be around Cabot, who was one of Duke's real good buddies and would play a supporting role in a lot of his movies. Cabot was from Carlsbad, New Mexico, and both he and Duke used to josh me about being from Texas. To me, it only seemed natural that a Texan would be working as a Western stuntman. *The Comancheros* turned out to be the last film Curtiz made.

I had been working in Hollywood for three years before I could finally afford to buy my own stunt horse. In 1960, I purchased a beautiful sorrel mare from Dyke Johnson. I named her Crawdad, after my horse from my childhood. Since Pam and I were still living in an apartment, I kept Crawdad out at Dale Robertson's place. One day I was out there when Dale's mother came out for a visit. She saw Crawdad and said that mare sure looked like she was putting on weight. About a month went by and Dale told me, "Dean, that mare's in foal." So I took her out to Buster Matlock's place out on the road to Malibu and let her stay there until she had her foal, a colt, which I gave away.

By observing other stuntmen I learned how to teach Crawdad to fall and jump over obstacles. I did different types of mounts and dismounts on her. She was a wonderful horse and I started using her in my movie stunts. It was unusual for me to have a mare on set. Most stuntmen wanted to use a gelding, since you can't have mares around other horses when they're in heat or all the studs will come horsing around. Most horses around movie sets are geldings, but that mare was the best falling horse I ever had.

Almost all Hollywood falling horses were trained to fall to the left. First you have to train in an area that has soft dirt or sand so as not to hurt your horse. To train a horse to fall, on the left side of the head stall you build a leather ring to keep the snaffle bit from pulling through the horse's mouth. Then you take a cotton rope, tie it around the horse's left fetlock, pull its leg up, and dally the rope around the saddle horn so the horse doesn't have the advantage of getting away from you. From the ground you pull the horse's head around with the right rein over its neck. After several repetitions you mount the horse and pull its head to the right until the horse drops its head and falls over. All the while you have to keep your left leg in a position so as not to get it broken or mashed. After more repetitions and when the horse gets used to the trick, then you take the rope off its leg and stand the horse in soft sand. Back on the horse and without its leg tied up, at a standing position you pull the horse's head around fast, which makes it fall. Then you do it at a walk, next at a trot, and finally at a run. This takes patience as well as lots of repetition and practice.

When a horse falls, a stuntman has to get his feet out of the stirrups beforehand or he could get tangled up with the horse when it goes down. In leaving the saddle, the way you want to go is away from the horse's feet, since the horse will start kicking its legs to get up after it has fallen. Don't try this trick without help from someone who knows what the heck he's doing and has a wagonload of practice.

For the fall 1961 season, they decided to expand *Tales of Wells Fargo* into an hour-long show. They also started filming it in color, since that's the way TV was heading. For the longer show, Dale's character had gone from being a traveling Wells Fargo trouble-shooter to a rancher with a spread near San Francisco, which was where Wells Fargo had its headquarters. He still handled cases for the express company, but now that he had a home life, the writers had more plot possibilities. The producer also added some extra actors, including William Demarest and Jack Ging. Demarest played the manager of Dale's ranch, and Ging, who had played football for the University of Oklahoma, was Dale's sidekick. Ging and I got to be good friends.

The other idea behind adding characters was to relieve Dale of having to do so much work, but he still carried the show. Before long, however, Jack was beginning to say he should be getting more screen time. One day, Dale said, "Give me that script," and tore out the pages where Jack had lines. That's how he wrote him out of the show. The fans didn't like the changes in the show any better than Dale did, and we only shot thirty-four of the hour-long episodes before the series got canceled.

In the fall of 1961, Michael Wayne and Cliff Lyons called and said that Batjac would be making a movie called *McLintock!* in Tucson. Since there still weren't many women who did stunts, they wanted me to double Maureen O'Hara, who would be Wayne's leading lady, and Strother Martin. I didn't mind playing a woman as long as the checks were good, which they were. I went over to Max Factor's at Hollywood and Vine and got fitted for a red wig that would look like Maureen's hair. At Western Costume, on Melrose Avenue across from Paramount, I was fitted for a dress, a padded corset, and bloomers. I took plenty of kidding, but when I had that costume on, I looked voluptuous—although I sure made an ugly woman.

Most of the cast and crew stayed at the Desert Inn in Tucson. From there, we'd go over the hill to Old Tucson, a replica of a frontier town opened as a movie set in 1939. The film was shot there and at various locations in the area.

The day before the big scene where Duke, me (as Maureen), and Loren Janes (as Yvonne De Carlo) fall down some stairs, I was talking to Wayne when I happened to look down at his nicotine-stained fingers. That got me thinking about things showing up in a scene that weren't supposed to be seen.

"Duke, I'm scared that the audience will see my pink tennis shoes when we do the fall."

"Oh hell, Dean, if they see those pink tennis shoes we'll give 'em back their nickels."

I soon forgot about those pink tennis shoes, which fortunately you can't see in the movie.

Since I was stunt doubling two people I made the most money of any of the stuntmen on that movie. But I took a lot of ribbing wearing those white tights when I doubled Maureen. Bad Chuck Roberson laughed and told Good Chuck Hayward, "In those silk stockings looks like Dean has walnuts in his socks." Duke laughed along with everyone—I really did look as odd as I felt.

I think we did that scene where I doubled Maureen twice, but the fall down the stairs only took one take. We spent the rest of the day doing bits and pieces to cover the scene.

I also doubled Maureen in a scene where she fell out of a second-story window. In that scene, I hit a breakaway balcony rail and tumble backward onto a couple of mattresses covered with hay. They had to shoot that one twice. Duke also went out the window, but he didn't use a stuntman since all he had to do was jump feetfirst and land in the hay. He was pretty handy and probably could have done more of his stunts if it hadn't

Dean doubling Maureen O'Hara in *McLintock!*, c. 1961.

Dean doubling Strother Martin in *McLintock!*, c. 1961.

been so important to keep him in one piece for the next movie. And for him, as long as he was breathing, there was always going to be a next movie.

This was the first time I'd met Maureen and she was just great, one of the boys. She did a few of her own stunts, including falling off a ladder and another where she's running down the street. She was a pretty gutsy gal, always wanting to get in on the action if she could. Director Andy McLaglen didn't want her to get crippled, but she was gung-ho. When we did the big outdoor fight scene, she and Duke both went down that mud slide.

I doubled Strother Martin in that scene. The scene looks great on the screen, and really added to the movie, but it was not as fun to film as it looks. A cold, blustery norther was blowing that day and that brown goo, which was oil field drilling mud, was not pleasant to be in. On top of that, there was so much of it flying in the air that I breathed some of it in, which got my nasal passages inflamed.

Strother was a damn good actor, very intense. He had been a national swimmer and diver as a young man, so we got along fine. In the movie he played the little twerp who was always the butt end of jokes.

One day while we were filming *McLintock!* a man showed up at the set and introduced himself to me as Lee McLaughlin. He said he was from Fort Worth and his brothers were Don and Gene McLaughlin, world champion ropers. Then he asked if I remembered getting hit with an egg at Hardin-Simmons back in 1955, and when I said I did, he confessed that he had thrown it. Lee had been in the college's Cowboy Band at the time. Well, it was a little late to worry about the egg incident, so I told him I had no hard feelings. We ended up becoming good friends.

With the money I made from *Comancheros* and *McLintock!* I bought my first house in 1961 for $25,000. It was a beautiful ranch-style home, on a three-quarter-acre corner lot in Woodland Hills. With that big a lot, I was able to keep my horses there. The place was near Pierce College (where I could work out, compete in all-comers track meets, and ride my horses on their acreage) and Taft High School (where Christine would later graduate). Our neighbors were Clint Walker, Peter Breck, Chuck Connors, director Bill Whitney, and stuntmen Red Morgan and Al Wyatt. I lived there for as long as I was in Hollywood.

You couldn't make a good movie, especially a Western, without stuntmen, but there was a lot of discrimination against us. Basically, producers tried to pay us as little money as they could possibly get away with. They would try to hire you as an extra horseman so they wouldn't have to pay you the big money required by the Screen Actors Guild. If they needed you to do a stunt that day, they'd just upgrade your paycheck for that day.

Another way our trade got the short end of the stick was when studios would take a stunt from one picture and splice it into another picture. Most of the time they'd lift that footage without giving the stuntmen involved a nickel. In other words, they were taking advantage of us.

In 1961, a group of stuntmen formed the Stuntmen Association of Motion Pictures. The idea was that the association would take up grievances with producers and the Screen Actors Guild to protect our rights.

We had our organizational meeting at the Hollywood Roosevelt Hotel. I remember being there with Jock Mahoney, who played Yancy Derringer on the Western series by that name. Frank McGrath, who played Charlie Wooster, the old cook on *Wagon Train*, was another of the organizers. What a character he was. That night Frank had a few drinks, so I drove him home. I had never seen anything like what I was fixing to see. He lived in an apartment with a big hall down the middle. Frank had one side of the hall just as he wanted and his wife had the other side. He was showing me all the pictures he had of him in various Ford and Wayne movies when his wife—from her side of the apartment—started raising hell and told him to quiet down since she was trying to sleep.

We started the stuntman association with only thirty or forty members. You had to make a certain amount of money each year to qualify to be in it, and you had to qualify as a stuntman or an actor. They set up an office in Sherman Oaks. A lot of times a stuntman got hired strictly as an actor, but we had our backs covered by being in the stuntman association. One of the first important things that happened was that the association worked with the Screen Actors Guild and various ad agencies to develop a standard residual contract for us. If we hadn't chartered that stuntman association, everything I did in Hollywood might have been for just a pittance. The association was in constant negotiation on our behalf.

Not too long after we organized, the association had a party at the Ambassador Hotel. Robert "Buzz" Henry, a famous Western stuntman who had also doubled for Frank Sinatra, got Sinatra to get Dean Martin to attend the party. At one point, I went to take a leak and found myself standing at the urinal next to Dean. As we took care of business, I told him my grandmother back in Texas thought he was the best thing since Post Toasties. He said, "You tell your little grandmother I said hello."

I met so many wonderful people and made many friends in that business. I remember my good friend and fellow Texan Dan Blocker, who starred on *Bonanza*, saying to me, "Dean, I know why I have done so well: I am big and ugly. You being little and skinny, it has to be hard." Some of my other friends in the industry were Bobby Fuller, Jim Drury, Alex Cord, Bing Russell (Kurt Russell's father), Guy Mitchell, Fess Parker, L. Q. Jones, Morgan Woodward, Lee Majors, Doug McClure, Michael Landon, and many more.

Not only did I work on movies and television serials, but I did a lot of commercials as well. They were great. Every time they would run a commercial I was in, I would get a nice check. My first commercial was for Coca-Cola in 1959. I also did commercials for Kellogg's Corn Flakes and Sugar Pops, Kemper Insurance, Bell Telephone, Pabst Blue Ribbon beer, Cudahy hot dogs, and Reese's Pieces. Commercials had a longer shelf life back then and I'd make money on them for a good while.

John F. Kennedy had been elected president in 1960. During World War II, he had pulled strings to get a combat command in the South Pacific and ended up skippering a PT boat that was rammed by a Japanese destroyer. Kennedy saved all but two members of his crew and managed to keep them alive until they got rescued about a week later. In 1961 Robert J. Donovan came out with a book called *PT-109* that pretty quickly was optioned by Hollywood. In 1962, agents Pat Holmes and Mary Ann Edwards, who had contacts at Warner Bros., got me an interview and I earned a part in that film. (A former Blue Bonnet Belle member at UT, Mary Ann had a little part in the movie *Giant* but didn't make it any further as an actress and became a successful Hollywood agent instead.)

The movie version of *PT-109* starred Cliff Robertson, who played Kennedy; Ty Hardin; Bobby Blake, whom I'd met when we did *Pork Chop Hill*; and others. The FBI checked us all out before we worked on that picture since we'd be filming it so close to communist Cuba.

In June we flew from L.A. to Miami, and then rode a bus to Key West. We went across a bunch of long, thin bridges across the Florida Keys before we reached the end of the line, the southern tip of the country. They gave the cast and crew a big welcoming party there.

Most of us stayed at the Holiday Inn at Key West. I had a great room: one side looked out on the Atlantic, the other side on the Gulf of Mexico. We were only ninety miles from Cuba and at night, I'd turn on the TV and there would be that crazy Fidel Castro on Cuban television, ranting and raising hell for hours. We didn't know anything about it, but while we were there, the CIA and exiled Cubans were busy planning to invade Cuba, the fiasco that came to be called the Bay of Pigs incident.

The PT boat I operated in the movie was the one that picked up Kennedy and the other survivors after the Japanese destroyer rammed it. I played PT-159's skipper, Lieutenant Lebanow.

Partway through the filming, we had a change in directors. Lewis Milestone, a veteran director, had started, but he was not very speedy. Two months after we began filming, they released him and got Leslie Martinson, who had done the Roy Rogers TV show.

We'd go out on a barge every morning to Munson Island, then owned by Monroe County Sheriff John Spottswood. The set designers had fixed it up to look like it was in the South Pacific. First thing they had to do every morning was fumigate it, because the danged mosquitoes would eat you alive.

My part was bigger in the book than it was in the movie. When they changed directors, the new guy started cutting the script and speeding it up. I think that if Milestone had stayed on, he would have covered my part better. Anytime they cut anything, it ain't gonna be the major actor's part.

I actually drove my PT boat when we were at sea, but they wouldn't let the actors dock them. They had separate boats for the cameras. On that film I did more silent acting than stunting. The few lines I had weren't hard to remember. One of them was "Stand by to strafe the starboard side!" That was done as a process shot back in Burbank on a sound stage that had a big boat. When they're doing dialogue it's easier to shoot it at the studio than outside on location. Time is money.

One Saturday Cliff invited me to go along with him to the Miss Universe pageant in Miami. They wanted him there for the publicity, both for the pageant and the movie. It was a fun side trip. I had never seen so many pretty, long-legged girls in my life.

After we finished the filming, Ty Hardin asked me to drive his new yellow Lincoln Continental back to California for him. I jumped at the chance so I could go back through Texas for a visit. When they wrapped up, we went back to Burbank and did the interior stuff. We hadn't been back a week when the Bay of Pigs happened. Just in case that started a war, which nearly happened, the area around the Holiday Inn where we had stayed had been surrounded by troops. We'd been down there for six weeks and left just in time.

My next movie was also filmed on the sea coast, but this time it was the Pacific. *Kings of the Sun* was made in 1962 at the western Mexican seaport of Mazatlan, a beautiful location. It starred Yul Brynner and George Chakiris. Good Chuck was the stunt coordinator and called me to be a part of the film. He said we would be working barefoot and in shorts.

I did some nondescript parts, mostly a lot of fighting on a Mayan pyramid and on the beach.

Brynner was a fine dramatic actor and very good to the stuntmen. We stayed at the Hotel De Cima, a very nice place. While we were there I ran into Patrick Wayne, who was in the navy at the time. His ship had just docked there and he had shore leave. All he had to wear was his uniform, so I loaned him some clothes, which were a tight fit. We went to the Festival of the Sea celebration, something like Carnival in Rio de Janeiro.

In 1963 I was back in the desert doing *Rio Conchos* at Moab, Utah. Directed by Gordon Douglas, this movie starred Stuart Whitman, Edmond O'Brien, Tony Franciosa, Richard Boone, and Jim Brown, the great football player. Stuart wanted me to double him and got me the job.

Me being an Olympic sprinter and Jim being a big football star, everyone on the set wanted us to have a foot race. The idea was, we would wear our US Cavalry costumes and race to the chow line. I beat him the first time, hands down. The second time, he threw his arm in front of me to trip me. But I still beat him. I knew that if I had my shorts and track shoes on he would never be able to beat me in a race. Of course, I would never be able to outdo him in football.

From the *Rio Conchos* location I went to Apache Junction, Arizona, to double Dale Robertson and be the stunt coordinator for *Blood on the Arrow*. By this time in my career, I had already seen and done a lot while overcoming a lot of difficulties. But the cholla cactus there in Arizona was the most vicious cactus I had ever run across. Wranglers were always out there with pliers picking the cactus needles out of the horses' legs.

My next movie was another Western: *A Distant Trumpet* starring Troy Donahue with Richard Farnsworth doubling him. Personally, I thought Richard should have done the lead. Suzanne Pleshette; Bobby Bare, who wrote the song "I Wanna Go Home"; and Claude Akins also had roles. I doubled for Akins. This movie, directed by Raoul Walsh, was shot in Gallup, New Mexico, and Flagstaff, Arizona. The other stuntmen were Red Morgan, Bill Hart, Neil Summers, and Erwin Neal.

While we were working around Gallup, all the horses got sick with influenza. I thought I was going to lose Crawdad, my wonderful falling horse. They gave the horses lots of medicine and after three weeks several survived, including Crawdad.

Stuntmen Bear Hudkins, Joe Lomax, and Buddy Sherwood, along

with wrangler Ace Hudkins and others wanted me to run a race with one of the local cowboys who was working on the movie. By this time, I knew better than to go to a shoot without my shorts and track shoes, but I never took part in the betting or accepted a kickback. Even though this particular cowboy had a reputation of being fast, the stuntmen knew the guy didn't have a chance against me with my prior experience as a sprinter. Just like the stuntmen figured, all the cowboy's buddies bet a lot of money on him. Of course, they kept quiet about my background so as to not spoil their winnings. I won and the stuntmen collected a good pile of cash.

A few days later we were doing a fight scene with a few of the local cowboys, including the big strapping kid I had beaten in the race. He came in and took me to the ground and was quite rough. I didn't say a word. I always wondered if the boy had any suspicion he and his friends had been set up.

Later the production crew moved to Flagstaff, where we did the movie's Indian battles. One day old man Walsh came over and had someone with the makeup department darken my teeth. He said the audience wouldn't be able to see Troy because my teeth were so white and bright. He said they took the attention off the actor and were a distraction. That was a new one on me, but I went along with it.

While we were in Arizona, John Ford visited the set. He told me he was scouting locations for his next movie. Not long after that, in 1964, I got a call from Wingate Smith, who said Ford wanted me to double Ben Johnson in *Cheyenne Autumn*. Turned out a trailer hitch had dropped on Ben's foot and broken it. Other than Ben, the cast included Dobe Carey, Richard Widmark, Jimmy Stewart, Carroll Baker, Ricardo Montalban, Patrick Wayne, Victor Jory, Dolores del Rio, and Sal Mineo. The stuntmen were Jackie Williams, Richard Farnsworth, Bear Hudkins, Jerry Gatlin, LeRoy Johnson, and three Indian actors, Many Mules and the Stanley Brothers.

This was my first time to work at Monument Valley, which is where Ford had filmed *Rio Grande* and *She Wore a Yellow Ribbon*. We lived in trailers and met in a large circus tent for meals. Those red buttes and beautiful sunsets were breathtaking. Ford and the other directors of that generation had a great eye for how magnificent the landscape would look on film. In a sense they were artists, never even using a monitor to look at a scene that had just been shot.

I was proud to work for Ford and never took my time when he asked me to do something. One time Ford told me to go get Ben Johnson's costume on. When I started to run toward wardrobe, Luster Bayless, who owned American Costume Company, said, "Just slow down, Dean. I can't get there before you, so take your time."

Much of the time on that film we were working in sand midway up to our knees. Ford asked me if I could run and do one of my scissor mounts behind Dobe on his horse. I told him I could but that I needed the set dressers to put down some plywood in that sand to give me better purchase. This was for a scene where Dobe and Ben are riding in a canyon and Sal's character shoots Ben's horse out from under him. When that happens, Dobe turns his horse around and, doubling Ben, I do a scissor mount on the horse up behind Dobe. After we got that far, we ran our horses fast through those sand dunes and I did a flying dismount and walked right up to Widmark and saluted him. Ford loved it, and I knew I had scored points with him again. But that turned out to be the last movie I ever did for Ford.

CHAPTER 12

BACK TO TV AND MORE WESTERNS

One day in 1965 I was home painting my bathroom when the doorbell rang. It was Bob Culp, whom I'd met when we worked on *PT 109*. He said they were fixing to do a new television series called *I Spy* with him and a new unknown actor, Bill Cosby. He said he wanted me as his double. Before I could say yes, he asked me if I knew how to do karate. I said, "What is that?" He told me it was a form of martial arts and that I needed to know how to do that to double him. Bob said he wanted me to go to a gym in Santa Monica run by a fellow named Earl Parker and learn karate, and that's what I did.

When I got acquainted with Cosby I found out he had attended Temple University and played football. He introduced me to Cicely Tyson, a beautiful lady who could really act. We were always kidding around with each other. One day I had to do a flat-foot standing jump. Cosby wanted to be in the scene, but when it came to jumping, he couldn't outdo me.

I Spy was the first TV series to have a black costar and became very popular. It was also the first time Hollywood used the buddy system in a television show, a formula that stayed popular for years after that. My only problem with *I Spy* was that I wasn't getting paid as much as I thought I should have been, even though I was in demand at the time and working regularly. At least I got some free karate lessons.

Also in 1965, stuntman Dick Crockett offered me a job on *The Great Race*, which Blake Edwards directed. The movie starred Tony Curtis, Natalie Wood, Jack Lemmon, Keenan Wynn, and others, a large cast and crew. We shot it at Warner Bros.

The highlight of *The Great Race* was taking part in the largest Western fight scene ever done. It involved about a hundred stunt people. For three weeks we worked on this saloon scene, throwing punches that looked real but didn't connect, crashing fake bottles over people's heads, falling off balconies or out of windows. It was a lot of fun to shoot, and it looked pretty convincing on the big screen.

I had first met Natalie and Lana Wood at the Pickwick Saddle Shop on Riverside Drive in L.A. They were prettier than two speckled pups, very nice, and I really liked them. During the filming my friend Good Chuck Hayward had to rescue Natalie on horseback. She was wearing black tights that showed her great figure. Chuck was so excited I thought he was going to fall off his horse. A few years later, Natalie and Lana wanted me to try out for the part that John Voight had in *Midnight Cowboy*, which turned out to be a very successful film. But I didn't want to portray a character like that and didn't try for it.

I was tuned in to *Gunsmoke* one night and saw a young actor named Alex Cord on the show. As I watched him, it occurred to me that I would make a good double for him. A few days later I heard that Alex would be starring in a remake of the 1939 John Ford classic *Stagecoach*. John Wayne had played the Ringo Kid in that movie, the role that made him a big star. Yakima Canutt, the greatest stuntman of all time, had doubled Wayne in the original. This time around, I wanted to be the one doubling the Ringo Kid.

The 1965 remake for Fox Films was produced by Marty Rackin and directed by Gordon Douglas, who had also directed *Rio Conchos*. The stunt coordinator was Dick Hudkins. In addition to Cord, the cast included Bing Crosby, Stephanie Powers, Ann-Margret, Red Buttons, Van Heflin, Mike Connors, Slim Pickens, and Bob Cummings.

By this time, I had been in the business eight years and had begun to get a pretty good reputation, but I wasn't in Douglas's or Hudkins's camp. I was missing working in Westerns, so I contacted the producer. Well, the guy was a real horse's ass, not to mention cheap. He was interested in me, but wanted me to work for less than Guild wages. Being taken advantage of was something I did not approve of, so I went to Fox Studios to find Alex Cord. I happened to be in the commissary and ran into him on the way out. I told him I wanted the chance to double him. I think he thought I was crazy as hell for believing I could do one of the most difficult stunts in Western filmmaking. But he didn't have a stuntman yet and said he would say something to Rackin and Douglas. When Alex told Marty, Mar-

Dean on the cover of *Parade* magazine. Picture taken in Colorado
on the set of the remake of the movie *Stagecoach*, where
Dean stunt doubled Alex Cord, January 1966.

ty said he had heard good things about me. But word that I was interested
in the job was not received as well by Douglas or Dick Hudkins. I had
gone over their heads. A lot of stuntmen wanted to do this picture, but
thanks to Alex I got the job. I left *I Spy* to go to work on *Stagecoach* for
more money.

Not only would I be better paid, but I would also get a chance to re-
create one of the most famous Western scenes ever filmed, the stagecoach
stunt that Canutt did in the original movie. I was proud to be the stuntman picked to do the scene, but it put me under a lot of pressure. For one
thing, I didn't want to mess it up, especially since I was working for a di-

rector and assistant director who hadn't been all that thrilled that I'd gotten the job doubling Cord. On top of that, I didn't want to get hurt or killed. To make things even harder, we were working at Caribou Ranch up above Boulder, Colorado, at about 7,500 feet. A bulldozer had made a path for the stagecoach and the camera car through this thick forest, and I would have only so much time to do the stunt before we ran out of road, though it wasn't much of a road to start with. If that happened we would have to do a retake. Directors didn't like retakes, because they cost money.

The original movie had been filmed in Monument Valley, Utah, and on the desert flats at Lucerne Lake in California. Ford had picked the flats so he would have a smooth, hard surface for the stagecoach and horses and for the big stunt scene by Canutt, who was with Duke on most of his early movies. Canutt had pioneered the use of mechanics in stunt work. That made the business safer and I am forever grateful to him for that.

When I found out I had the job, I went to my friend and mentor Cliff Lyons at Batjac Productions. He was always wonderful to me. I visited with him and asked how to rig the mechanics for the big stunt, which was to stop a runaway stagecoach. Cliff told me to get spreader bars to put in between each of the paired horses so they would be a little farther apart. Once I did that, I wired up the straps on the collars and hames (the curved supports attached to the collars) so they would not snap under my weight, which would not be a good thing to have happen.

When it came time to do the stunt, I did a final inspection, got inside the stagecoach, and said a little prayer as one of the wranglers got the six horses running. With the stagecoach rolling at top speed with a bunch of Indians chasing us, I climbed out on the top. Then I jumped down between the first two horses, known as the wheel horses. After I landed on the spreader bar between the horses, I jumped out to the next two horses, the swing team. To do that, I had to cover a very dangerous dead space between each set of horses to get to the next spreader bar. As I left the swing team for the lead horses, I grabbed the mane of one of the swing team horses and, with my foot on the spreader bar for purchase, I threw myself forward and jumped high so as not to catch my foot on the reins. The shot ended when I got control of the lead horses and brought the stagecoach to a stop.

I did the stunt in one take. I guess all the time I'd spent running the

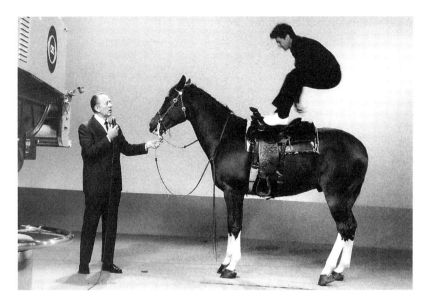

Dean jumping up on Sox on live TV during the
Art Linkletter television show, 1960s.

100-meter dash and rodeoing had helped keep me in pretty good shape. My adrenaline was flowing like a blown-out oil well. It was one hell of a thrill. The Lord was in my corner looking after me, but by planning things out beforehand, I had made my own luck. I'll never forget the expression on everyone's face after it was over. When I did that stunt successfully, the director and stunt coordinator finally realized that Alex Cord had picked the right guy as his double.

One of my favorite memories from this production was meeting the artist Norman Rockwell. He asked me to model for him, having me do all kinds of things like throwing lances and riding horseback. His little wife was with him and she never left his side.

When we broke for lunch one day, the Indian actors on the film went down the hill to a beer joint. They got drunk and couldn't work. That changed the schedule around and I got to spend the afternoon visiting with Bing Crosby. He was a very nice man and never acted like a big star. It seemed like we talked about everything, from show business to politics. He was married to Kathy Grandstaff, who had been a freshman at the University of Texas in 1950, the same year I started there. She was thirty years younger than Bing, but they had three children together and stayed married until he died.

As a small perk of doing these big-name movies, I was invited on *Art Linkletter's House Party* twice during the 1960s. The show ran thirty minutes after lunch on weekdays. On my first appearance I asked if there was anyone in the audience who wanted to do a stunt fight. I picked a woman and when she came up I explained how we were going to do the fight routine. She flipped me over her shoulders and then I got up and knocked her over the table. We finished and it was a great scene. Of course, she was a ringer, stuntwoman Sharon Lucas. I later learned that as she had gone over the table, she had hit her shoulder on its leg and broken her shoulder. She never gave any indication on stage, though it must have hurt like hell. She was a true stuntwoman.

For my second appearance with Linkletter I was his first guest, followed by Lena Horne. It was a treat to meet a classy, talented lady like her. After the show, while still at the studio, the famous Hollywood columnist Hedda Hopper came up to me. She complimented me on how I had worked my horse on the show, and added, "I don't know why you are not doing leading parts in movies." That sure put a smile on my face. Her next article reported what she had said to me and how she felt. I still have that article in my scrapbook.

I had a great year in 1965. Out of the blue I got a call to be in *In Harm's Way*, directed by Otto Preminger and starring John Wayne, Kirk Douglas, and Patricia Neal. It was a black-and-white film about Pearl Harbor shot in Hawaii. The cast, including Wayne, stayed at the new Ilikai Hotel, the first luxury high-rise hotel on Waikiki Beach. They weren't even finished with it yet.

Stuntman Hal Needham and I would be doing a fight scene with Kirk Douglas. We were told by fellow stuntmen that Kirk was notorious for nailing stuntmen with his punches. Knowing that, I told myself I'd watch him and give him plenty of room. But neither Hal nor I got hit by Kirk, no matter how real our fight looked in the movie. He was great to work with.

This was my second time in Hawaii. When I was in the service back in 1956 I ran in a track meet at Punahou School, a prep school on a large campus in Honolulu. When I first found out about *In Harm's Way*, I was with Mama, who was hospitalized at Breckenridge. She had been having a lot of pain in her hip, but the doctor said she would be all right, so I went on to the location. They ended up replacing her hip and she did fine.

In 1966 we did the pilot for the series *The Iron Horse*. Dale Robertson had been doing the TV show *Death Valley Days* for quite a number of episodes after Robert Taylor had died. Then Columbia asked Dale to do a series about a flamboyant gambler turned railroad man. The part was made for Dale. The show also starred Gary Collins, Roger Torrey, and Bobby Random. Earl Bellamy, a truly kind man who had become a good friend, directed the show.

We shot forty-seven one-hour shows, but Dale was disappointed in the production. For instance, they had put rubber tires on one of the trains they used and ran it all around the Columbia set. Having a train that wasn't on rails just didn't seem right for a show about trains. We did go on location a couple of times to Sonora, which is where we should have been working all along. In one scene where I doubled Strother Martin, I ran seven black horses down chasing that narrow gauge train at Sonora before we got it right.

While we were doing *The Iron Horse*, Dale, Jimmy Durante, myself, and several others spent a day at the Ambassador Hotel raising money to benefit Armenian refugees. When the event was over, Dale asked me to take Jimmy back home to Beverly Hills. As I drove down Wilshire Boulevard, Jimmy said, "Are you hungry, Dean?" When I said I was, he said, "Let's stop at the Brown Derby." In the restaurant he said, "I'm going to have a Cobb salad, Dean. It's real good; you oughta try one." After that I ate a lot of Cobb salads at the Brown Derby until one by one they closed all the locations.

Thanks in part to *The Iron Horse*, I was able to buy from Rex Allen my second movie horse, a gelding sorrel with white-stocking legs that I named Sox. He had a lame front left hoof, but as long as he had some medication he worked great. I made more money off him than any other horse I ever had.

While still working on *The Iron Horse*, I read in the *Daily Variety* that Howard Hawks would be doing a movie called *El Dorado* with Duke, Bob Mitchum, and James Caan. I wasn't able to get an interview, so I went to Paramount and slipped into Hawks's office right before lunch. I told him how much I wanted to work on the picture. He said he would test me for the part of Charlie Hagan. I landed the role and beat out some pretty good actors, playing opposite of Caan. I got killed off early in the story, but it was a fun picture and brought me lots of recognition.

Not long after *El Dorado* hit the theaters, I was on a one-hour nighttime show Art Linkletter did called *Talent Scout*. The show featured guests who wanted to become actors, and they wanted me to stage a fight scene. I got to hire ten stuntmen, including my friends Chuck Roberson, Bill Hart, Chuck Hayward, and Red Morgan. The show opened with me being thrown out a fake saloon window. Then Art introduced me and we did the fight scene in the saloon set. They ended the segment with the clip of me being killed by James Caan in *El Dorado*. If it hadn't been for Howard Hawks and that part in *El Dorado*, I wouldn't have gotten that much exposure. I'll say it again: Hawks was one of the nicest men I've ever met.

Otto Preminger, on the other hand, was a little unusual and would intimidate you if you let him. The second time I worked for him, they called me to Baton Rouge, Louisiana, to set up a fight scene on the movie *Hurry Sundown*. I had to hurry, too, since I had only a week before I had to get back to work on *The Iron Horse*. I took stuntman Bill Hart with me. The movie starred Jane Fonda, John Phillip Law, Faye Dunaway, and Michael Caine. Faye Dunaway's room was across from mine.

The script had the two characters Bill and I played starting to fight near a Confederate monument. They didn't have all the stunt people they needed for the scene and we had to work with the actors. I was supposed to whip Bill and then run fifty yards to Faye Dunaway while she and Phillip Law were having a squabble in front of the courthouse. Law was supposed to throw a punch at me. Each time I made that run, I would get there, Law would take that punch, but he would fail to make it look like it had connected. A fake punch is routine stuntman stuff, but he was an actor and just couldn't execute it. We did that scene twenty times before he got it right, and it was hotter than hell on the set. At one point, Dunaway said, "Oh, Mr. Preminger, I'm so hot I feel like I'm going to faint." He said, "Oh hell, go ahead and faint." Eventually we finished and I made it back to *The Iron Horse* on time.

Also in 1966 I was in *Camelot*, which starred Richard Harris and Julie Andrews. We did a lot of click-clacking on stage at Warner Bros. During one sword scene, stuntman Jimmy Sheppard hit me right on my knuckle and split it open. They took me to the hospital in Burbank where a doctor sewed it up and gave me a penicillin shot. I went home and started breaking out on my chest from an allergic reaction to that shot. We went back to the emergency room and I had to be treated for that. My knuckle didn't heal well and I had a problem with it for a good while after that.

In 1967 Dale Robertson had a great little black horse named Joe Thunderbird, and Dale told me I could have him. (Dale knew Jim Wells who owned the Thunderbird Hotel on the Las Vegas strip, and he named the horse after that.) I renamed the horse Choya and trained him to do several stunts. He could lie down, do a fall, and jump like a deer. One of my greatest horses, he later doubled in *The Black Stallion*. Twenty-one years after I got him, when he started having back trouble, I sent him home to my ranch in Texas. He lived a couple of years longer and we buried him on the ranch.

The same year I got Choya, I started a stunt job on the *Scalphunters*, a film directed by Sydney Pollack and starring Burt Lancaster, Dabney Coleman, Ossie Davis, Telly Savalas, and Shelley Winters. Tony Epper, who doubled Lancaster, recommended me for that job. The other stuntmen were Bad Chuck Roberson, Tom Sweet, Jack Williams, and Joe Canutt. We went to Torreón, Mexico, on location. I was still having trouble with my knuckle, but my doctor said I could work as long as I put a condom on my finger. I doubled Coleman, a former student at the University of Texas.

My stunt was to be in a stagnated pool of water holding ten wild mustangs. The script had the horses eating loco weed and going berserk at a water hole. I was holding these scrawny mustangs in that nasty water, which was real, and the wrangler came by and squirted an irritant all over their backs and legs. That stuff took effect pretty quickly and those horses started rearing and pawing and going crazy with me hanging on.

While in Torreón I had a pleasant surprise, running into James Garner at the marketplace. He was there making another Western. I also took in some bullfights while I was there. That was an experience. When a bull gored a horse they would stop the fight, poke his entrails back in, sew him up, get on him, and head back to the fight. When it was time to leave Mexico, Shelley Winters sat next to me on the plane and we had a good visit on the long flight back to California. She talked like a sailor—I don't think her mother ever washed her mouth out with soap when she was little.

After *The Iron Horse* had been dropped in 1967, Don Murray (who had done *Bus Stop* with Marilyn Monroe) came to see me about doubling him and doing the stunt coordinating on a TV series called *The Outcasts*, a Western about an integrated bounty hunter team. Don would be costarring with Otis Young, a black actor. I went to the studio to meet production personnel and decided to take on the job.

Back then, there weren't any black stuntmen, but I had to get some doubles for Otis. I had a casting call at Columbia for black men wanting to do stunts. I got them to demonstrate their athletic talent and finally hired Wayne King to do the fight scenes for Otis. I sent him to a gym run by stuntman Paul Stader to learn to do movie fights. For the horseback scenes, I hired Eugene Smith, a former rodeo steer wrestler. Both men did a good job.

One day, we had just finished shooting a chase scene where I was doubling Don and Eugene was doubling Otis when I got called to the office to see the editors. One of them said, "Why is Eugene holding his arm out? It looks like he's waving a lantern." I explained that he'd been a steer wrestler, where he'd have his arm stuck out to grab the horns. I had to go back to Eugene and coach him to bring in his arms when he did a running scene. He was a quick learner and stopped doing that.

On another episode, the script called for Otis's character to fall from his horse. Good as he was on a horse, in that short time Eugene didn't have enough experience for that stunt. So since I was responsible for making the stunts look good, as well as keeping the other stuntmen from getting hurt, I decided to cover the horse fall for Otis. I had the makeup department darken my face and give me a wig, and I used my horse Choya to do the stunt.

I don't know who snitched me off, but the NAACP came out and raised hell about me doing the horse fall instead of Eugene. I told them I didn't know what the problem was and explained that Eugene was not qualified to do the stunt and that I hadn't wanted him to get hurt. I explained why I had done what I did and they accepted that. It blew over without making the newspapers. I was one of the first stunt coordinators to get men of color in the stunt business. In fact, while doing *The Outcasts*

I was the one who hired O. J. Simpson and other USC football players to work in the background as settlers. That was the beginning of O.J.'s Hollywood career.

After a few episodes, the production company started trying to get me to work cheaper. They were even pushing me to get the black stuntmen to work for less than the whites. I said no and told that production guy to take that job and shove it. I wouldn't work cheap and I wasn't going to screw black stuntmen out of money. If someone is working for me, I want them to get paid for what they did. *The Outcasts* lasted that season and part of the next before getting canceled, but I was long gone by then.

In 1968 I got to work with Elvis Presley in *Charro!* Of Elvis's thirty-one movies, this was his only non-singing, dramatic role and he turned out to be pretty good at it. It was also the only time he wore a beard, even if it was mostly just a five o'clock shadow. They filmed it at Apache Junction, Arizona. Other than Elvis, the movie starred Ina Balin, whom I'd doubled before, Lynn Kellogg, and Victor French, whose dad was an old cowboy actor in the movie business in the 1930s and '40s. The cast and crew stayed at Superstition Inn there at Apache Junction.

Though Elvis had been a heck of a lot more successful than me when it came to making money, we were almost the same age and got along fine. I had some good visits with him and Colonel Tom Parker, his manager. In fact, all the stuntmen had good camaraderie with the cast and crew.

One day I was in my trailer and had just taken off my britches to change into my costume when Elvis threw a string of lighted firecrackers inside and shut the door. He and all his friends were outside laughing their asses off when I came out. My ears rang for a while, but we all got a big kick out of it. He was a prankster and liked to have fun. I enjoyed working with him, but the production company was a little too cheap for me.

This was one of many low-budget pictures that Elvis did, everyone working for hardly anything. I was a professional stuntman going by SAG rules, but there was a production man who was trying to cheat all the younger cowboys money-wise. He was not doing the right thing and I told him I'd better head for home. I was not going to risk my neck for that kind of money. SAG raised hell and the guy, who was notoriously deceitful, was fired and never worked again.

I was having a little trouble with my leg during that shoot. The guy who would work on my leg also worked on Cyd Charisse, a famous dancer. He worked on her, then on me. She just happened to be in Arizona taking it easy. When I got a chance to talk to her, I told her I was a Texas boy and she said she was raised in Amarillo, but didn't stay too long. She was sure a pretty woman and talented, too.

Elvis, a real Southern gentleman, was down to earth and just one of the boys. About the time I was getting started in Hollywood in 1957, Elvis was traveling from gig to gig with his band. He made one of his stops in Breckenridge, where he played at the auditorium. He even had a date with a local girl, and people still talk about it.

I first met Colonel Parker when I was down in Palm Springs staying at a spa, taking a break. He was a grand old fellow who could sell ice cream to an Eskimo. I was in the steam room and started carrying on a conversation with this heavy-set guy. Turned out he was the colonel. Later, I got to spend some more time with him when he came to visit my next-door neighbors in California, Hugh and Barbara Gibb, parents of the three Bee Gees. While we were there, Parker got up to do something, went two or three steps, and slipped. Luckily, I was fast enough to grab him before his head hit the floor.

In midsummer of 1968, George Roy Hill started work on *Butch Cassidy and the Sundance Kid*, starring Robert Redford, Paul Newman, and Katharine Ross. Jim Arnett, a good stuntman friend who was stunt coordinator and would be doubling Paul Newman on the movie, called and wanted me to go with him to scout locations for the movie. When they started shooting, I would double Redford. We flew from L.A. to Denver and then drove to Durango. I read the script on the plane and considered it the best script I had ever read. We rode on the narrow gauge train in Durango, visiting Silverton and several other locations up there in the mountains looking for good places to shoot. After that I went home and they paid me for my time. It was a month before production and I thought they should have kept me on salary, but they didn't. They ended up shooting at most of the locations Jim and I picked.

That fall I went with Dale Robertson to San Antonio where he would be making an appearance at Hemisfair. When I called my answering service after we got off the plane I found out that Henry Hathaway was trying to reach me. As soon as I could get him on the phone, he told me he was making a movie called *True Grit* with Wayne, Glen Campbell, Robert Duvall, and Kim Darby. Henry offered me the job of doubling Bob Duvall and said he would give me a part as well.

I already had the job on *Butch Cassidy and the Sundance Kid*, so it was a hard decision to make. Both projects were tempting. But Duke was a bigger star than Redford, plus he was like family. I finally decided I'd be better off with the old crew. Financially, that turned out to be a bad decision. The stuntman they hired to double Redford instead of me made $20,000 while I only got $5,000 for my work on *True Grit*. The acting part I got was as a telegrapher, but you only see my back as I tell Kim Darby which train leaves and when.

We filmed *True Grit* in Montrose, Telluride, and Durango in Colorado and in Bishop, California, up above Mammoth. The locations had the prettiest country I've seen, and seeing the changing colors of the aspens in the mountains of Colorado was breathtaking.

Hathaway was an old, crotchety fellow but a good director. On one occasion he was hammering on Duvall on this one certain scene. Bob blew up and told him, "I can't do the scene like Martha Graham you old ——!" I looked at Duke and never had seen him speechless before. Hathaway just sat there and took it, but he eased up on Duvall. Bob is a fine actor and a good friend.

I enjoyed working with all the cast and crew, especially Duke. In the evenings, he and I watched the 1968 Olympics on TV in his room. One morning, as I went to the Red Barn for breakfast, it looked as if the army had descended on Colorado. It was deer season and the Texans had come to hunt. I have never seen so many trucks and Jeeps in all my life.

My next movie job was in 1969 on *Stalking Moon*. The film starred Gregory Peck, Eva Marie Saint, and Robert Forster, whom I doubled. The stuntmen I worked with were Richard Farnsworth, Red Morgan (I used Red's falling horse Chips in the movie), Jerry Willis, and Buddy Van Horn, who doubled Peck. We worked on location at Valley of the Fire, an area of beautiful rock formations north of Las Vegas. We stayed at Echo Bay. It was a great pleasure to double Robert and we became friends.

Not much later, I was asked to double John McMartin in *Sweet Charity*, a film directed by Bob Fosse and starring Shirley MacLaine, Paula Kelly, and Chita Rivera. My biggest stunt came in a scene where Shirley is on the railing of a bridge, looking like she is about to jump. On cue, I run over to save her. But at the last moment, she moves and I go over the railing and fall twenty feet to the water below.

One day during the filming, Chita said to me, "You got a great set of legs, kid." All three of those women in that movie were dancers and had great sets of legs themselves.

I was also in *The Legend of Nigger Charley*, starring Fred "The Hammer" Williamson, who had been a star defensive player for the Kansas City Chiefs. They shot that movie in Santa Fe, New Mexico, on the J. W. Eaves Ranch. We did a lot of stunts, including one shot of me running my horse and getting jerked off it with a cable. There was a guy already on the ground whom I was supposed to jump my horse over, but when I did, the horse stepped on his head and broke his nose. They only needed me on location for about two weeks. The movie did really well at the box office when it came out in early 1972. When it ran later on TV, they changed the name to *The Legend of Black Charley*.

In the summer and fall of 1969 I worked as a stuntman during the filming of *Little Big Man* in the rolling hills of Montana. The movie—part drama, part comedy—starred Dustin Hoffman as Jack Crabb, a man who was around when George Armstrong Custer and his men were massacred in 1876 and lived on to be 121. They kept it quiet, but at one point during that production some of us stuntmen ended up in a real cowboys-and-Indians fight. They used local Lakotas as extras on that picture, most of them teenage boys. The prop department had issued these young Indians authentic-looking bows and arrows, but the arrows had rubber tips. Teenagers being teenagers, the Indians started harassing me and some of the other stuntmen in US Cavalry uniforms, circling us on their horses and shooting those rubber-tipped arrows at us. They were just having fun, but it got more serious when they started breaking the rubber tips off their arrows. To protect ourselves, we started shooting the bellies of their horses with blanks. When a wad hit a horse, the horse would start bucking, and usually the rider got thrown off. Unfortunately, one of those jagged-ended arrows caught my friend and fellow stuntman Gary Combs in the face, taking out one of his eyes. Roydon Clark and I were the first to ride up and help him until they could get him to a hospital. Gary never let that incident get him down. He went on to become a successful stunt coordinator.

In 1969 Paul Helmick, associate producer to Howard Hawks, called and told me they were doing *The Cheyenne Social Club*, a movie directed by Gene Kelly, the dancer. This was the first and only Western that Kelly ever directed. The actors on that production were Jimmy Stewart, Henry Fonda, Shirley Jones, Sue Ann Langdon (a Texas girl), and a cast of lovely ladies who played the girls working at the brothel inherited by Stewart's character. Paul offered me a part playing one of the Bannister gang.

We did the filming on the Eaves Ranch. In the movie, the character Jimmy Stewart plays inherits a "social club" from his brother. He and Henry Fonda move from Texas to Wyoming to run the club, not knowing it's a whorehouse. When things get heated after Stewart says he is going to get rid of the club, Fonda's character decides to ride off. That's when he runs into the outlaw Bannister boys. Stewart's character had killed one of their brothers and they had come back for revenge. I play the only Bannister who makes it into the bordello to try and shoot Stewart's character. But before I can, Shirley Jones shoots me.

As always, I seemed to bring out the gambling in the wranglers. They bet that I could not outrun the cattle and get to the bordello before the cattle ran across the front. I won.

It was great to get to work with Stewart and Fonda on this film. And I got a kick out of watching them together. Both were always cracking jokes. Although Fonda was liberal and Stewart was conservative, their friendship of many years never suffered from that.

I liked acting, and as I got older, I hoped I'd get to do more of it. One time when we were on location I was talking to Fonda and asked him something that had been on my mind.

"When you act, Mr. Fonda, do you get nervous when doing your lines or have you done it so much that you never get nervous?"

"Dean," he said, "I want to tell you something. No matter how many pictures I've done, I would still be nervous. It's the unknown until you get comfortable."

CHAPTER 13

DOUBLING THE KING OF THE COWBOYS

In 1970 I was thirty-eight and still competing in track meets. At an all-comers track meet at Pierce College, I ran against a sixteen-year-old named Ron Gaddis. He was an All-State quarter-miler at San Fernando Valley High School. The young man didn't realize I still had plenty of gas in my tank and it took him by surprise when I beat him. We went on to become close friends. Ron helped me stay in shape while I was running in those senior track meets. We're still friends, though he has been more like a son to me than a friend.

My first movie of the new decade was John Wayne's *Rio Lobo*, which we shot in the beautiful city of Cuernavaca, Mexico, and at Old Tucson in Arizona. Aside from the scenery, they chose Cuernavaca because a narrow gauge railroad operated out of there. Howard Hawks directed the film, which turned out to be his last. Wayne's costar was Chris Mitchum, actor Robert Mitchum's second son. I was up for one of the leading roles, but I didn't get it. Hawks called me in and said he wanted me to teach Chris to talk like a Texan. For every line Chris had, I had one, too. My character, a young Confederate named Bide who wore a stovepipe hat, was not in the original script but Hawks had it written in for me.

Hawks loved tall, long-legged, beautiful women. For *Rio Lobo* he had models Jennifer O'Neill and Sherry Lansing (who later became head of Paramount Pictures). Other actors in that movie were Mike Henry of Lodi, California (he had been a linebacker for the L.A. Rams in the late 1960s and had also played one of the Tarzans); Jorge Rivero ("Mr. Mexico"); Jack Elam; and Victor French.

Yakima Canutt directed the second unit. The stuntmen I worked with on that film were Bad Chuck Roberson, who doubled Duke, Joe and Tap Canutt, Mickey Gilbert, and Terry Leonard. A country boy from Wiscon-

Dean as the character Bide, listening for the train in the movie *Rio Lobo*, 1970.

sin, Leonard went on to become one of the top second unit directors and directors in the business. He was stunt coordinator for *Apocalypse Now*. I had given him some of his first work, and we've stayed good friends all these years.

Working under Canutt, I did a lot of train scenes—either chasing them or jumping out of them. I doubled Mitchum and Rivero. In one scene, we were working in a mine shaft not far from downtown Cuernavaca. While we were there, a woman who lived in a cabin near the mine entrance lost a child at birth. Duke was very gracious about it and the company took up a collection for her family.

A jockey and stuntman named Danny Sands, who had once worked for my cousin Silas Hill back in Texas, had a bit part in the movie. One of his lines, which I still remember better than he did, was, "Hey, you in the jail, got a message for you." I bet they did fifteen takes on that SOB before Danny got it right. We all loved working with Danny, and Hawks always gave him work.

Cuernavaca had a great night life to offer—live bands and good food, especially at Las Maginitas. It was a beautiful place, with flamingos walking all around. We ate there every night. The food was excellent, and we were comfortable that it was safely prepared. No one in the company wanted to get sick, since that would mean lost production time. While we ate, Hawks would talk about his long career. He had worked with Duke and Montgomery Clift in *Red River* and Gary Cooper in *Sergeant York*.

One night Terry Leonard and I ate at this real fancy nightclub and restaurant that had a big copy of the Venus de Milo in the courtyard. As usual when we were out and about, I was the more sober member of our party. I could have a drink or two and have as much fun as those who had a dozen drinks. Well, after a few more drinks, Terry, feeling really good, grabbed that topless gal on the pedestal and was pretending to dance with her. Unfortunately, she came off her base and broke in half in Terry's arms. Terry had spent some pleasant time with the señorita who managed the place and needless to say lost that friendship over that broken piece of art.

We wrapped up in Mexico after about a month and went to Tucson for the rest of the shooting. During the filming around Cuernavaca, I had been real careful about what I ate and drank and had no problems. Not thinking anything about it, I had a Mexican Coke in the lounge at the airport before we left, and not long after we arrived in Arizona I got sick. I guess the ice in it had been made with bad water. I was rooming with Terry. While on the commode, I was throwing up in the trash can. They finally took me to St. Mary's Hospital, but they weren't able to do anything to make me feel any better. The next morning Chris Mitchum came to me and said to go with him. His dad thought he had something that could give me some relief. Bob gave me some Lomotil pills and within a couple of days I was back in action, jumping over fences and doing some really good stunts. After that, I never went anywhere without some Lomotil in my suitcase.

George Plimpton had a small bad-guy part in *Rio Lobo* while doing research on how to be a cowboy actor for a TV documentary called *Shoot-*

out at Rio Lobo. My job, working with stuntman Mike Henry, was to show George how to jump on a horse, spin a six-gun, and shoot. The hourlong special turned out really good. It aired on ABC on December 9, 1970, about a week before the movie premiered.

One night Terry, a couple of film editors, and I went bar-crawling in Terry's Lincoln Continental convertible. I was the designated driver, but even though I was supposed to be the sober guy, Terry kept trying to get me drunk on Black Russians. It wasn't working, but Terry always thought it would be funny to get me tight. After four or five different stops we ended up at a saloon called the Dunes. It looked pretty rough from the outside, but I was the only one sober enough to notice or care. Terry and the other boys started playing pool while I went to the restroom. As I walked back to the pool table, all of a sudden some fellow hit Terry over the head with a pool stick and the wreck was on. Everyone started fighting, but unlike the kind of fights we staged for a living, nobody pulled any punches. I pushed several guys aside, grabbed Terry, and headed to the door with him, with the film editors following close behind me. Terry outweighed me by forty pounds, and moving him along was like pushing a yearling bull. On the way out Terry picked up a chair and threw it across the room. It hit a woman in the leg and she started screaming like a banshee. About the time I got Terry to the door the bartender, a real skinny guy, came up and said something. Terry, who weighed about 210, must not have liked what he heard because he shoved the guy against the wall and he slid down that wall like running paint. Outside I herded everyone toward Terry's Lincoln. I had everyone inside except for one of the film editors when the police showed up. That film editor started mouthing off to the officer, who handcuffed him and put him in his patrol car.

"Sir," I said, "we didn't want to cause any trouble. We just wanted out of there. If you'll let me get him in my car, we'll take him back to the hotel."

The police officer took me at my word, turned the film editor loose, and let us go. It must have looked like a real Wild West show there for a while. We were lucky we all didn't end up in jail, but I got everyone back to the Desert Inn without any further trouble.

I woke up the next morning sure feeling a whole lot better than Terry. Meanwhile, the Tucson paper had a big headline saying something like "John Wayne's Stunt Double in Fight at Hotel." Later that day Terry and I ran into Duke and Roberson, who both had seen the Tucson paper. "I hear you are the real John Wayne," Duke said to Terry. He wasn't mad about it, but he and Bad Chuck said they sure were glad they hadn't gone out with us that night. We stayed around the movie set for the rest of the filming.

The next afternoon, after we had finished shooting for the day, someone knocked on our motel room door.

"Is Mr. Terry Leonard here? I'd like to say hello to him."

Terry opened the door and this guy stuck a subpoena in his hand. The owner of the bar was suing him for the damage he caused during the fight. Terry had to hire a lawyer to get it behind him.

Hawks had me on a stuntman's contract as well as an actor's contract. The production people didn't like that at all, and Hawks didn't dig the production folks. The studio didn't think it had to pay me two checks, but after much grumbling they finally paid me the money they owed me.

Being a member of SAG, I noticed that every time stuntmen would get a raise in the business over the years, we got less and less work and the less the producers would take Westerns on location. The idea, of course, was to make more money for the big boys.

Duke, who had taken to calling me "the Kid," had a ranch in Arizona, and he spent a lot of time there when he wasn't needed on the set at Tucson. Sometimes he'd invite me out for a visit, or he'd come by the set to see how things were going. He had a great sense of humor and liked to josh and carry on. He knew I wanted to graduate to more acting.

We were working on *Rio Lobo* when Duke got his Academy Award for his role as US Marshal Rooster Cogburn in *True Grit*. When we were talking about his nomination before the award ceremony, I told him I was sure he would be getting that Oscar.

"Well, Dean, it would be great to get this award, but it doesn't matter," he said. "I've worked hard all my life on these Westerns. I've been blessed and been able to do a lot of great things." Duke was a modest, humble fellow.

The next day, after he got the award, we were on the set at Old Tucson. Luster Bayless, Duke's wardrobe person, gave us all a black eye patch to wear when he arrived from L.A. All of us were sitting there by this big cactus looking like Rooster Cogburn when he showed up. He got a big kick out of that.

It was about time he got an Oscar. When Wayne worked, he wanted it to be the best. And if you worked for him, he wanted you to put on a show. He loved Western movies as much as any of us. That was his way of life. If you worked for John Wayne, you had a good reputation. I liked all the people associated with him. It was like family.

In the summer of 1970, Cliff Lyons and Michael Wayne called me to be in the latest Batjac production, *Big Jake*. George Sherman would be directing it. Chris Mitchum would have a starring role again, along with Richard Boone, Glen Corbett, Bruce Cabott, Greg Palmer, Ethan and Patrick Wayne, Bobby Vinton, and Maureen O'Hara. I would be playing Kid Duffy, one of the bad guys in the gang led by Boone's character, John Fain.

Duke really liked working in Mexico. He loved the people there and they loved him. We filmed *Big Jake* in and around the old colonial city of Durango. They had been making movies there since 1912, and no wonder. It was the most beautiful country you ever saw, but it did lack some of the comforts of home. When we landed at the airport on a charter plane from L.A., the pilot found out that when they built the airport, they hadn't included a lighting system.

In this movie, Duke played Jacob McCandles, a man everybody called Big Jake. Just like in *McLintock!,* Maureen O'Hara played his wife. The script had them at odds, with Big Jake having been away from the ranch for ten years. But when a bunch of outlaws called the Fain gang kidnapped their grandson, Big Jake's estranged wife called him back to help. The story went on from there, with plenty of action. Ethan Wayne played the grandson, and Patrick Wayne and Chris Mitchum played McCandles's two sons. The movie was set in 1909, when cars and motorcycles were beginning to edge in on horses. Most of the characters stuck to horses, including Big Jake, but Mitchum's character rode a motorcycle when they were on their way to Mexico to rescue the grandson. And the Texas Rangers in the script preferred cars to horses. I always felt more comfortable on the back of a horse than on the seat of a motorcycle, but I did several stunts on two-wheelers. I doubled Corbett for a scene where Everett Creach, who doubled Mitchum on the motorcycle, ran over me with a motorcycle and knocked me down. In another shot, I'm running from a motorcycle when it bounces out of control and knocks me down.

At Durango we stayed at a collection of little bungalows called the Campo de Mexico Courts. I found a high school track across the street, and when I wasn't working, I'd go over there and run laps to stay in shape. When a lot of the other stuntmen would go out for drinks I made it a practice to exercise and keep myself agile and quick.

During the filming of *Rio Lobo* the company had managed to avoid getting "the turista," but not this time. It seemed like everybody in the whole company got sick sooner or later, and it was a big company. We took all our water out of five-gallon bottles provided by a guy named Hercules, who managed the bungalows, and thought it was safe to drink, but it turned out it was just tap water full of the bad bugs that cause diarrhea. When they discovered that old Hercules had been cutting corners with our water, someone went and checked out his kitchen. It was awful. They threw away rotten potatoes and a lot of contaminated food and we all started getting better. After that, we ate a lot of our meals at the Benavides drugstore, which always did a good job for us.

On a movie set, not everyone's busy at once. When he had any free time, Duke loved playing Hearts. We'd sit in one of the trailers and play that card game until they called for a scene we were in. Bad Chuck was another big Hearts player. Duke was good, but I got pretty good myself.

We were on location around Durango for better than six weeks, doing most of our shooting on a large ranch nearby. At the end of the day out there in the desert, I'd sure be ready to come back to those bungalows in town for a hot bath. Finally, when a big suite became available, I took it over. It had a dinette and I could do some of my own cooking. When Maureen O'Hara came down to shoot her scenes, she didn't have access to a suite, so I took one of the little rooms again.

My big scene took place in the bell tower of an old Catholic church. I didn't have any lines in this bit, but I got a lot of visibility. This church was the real thing, not something built by a set designer. At the beginning of the scene, I was on top of that tower with a scoped rifle, trying to keep an eye on the kidnapped boy played by Ethan. If Big Jake and his family tried to do anything funny, Fain told Jake I'd shoot the kid at his order.

Naturally, Duke's character had no intention of paying the ransom. When Jake got the drop on Fain with a double-barreled shotgun, Richard Boone's character yelled for me to shoot the kid. Then the script had me firing and missing. That was just about my last hoorah. Big Jake had sent Mitchum's character up into a nearby water tower with instructions to kill me. He shot at me and missed, but that was just to add to the action. When he shot again, my job was to look like I'd just been hit, stumble into the bells, and fall from the tower. The close-up shot would be filmed at a mockup back at the studio, but my fall would be done on location. I would be falling fifty feet, hitting a dirt area surrounded by a rock fence. That's the equivalent of going off a five-story building.

Of course, I'd be landing on a layer of pads hidden behind that fence. In preparation for the scene, the prop men had dug a twenty-by-fourteen-foot pit deep enough to handle three-plus feet of padding. They wanted to make sure the pit was big enough not to miss. While digging the pit, they dug up the skeleton of someone who had been buried in the church cemetery for so long there wasn't any kind of marker left. Some smart guy joked that the skeleton had belonged to the last guy who tried to jump out of that tower.

We did the bell tower scene at 2:00 a.m. when the moonlight would be just right. God added nice special effects by throwing in some lightning in the distance. To break my fall they used four rows of compressed cardboard boxes with ropes tied around them and then put a big mattress called a catcher on top. I had inspected it before the shot, but after I'd climbed up in that tower, it looked a whole lot smaller than it had when I checked it out. Today, they'd use an inflatable bag four times as big, which is a whole lot safer.

On cue, I staggered to the edge of the tower and went over the side. Next thing I knew I hit that pad and sank into it like a fist slamming into a pillow. Fifty or sixty people came running over to see if I was OK, which I was. Then I realized I had just barely missed hitting my head on a corner of that rock wall, which would have finished my career right quick. The director liked the first take, thank goodness. Kid Duffy was gone and he wasn't coming back.

When *Big Jake* came out in 1971, some reviewers tagged it as too violent, but it did well at the box office, which is what really counted as far as we were concerned. *Big Jake* was the last film I did with Duke. He only filmed three more movies after that, and none of them were really a fit for me and my stunt skills.

In 1971 I was hired to double Robert Redford in *Jeremiah Johnson*, a movie where he played a mountain man. But before I could get to Utah,

Dean doubling Robert Redford in *Jeremiah Johnson*, 1972.

where the filming would take place, my dad became very ill and I had to go to Texas to have him admitted to an extended care facility in Fort Worth. As soon as I was sure he would be taken care of, I flew to Salt Lake City where someone picked me up and took me to Heber City, Utah. The movie production crew was staying at a nice hotel there, but they didn't have any rooms left. They stuck me across the road in a run-down hotel in a room with Redford's stand-in. (A stand-in literally just stands there for an actor while the scene is being lit. A photo double does riding or walking scenes, but not stunts. Stunts are done by a stunt double.) This kid turned out to be a marijuana user. That didn't sit well with me, so I went out and rented my own room a few miles from the main office.

I had also found out that Redford had grown a full beard for his part.

That made me mad because I had to show up at makeup at 4:30 every morning to have a full beard glued on, which was very uncomfortable. They could have told me earlier and I would have gladly let my own beard grow out.

As the shooting began, I started to realize that I was not working with the same kind of people that I had worked with during the previous fourteen years. The Vietnam War was going on and a lot of the college kids were protesting it and generally raising hell about everything from women's liberation to whales. I did not think much of those who spoke ill of our military, weren't supportive of our troops, and bellyached. On the *Jeremiah Johnson* company there were those who were cussing our military, and let's just say it inflamed my butt. They would also put down some of those in Hollywood who were supportive of the war, particularly my friend John Wayne, who a few years earlier had done the movie *The Green Berets*. All of this left a bad taste in my mouth. This was the first movie set I was on where I noticed the drug culture. I won't name names, but some of the cast and crew were doing drugs. They didn't drink out of the same water fountain as I did, so to speak.

I do respect Robert Redford and made three more films with him. I was a good double and was left-handed, as was he. But he wasn't very friendly to me.

While we were filming in St. George, a few of the stuntmen approached me with a familiar request: they wanted me to run a race. Walt LaRue, Tony Epper, and Fred Learner got up a foot race between me and a young man at the high school there in St. George. He looked nineteen but might have been younger. Since he seemed to be a good athlete, I wasn't going to take any chances. I had these bloomer-legged pants on from the movie. I pulled out my pocket knife and cut them off to make shorts out of them and put on my tennis shoes.

Quite a number of people showed up to bet on the race. We ran about seventy-five yards on the football field and I outran the guy fairly easily. The money changed hands and I went back to my room. When I got to work next morning I had to explain to the wardrobe guy why I had cut the pants. They replaced the pants with not much said.

I had started my career working as a Western stuntman and double, but with fewer Westerns being made, I was doing more and more contemporary stunt work. Instead of cowboy outfits, I wore modern clothing, sometimes even coats and ties. No matter what kind of costume I had, I still ran and did fights. I also started doing stunts in cars. I was not into car stunts as much, but I could do the same thing with a car as I did on a horse if you told me what to do.

One contemporary TV show I did a lot of work on was *Streets of San Francisco*, a television series starring Karl Malden and Michael Douglas. The show, produced by Quinn Martin, debuted in the fall of 1972 on ABC and made it for nearly five years. Karl played a longtime detective lieutenant named Mike Stone and Douglas played his young, inexperienced partner, Inspector Steve Keller.

I doubled Douglas some whenever I'd be available. For one episode, I was at the University of San Francisco running across the top of a big building. I ran through airports and did a bunch of car sliding and spinning in some of those big warehouses in the Bay Area. You'd be surprised how loud screaming tires sound inside a building.

Michael was a real nice guy and very intelligent. He went on from *Streets of San Francisco* to be a big-time producer and actor. I doubled him in fights, mostly. Billy Burton would also double him. Karl was always very personable and a terrific actor. He could get into character and scare you half to death. I'd first met him on *Cheyenne Autumn* in 1964. He always referred to me as "that fleet-footed kid from Texas" and was very complimentary of my abilities.

For one episode, I was standing outside on one of those steep San Francisco streets and had to dive headfirst into a parked Mustang with an open door just as a car passed and sideswiped it. The car took off the Mustang's door, which sent a nut from one of the door hinges flying off like a bullet. It hit me in the butt as I made my jump and left a big bruise. They hadn't figured on that nut coming off, but the scene looked good on TV.

One nice thing about working in California—I could usually commute. Whenever I had a stunt to do, I'd fly to San Francisco from Burbank, work during the day, and then go back home that night. It was only a thirty- or forty-minute flight. Of course, if I needed to be there longer, they'd put me up in a motel. On episodic TV, there's no telling when they'll need you. It's like a revolving door.

Judge Roy Bean was a real-life Texas character who ran a saloon and served as justice of the peace in the little West Texas railroad town of Langtry in the 1880s and '90s. In 1972, old man John Huston directed a picture loosely based on Bean's story called *The Life and Times of Judge Roy Bean*. They hired Paul Newman to play the judge. I got cast as a nameless outlaw along with my friends Richard Farnsworth and Terry Leonard, among others.

Though the story was supposed to be taking place in Texas, we shot the exteriors around Tucson and Benson, Arizona. It would have been nice to shoot in Texas, but I always liked working around Tucson. Whenever I had any spare time, I'd go to the University of Arizona and work out.

The big action scene in the movie comes after Bean has supposedly been killed after the bad guys tied a rope around his neck, tied the other end around a saddle horn, and sent the horse running off into the brush and cactus with Bean dragging along behind. That would be enough to kill a man in real life, but not in the movies. Bean survived and showed up at the brothel-saloon where the outlaws who did it were hanging out. Naturally, he was a little irritated.

When the big scene opened (we did it back in L.A. at the Warner Bros. studio), I was sitting inside that saloon with a bunch of other drunken outlaws and good-looking dance-hall girls. Bean walked in, all bloody from being dragged by that horse, and started shooting everybody in sight. I had Margo Epper, a stuntwoman from Hollywood's biggest stunt family, sitting in my lap. She was playing one of the dance-hall girls. (Her dad, originally from Switzerland where he had been a cavalryman, had a line in the movie *Charge of the Light Brigade*: "Get your rusty ramrods, we're riding." But every time he said it, it came out, "Get your wusty wamwads, we're widing.") Newman got too close to her during the shooting and shot her in the back of her shoulder. The wadding from the blank had enough velocity at that point to penetrate her skin. It wasn't going to kill her, but it sure hurt. While it was bad luck for her, if I hadn't been staring at her cleavage, the shot would have blown my eyeballs out.

Meanwhile, I got up to start shooting back. The script called for my pants to be about half down, since I was supposed to have been getting pretty friendly with that dance-hall gal. I pulled two six-guns and spun 'em. Well, while I was showing off, Bean shot me with his shotgun. As the load hit, I did this funny bit and then they used wires you can't see to jerk me through a fake wall as if the force of the blast had blown me through it. I landed on the porch outside the saloon.

We stayed in Arizona for a week or so. One night at the Hilton, Margo and her sisters Jeannie and Stephanie Epper, and all the other stuntwomen who played dance-hall girls, started dancing on tabletops in the hotel bar. For a while there, I thought we were all going to get thrown out of that hotel, but it was just innocent fun. We also had a good time riding around the hotel in electric golf carts, crashing them around like bumper cars at the state fair. On a lot of movies, we did about as many stunts off-camera as we did on-camera.

About this time in my life I was working a lot and things at home were not the same. I began to suspect that Pam might be seeing someone. But before I could confront her, I was gone again on another shoot.

With Darryl Zanuck as producer, a young filmmaker named Steven Spielberg started putting together a project in 1972 that would be his first full-length feature film, *The Sugarland Express*. The screenplay, which Spielberg worked on with Hal Barwood and Matthew Robbins, was based on a spectacular criminal case that actually happened in Texas in 1969: a woman helped her husband escape from a minimum-security prison and they ended up kidnapping a highway patrolman and leading 150 or so officers on a long chase that got national and even international news media attention.

Spielberg was still more than a year away from *Jaws*, his breakthrough blockbuster, but he put together a good cast for *Sugarland Express*. The biggest names were Goldie Hawn and my old friend Ben Johnson. Goldie would play the wife of the convict (William Atherton), and Ben would play Highway Patrol Captain Harlin Tanner. Ben had to wear a suit for his part. The wardrobe people wouldn't let Ben wear his world champion rodeo buckle, but he wore one of mine with a longhorn on it.

I was hired to play Russ Berry, a TV reporter for Big 6 News in Houston, a part that required both stunt work and acting. Beyond my role, they wanted me to coach Goldie in sounding like a real Texan. Like just about everybody else in America at that time, I had seen Goldie on *Laugh-In*, a really popular comedy show in the late 1960s and early '70s, but this was the first time I had met her. She turned out to be just wonderful to work

Dean and stuntman Teddy Grossman in *The Sugarland Express*, 1974.

with. I would meet up with her, sit in a car, and coach her on talking Texan. She'd giggle and carry on while we went over her lines, but she got pretty good at it. The main thing I had to do was get her talking through her nose. She made a good Texas girl. Goldie had fun being an actress and it showed in her work.

We started filming at the Texas Department of Correction's prerelease center at Sugarland on my forty-first birthday, January 15, 1973. While we were working in the Houston area, we stayed at the King's Inn. We were down in that part of the state for eight weeks or so.

By then I had started performing every once in a while in stunt shows, sort of a modern combination of the old Wild West shows and rodeo. While we were shooting *Sugarland Express*, Bennie Dobbins and J. R. Randall scheduled one in the Astrodome at Houston during their big fat stock show. They organized a good show, an extravaganza with cowboys and Indians. What they didn't plan on was snow. The day of the show, Houston got hit by the damnedest ice and snow storm you could imagine. I bet we didn't have 500 people show up. Anyway, those folks who braved the weather got to see a pretty good show, including me chasing a stagecoach. At least I got to see my name in big letters on that famous scoreboard in the Astrodome.

Sugarland Express had more cars in it than any other movie I was ever involved with. When we moved locations, just about everyone in the whole company had to drive a car, including cars that had been painted to look like Texas Department of Public Safety Highway Patrol units, and that's what I drove. We were supposed to have a card in the window saying "Not in Service," but we made a lot of people pretty paranoid when we caravanned across Texas. People thought, *Oh my gosh, I'm going to get a ticket.*

I had some fun lines playing the TV guy. Carey Loftin, the greatest car stuntman of his day, set up the scene and also did the driving. Stuntman Teddy Grossman, a good friend of Spielberg's, was on top of a TV station panel truck running a camera. I was inside the back, wearing a coat and tie and holding a big boom mike. We drove up along Goldie and William Atherton and I started talking to them as we're going down the highway.

"Can I ask you some questions? I want to get an in-depth interview for my station," I said.

"How much you paying?" Atherton asked.

"I guess that can be negotiated," I said.

While all this was going on, I could see Spielberg in the camera car laughing. He laughed so hard I thought he was going to fall out of that car. But the scene got funnier.

Ben (as Captain Tanner) got fed up at the TV crew interfering in the situation and shot out a tire on the truck, causing it to go out of control. When that happened, I flew out of the van and landed in a stock tank. The last time the audience saw me, I was sticking that microphone out of the water and rising up soaking wet as water from the microphone rained down on me.

From southeastern Texas the company moved on to San Antonio, where we stayed at the downtown Holiday Inn. I had a lot of friends in

San Tone, dating back to when we did *The Alamo*, so it was always a pleasure to spend some time there. The Buckhorn Saloon threw a nice party for us. After hours, I'd work out at Alamo Stadium, where I'd won the junior AAU track meet when I was a freshman at UT. Of course, I always enjoyed working in Texas, no matter where we were. From San Antonio, we went to Del Rio, where they wrapped up the filming.

After *Sugarland Express*, when I returned home I found out that Pam was for sure involved with someone else. Only it wasn't with a man. It turned out to be a woman she always said was just her good friend. I realized it was time for Old Deano to clear the air. I hired Roy Rogers's attorney and got out of the marriage as quickly as I could so I could get on with my life.

That winter I went to Chicago for about three weeks to double Redford in *The Sting*. We stayed at the Lakeshore Inn. I thought I'd seen some hard winters in northwest Texas, but Chicago was one cold son of a buck during the time we were shooting the exteriors. A few of us took a tour of the Playboy Mansion while we were there. I got to shake old Hugh Hefner's hand, but we were more interested in the Playmates in the bunny suits than him. I did all of Redford's running and jumping off buildings in that movie, all kinds of activity. In one scene, I ran under the electric railway track at the LaSalle Station at Forty-third and Calumet. Charles Durning stripped the clutch out of an old Ford trying to catch me. *The Sting* turned out to be a real big picture.

In 1974, I did one more picture where I doubled Redford, *The Great Waldo Pepper*. Redford was at the height of his career, and he did very well in this film. In one scene, I was in a crowd at a carnival when Redford's character landed his plane. As he was landing, it got hooked on some banners and spun around out of control. My job was to outrun it without getting killed. The real pilot was Frank Tallman, a terrific stunt pilot. We did that scene on the edge of San Antonio, though most of the exteriors were shot near Elgin, closer to Austin. I did other stunt work as well in that film.

Nineteen seventy-four held another kind of challenge for me. My grandmother had broken her hip in the early 1960s and that set her back some, but she lived for more than another decade with her son King and his wife, Teena, on the old home place. They were so good to my grandmother while I was in Hollywood working in pictures. She passed away from congestive heart failure on June 16, 1974. I was in California at the time, but I had talked to her the day before. I rushed back to Texas and we buried her next to Grandpa Pink in the Eliasville Cemetery. Being raised by my grandmother was the best thing that ever happened to me in my life, a true blessing. She was a wonderful role model with sage advice for life, and she still lives within me.

The following year, Art Rush called me and asked if I would like to double Roy Rogers in a picture called *Macintosh and T.J.* that he was going to shoot in Texas. Well, like the old saying goes, does a bear you-know-what in the woods? By this point in my career, I had met Roy, but this was the first time I had been asked to double the King of the Cowboys, my boyhood hero. I said you bet, and reported to Dickens, where we would shoot on the 208,000-acre 6666 Ranch at Guthrie, one of the largest in the state.

In the movie, Roy played an aging bronc rider breaking horses on the 6666. He also became a mentor to a kid named T. J., played by fourteen-year-old Clay O'Brien Cooper, a seven-time world champion heeler. Clay had done *The Cowboys* with Wayne, and his dad, Gene O'Brien, shod my horses in California.

Most of the cast and crew stayed at the Holiday Inn in Lubbock, but that was seventy miles from Dickens and even farther from there to the 6666 Ranch. Roy and I didn't want to do all that driving back and forth every day, so we stayed in Dickens at the Double L Motel, the only one in town. It wasn't the grandest motel in the world, no television in the rooms, but with our being country boys it didn't bother us.

What did annoy Roy was that every afternoon when he called to check in with his wife, Dale, the gal at the front desk would listen in on their conversation. As soon as he figured that out, he started borrowing my pickup to drive to the nearest pay phone, which stood outside the court-house.

I enjoyed working with Roy. He was as pleasant in person as he seemed on camera. He never acted like he was as famous as he was. He and Dale were very religious, one of the nicest couples I'd ever met. You couldn't help but love and respect them. Later, I also got to know Roy's son, Dusty; Cheryl Rogers, his daughter; and her husband, Larry.

Aside from the Big Bend and Trans-Pecos, the country around Dickens is some of the most wide-open, wild landscape in Texas. The ranches are big and the few towns are small. All that mostly empty country really appealed to Roy.

At night, he and I would drive the dirt roads in a new green Dodge pickup that belonged to Dale Robertson, who was getting ready to move from California back to Oklahoma. I had been using Dale's truck and a trailer to move my late grandmother's stuff from my Uncle King's place back to my home in California. Roy and I would eat an early supper, and then go coyote hunting. I had been an expert rifleman in the army, but Roy could shoot the eye out of an eagle at a hundred yards. He was probably one of the best shots in Hollywood. He had a rifle with a scope and I used an open-sighted, lever-action .30-30. Roy had a coyote call and was pretty good at calling them up. After we shot them, we'd hang 'em up on a barbed-wire fence. We also did some target practice. We did that for several weeks, just me and him.

I was forty-three, Roy in his sixties. We'd stay out for an hour or hour and a half. He'd talk about when he was a boy, growing up in Ohio living on a riverboat. After a while, he'd start singing and yodeling as I drove us around out in the middle of nowhere looking for coyotes, humming along with him. I think he really enjoyed being able to get away from everybody. It seemed like we had all of West Texas to ourselves. Of course, it's against the law to shoot from a public roadway, even if it's unpaved, and I doubt Roy had a Texas hunting license. I know I sure didn't. If a state game warden had run up on us, I guess we would have gotten tickets and maybe gone to jail.

We stayed in Dickens about three weeks, driving from there to Guthrie each day. It was while we were doing this movie that I got to be friends with the other Larry Mahan, the rodeo star, as well as Dallas Cowboys star running back Walt Garrison, who also rodeoed.

I did one scene where I had to play an ND cowboy and rope and saddle a bucking horse furnished by Clay O'Brien's dad. They shot it at a big, round, wooden pen at the 6666 headquarters using local cowboys as extras. Since I couldn't be two places at once, they hired a local cowboy to double Roy in that scene. When the director yelled "Action!" Gene O'Brien and I flanked the horse at the snubbing post, pulled a sack off its head, and turned it loose. Well, that horse bucked that cowboy off and the fall broke his neck. They rushed that guy off to the hospital (he made a full recovery) and found another local cowboy, even younger, to finish the scene. Fortunately, he got the job done. Had I been in charge of the stunts, I would have hired a pro bronc rider to double Roy, not just some cowboy who thought he could ride a sun-fishing horse.

J. J. Gibson, who went to TCU, was ranch foreman. I took Gibson's boy down to the high school track at Guthrie and showed him how to run. Mrs. Anne Burnett Tandy, granddaughter of legendary ranch founder Burk Burnett, was still living in the big stone mansion her grandfather had built in 1918 on the side of the hill overlooking Guthrie. When we wrapped up the filming on the 6666, they threw a big party for the company. Someone who came in for the party landed a plane nearby and annoyed Mrs. Tandy, but it all worked out.

I wish I could say I worked with Duke on *The Shootist*, his last film, but I didn't. The principals, mainly Duke and Richard Boone, didn't need any doubling until the final shootout. Chuck Roberson did the heavy lifting in that scene, mainly where Duke's character dives over a bar. Chuck, who was getting up in years himself, looked like a porpoise going over the countertop.

In the late spring of 1975, just to see Duke, I did go over to Warner Bros. when they were filming *The Shootist* on part of the back lot. I knew Duke had lung cancer, which he was first diagnosed with during *McLintock!* He was a tough SOB who stayed the course as long as he could, but this time, the clock was ticking pretty loud.

I talked with Duke and we discussed Bad Chuck Roberson, who had just been involved in a car wreck. Duke asked me if I'd heard about it, and I said I'd already talked to Chuck and that he had told me he'd had a little too much to drink. While we were talking, Chuck walked up and we all had a good laugh about his latest real-life stunt. That was the last time I saw Duke. I'm glad it ended with a laugh.

The Shootist got good reviews and, as far as I was concerned, it was a hell of a movie. I think Duke knew it was going to be his last film and it was. I watched Duke on TV when they presented him with the Lifetime Achievement Award at the Academy Awards. He had lost a lot of weight by then, but he still had that sparkle in his eyes and that sense of humor. With that big Roman nose, he looked a lot like my dad when he got real thin. As much time as I spent in Hollywood, I never went to the Academy Awards in person, but some of the pictures I did stunts in either won Oscars or were nominated, including *The Sting*.

By this time in my career, I had been in so many movies I had begun thinking about doing one of my own. I was trying to raise money to do the story of Tom Mix and at the same time searching for an exceptional-looking horse resembling Tony, Tom's horse.

In 1976, I got a call from Rose and Richard Lundin. Richard had been head wrangler on some shows I had done. They said they knew where a two-year-old stocking-legged sorrel horse like Tony could be found. We went to Northridge near the San Fernando Valley to see the horse. He was beautiful and I wanted him. The owner wouldn't take a personal check, so I left and came back with a cashier's check for $2,500. Rose called later

Dale Robertson, Glenn Randall, and Dean, c. 1978.

and said that after I had driven off with the horse another lady came by wanting to buy him. She and the woman who had just sold the horse to me had nearly gotten into a fistfight over it. When I got home with the horse, which I named Sunday, he managed to get out of the stall and into my yard and tore the hell out of it. A month later I took him to Glenn Randall's ranch in Newhall to be trained by Glenn, one of the best trick horse trainers in the business. He had trained Roy's famous horse Trigger, the horses used in *Ben-Hur*, and many more. I wanted my horse to be magnificent and he was. One year later I had every trick in the world on him. In 1990 he was voted most clever horse in the movie business and beat out the Black Stallion and many more great horses at a competition at Universal Studios.

About the time *The Shootist* came out in 1976, I got a call from Everett Creach, a stuntman I had worked with in several John Wayne pictures. He wanted me to go to Miami, Florida, to work for John Frankenheimer in a movie called *Black Sunday* and double Bruce Dern. Everett also wanted me to run in an exhibition race against Nat Moore, a wide receiver for the Miami Dolphins. Having a race between a forty-four-year-old Olympic gold medal winner and a twenty-three-year-old hotshot football star wasn't part of the script, but Everett figured it would draw a crowd that could be used in the movie.

For one scene, they had me inside a mockup of the Goodyear blimp, hanging from a crane about 200 feet above the Orange Bowl. It would have been a whole lot safer to have been up in the real Goodyear blimp, but seeing the Orange Bowl from my viewpoint was breathtaking. The scene called for me to get shot and then hang precariously out the door of the mockup with fake blood all over my white shirt. In setting it up beforehand, I had tied a wire connecting a brace inside the mockup to a strap on my leg. It was pretty spooky dangling in the air that high over the football field pretending to be dead while wondering if the strap I'd tied would hold.

After they had that big scene in the can, we did the race. Dolphins coach Don Shula and a lot of his players were there to encourage their guy. When the starter gun went off, I jumped ahead and poured it on for forty yards, beating their speedy receiver by about half a step. I don't think he liked an old cowboy outrunning him like that. "Dean, next time you

Dean, age forty-four, outrunning Nat Moore, age twenty-three, of the Miami Dolphins football team at the Orange Bowl, 1975.

come back to Miami, you better bring two pair of starting blocks," he said. I said, "You know, Nat, I ain't never coming back."

In 1977 I worked on *How the West Was Won*, a TV series starring *Gunsmoke*'s Jim Arness and a younger actor named Bruce Boxleitner. Ricardo Montalban was also in it. I remember we were getting ready to fly to Canyon City, driving down the San Diego freeway from MGM, when I heard on the radio that Elvis had died.

We did most of the shooting in Colorado that summer on into the fall. I was stunt coordinator, setting up fight scenes and wagon wrecks. I also did stunts and parts, mostly horse scenes.

I had met Jim Arness through Dennis Weaver when I first got into pictures. Dennis played Marshal Matt Dillon's crippled deputy, Chester, on *Gunsmoke*, but his limp was as phony as a $3 bill. Actually, he had been a great track man and was still in fine shape. He came close to making the 1948 Olympics, but came in fourth during the trials. When I bought my house in L.A., I discovered he lived nearby.

Ben Bates was Arness's stuntman. A great big old boy, Ben was a terrific double for Jim. He could handle a weapon and throw a good punch. He was also a humorous kind of guy, which is something he had in common with a lot of Western stuntmen. When I left the series, Ben took over as stunt coordinator. I had other things I wanted to do and Ben was on salary doubling Arness. They didn't want to keep me on salary.

I worked on the television miniseries based on Alex Haley's book *Roots* staring Olivia Cole, LeVar Burton, Ben Vereen, Louis Gossett, Jr., John Amos, Richard Farnsworth, Gary Collins, and many others. I was doubling for Collins, an old friend I had met years before when he costarred with Dale Robertson on *The Iron Horse*. He is married to Mary Ann Mobley and they are a great couple. In the miniseries, Collins and Farnsworth played slave catchers. In one scene, Farnsworth and I were on horseback and threw a net over John Amos's stunt double to catch him. For the next take John got under the net on the ground surrounded by our horses so they could get a close-up of him. He was getting into character, thrashing around like a caged animal, when Farnsworth's horse's hoof hit him in the head and took some of his hair off. He got very mad and aimed it all at Farnsworth. I had to step in and referee, telling him that Farnsworth hadn't done that on purpose. Sometimes when you're in character it takes you over, but when you get hit in the head it makes you fighting mad.

I did a couple of episodes of *Young Maverick* for TV at Warner Bros. in 1978 as stunt coordinator. They also had me doubling Charles Frank, the actor who played Bret Maverick's young second cousin, Ben Maverick. They did the exteriors at Vasquez Rocks State Park. In one scene, I got off my horse at the foot of a rock, climbed up, and jumped down and on this gal who had been following Maverick. I took her off her horse. When the scene was over, I realized my horse had followed me up on top of that rock and fallen off. It stove him up for a while, but he recovered.

The same year, I did a big fight scene in San Francisco with George C. Scott, who was starring in a movie called *Hardcore*. He played a guy from the Midwest whose daughter had gotten pulled into the porn industry. My old friend Terry Leonard was the stunt coordinator and directed the second unit. He called me in to double Gary Graham for this particular scene. As its title suggests, *Hardcore* had some real adult stuff in it and I wondered if I should do it, but it was about a guy trying to do the right thing, even if it did have a lot about the porno world, so I agreed.

When I got to San Francisco, they were shooting on one of those famous steep streets. Wardrobe put me in an urban cowboy–style getup with a shiny silver shirt, fancy britches, and silver-tipped boots. I looked like a real piece of work. My job was to lose a big fight with Scott, who wanted to do the scene himself rather than use a double. When that camera started rolling, we fought up and down that hill. Trash cans flew as we crashed into them. Old George C. hung in there and we did the whole fight together. But at one point, he threw a punch, slipped, and sailed over me. I thought it had killed him, but he got up and we kept going. In the movie, it looks like Scott beat the crap out of me. Scott was a great actor, and a good ol' boy at heart. After we did that scene, he invited me into his dressing room and we discussed it. He had his wife, Trish, there. She was also an actress.

Also in 1978, Dale Robertson did *J. J. Starbuck*. We shot the pilot in L.A. but traveled to Vancouver, Canada, to do the series. Between the pilot and the start of production, Dale had been doing a commercial for the Steiner family in Austin at his farm in Oklahoma. He was on a young colt when the head stall (bridle) came off and the horse bolted. Dale jumped off to save his neck but broke his hip. After he healed up, we headed for Canada.

From the start, Dale wasn't happy with the series. It was a contemporary show, supposedly set in Texas and Oklahoma, but here we were doing it on a ranch in Canada. Dale wanted to do it back home, since Vancouver didn't look much like the Southwest, but they wouldn't listen. Beyond that, they had rules in Canada that we didn't care for. For one thing, they wouldn't let too many of us go up there. We had to have work permits. A Canadian was doing a lot of the stunt coordinating, and it was chaos. On top of everything else, it was colder than the devil.

Dale didn't even like the hat he had to wear, which he said made him look like Yosemite Sam. He just didn't have his heart in it and the show ended after only a dozen episodes. None of us who had worked during the golden era of the Western liked that they were doing so many movies in Canada. Westerns started here and should be made here.

My next movie, *1941*, was a comedy. This Steven Spielberg film was loosely based on an air-raid scare Los Angeles had in 1942 during World War II and the shelling of a California refinery by a Japanese submarine. The writers took those two events and a few other actual incidents and produced a script on an outbreak of panic in L.A. shortly after news of the attack on Pearl Harbor reached the mainland. Though the film had a lot of star power with John Belushi, Dan Aykroyd, John Candy, and others, at the box office the movie bombed bigger than Pearl Harbor. And it nearly marked the end of my career.

At the MGM studio, stuntman Bobby McLaughlin (my old friend Lee McLaughlin's half-brother) and I were in a scene showing the aftermath of a Japanese torpedo hitting the Santa Monica Pier. We had been on the pier before it blew up and now we struggled in the drink, a large tank with agitators and wind machines going full speed to make the water rough. I had been wearing a trench coat and all of a sudden the water started getting the best of me. Bobby realized I was in trouble and helped me stay upright so I wouldn't drown. If I had any lingering anger over his brother having hit me with an egg more than twenty years earlier, it sure went away after that.

Any time I could get to Texas, I went to see my dad and buy him new shirts. By this time, he didn't recognize many family members but he always seemed to know me. On August 18, 1978, Uncle King and Aunt Teena called to tell me that Dad had died. He was the type who would give you the shirt off his back. When he'd quit drinking for a year or so you couldn't have been around a nicer fellow. He could have done just about anything with his life, but his alcoholism denied him that. I think I tried to make up for some of that in my life. But there is one thing that he told me: if he never did much for me other than giving me life, at least I would never be an alcoholic. How he knew, I don't know, but he was right. I loved my dad very much. Sometimes we don't realize why things are the way they are, but that's the way they are. We buried him next to Grandpa Pink and Mama in the Eliasville Cemetery. Since cowboying had been such a big part of his life, I had a horse engraved on his grave marker.

Not long after that, I lost someone else important in my life. In 1979, when I heard Duke Wayne was in bad shape, I went by the UCLA Medical Center and talked to the family, but Duke was doing too badly for me to see him. I was at home in Woodland Hills on June 11 when I heard he had died. The family wanted his services to be very private, so I didn't go to the funeral. For some reason, they were afraid someone might try to steal his body, so they buried him in so much concrete nobody could disturb his grave.

CHAPTER 14

IT'S A WRAP: BACK TO TEXAS

ollywood is not all sunglasses and autographs. Life as a stuntman is chicken one day, feathers the next. But by 1981, I had nearly twenty-five years in the business and at age forty-nine could afford to be a little choosy. So when John Stephens, the director I had worked with on *How the West Was Won*, called and asked if I'd like to be stunt coordinator for a new television series he was doing for Universal called *Simon and Simon*, I didn't say yes as quickly as he probably thought I would.

John told me that Jameson Parker and Gerald McRaney would be playing brothers who ran a private detective agency in San Diego. One brother was a streetwise Vietnam veteran, the other a book-smart college graduate. In addition to the action-filled cases the two main characters would take on, the series would draw energy from the conflict caused by the differences between them. Though both actors were only in their early thirties, John wanted me to be their stunt double. My young friend Diamond Farnsworth would double Jameson some, too.

I finally told John I would do it but that I wanted to do it my way. I didn't want anyone working for me who wasn't a professional, which meant I also wouldn't tolerate any drug use. At that time in Hollywood drugs had become pretty prevalent, and I didn't like it. It seemed like just about everybody was smoking pot and snorting coke. John agreed to my ground rules, and I went to work for the series.

CBS premiered the show November 24, 1981, and we went on to shoot twelve more one-hour episodes. *Simon and Simon* had plenty of action, but it didn't do too well in the ratings. For its second season, the network put it behind *Magnum, P.I.* on Thursday nights, but I was not asked to come back. Later, I heard that the drug use on the show was bad. It was not Parker or McRaney doing the drugs, though. They were good men and a pleasure to work with. The series did better on Thursday nights and it ended up running more than seven years.

I happened to be home in Texas working on my ranch when I heard that Coach Clyde Littlefield had passed away on May 20, 1981. His family asked me to be one of his pallbearers and I was honored to help lay Coach to rest. He had been more like a father to me than a coach. Aside from teaching me to be one of the best sprinters in the Southwest, he had always been there for me in every other respect. I was the only runner he ever had to get a gold medal at the Olympics and the first-ever gold medal winner from UT in track and field.

I won my first high school meet on UT's Memorial Stadium track. My good friend and teammate Charlie Thomas and I would spend most of our time on the track in Memorial Stadium; there we won many, many events. I want to thank UT for remembering Coach Littlefield and recognizing him with a bronze plaque, which is placed in the new track stadium southeast of Memorial Stadium. Also in recognition of Coach, UT changed the name of the Texas Relays to The Clyde Littlefield Texas Relays. This event is one of the great track and field meets, comparable with the Drake, Penn, and Coliseum Relays. Coach Littlefield was the one who put track and field on the map in the Southwest, and I am so lucky and proud to have had a man of his stature in my life. My philosophy in life is, "don't forget who brung you to the dance."

After living alone for more than seven years, I met a pretty Italian woman at a country-western dance hall in Woodland Hills called The Yellow Rose. I asked her to dance and our courtship began. She was Anita Scaramoza Adams, a divorced mother of two girls, sixteen-year-old Deborah and fifteen-year-old Laurie. A smart, sophisticated lady, she lived and worked as a secretary in Woodland Hills. After dating for a little more than a year we decided to get married. She was from Hamden, Connecticut, near New Haven and came from a nice Italian family.

We got married in the fall of 1981 at Woodland Hills Methodist Church. Dale Robertson was my best man, and my childhood friend Larry Mahan was there, too. After marrying, Anita and I went back to Connecticut to see her family. Four months later we had to return when her father died unexpectedly. Less than two years later, my half-brother Gerald Smith died in Dallas on July 16, 1983.

In early 1984, Diamond Farnsworth told me about a part in the film *Rhinestone*, a comedy starring Dolly Parton, Sylvester Stallone, Richard Farnsworth (Diamond's dad), and Ron Leibman. I got the gig and had a few lines in the picture, where I rode a white horse with a silver saddle and lights all over it. It was the first picture I ever had to say a cuss word in: "Come back here, you son of a bitch." To add even more to the scene, the director had me throw my hat down with the "son of a bitch" part.

The movie had a fun story line, with the country singer played by Dolly betting her manager her next contract and her body that she could turn any fool into a country singer. The manager picked a New York cab driver played by Stallone, and Dolly had two weeks to make him a country star. But when the movie came out that summer, it flopped. They spent $28 million making it but it grossed only $21 million and change. At least I got my money and had fun working with Dolly, whom I'd met earlier at Fox Studios. She was one of the most talented people I had ever met.

Art Rush, the longtime manager for Roy Rogers and Dale Evans, not to mention being Roy's best man when they got married, called me in 1984 and asked me to double Roy for an episode of the television series *Fall Guy* starring Lee Majors, Douglas Barr, and Heather Thomas. Rush had represented Dale Robertson for a time, which is how we met. The series had been on the air since 1981, and I had already been on the show a few times doubling Majors, whom I'd also doubled in *The Big Valley* back in the late sixties.

In *The Fall Guy,* Majors played a Hollywood stuntman who specialized in automotive stunts. To make things interesting, when not on a movie set, he made his living as a bounty hunter. Each show would start with a big stunt—usually involving his pickup truck—for whatever movie he happened to be working on, and then go into his search for some bail skipper. Part of the show's shtick was to have a lot of cameo appearances by big-name stars. That's where I came in this time, since they were planning an episode where the King of the Cowboys would have a part.

Naturally, I jumped at the chance to double Roy again. Roy was everything a person would expect his hero to be. He treated me like family. This turned out to be the last time Roy did any acting work, and I was the last man in movies or television to double him.

They shot the exteriors for this episode at Agua Dulce, near Newhall,

Dean doubling Roy Rogers in the TV series *The Fall Guy*, 1981.

California. For the show featuring Roy, we were working again at Vasquez Rocks State Park, where the famous outlaw Joaquin Murrieta used to hang out. Many a Western film or series has been shot there. Doubling either Roy or Majors, I did a fight and a horse chase, and I had to outrun a Brahma bull.

Every day during the shoot, Roy drove from his place at Apple Valley to Vasquez Rocks. One morning, I got there early, before Roy or Art. When Roy finally pulled up and got out of his car, it looked like something must be bothering him.

"Roy, what's wrong?"

"Oh, I had to pull off on the side of road for a while. One of my eyes got a floater behind it, and I couldn't see."

"Roy, when Art gets here, I'd better tell him."

"Oh, hell, Dean, don't tell him. Art'll shut this shoot down and we'll have a problem."

I decided to keep quiet about it and we went ahead and finished the show.

By this time, Roy's famous horse Trigger had died. They used another Palomino, a sixteen-hand horse, as Trigger. In doubling Roy, I had to do some chases on that big horse. Roy still rode, of course, but he was getting old and so was his saddle. One time when Roy stood up in the saddle, one of the tapaderas—the leather covering on his stirrup—broke and liked to have dumped him. The silver-studded Edward H. Bolin saddle that we used was fifty years old and I had to replace the rigging with a plastic strap since the leather had been sitting up so long. The tapaderas were so heavy the old straps couldn't hold them, but the saddle worked fine after I added that heavy-duty plastic.

For one scene, I had to get a Brahma bull off a guy in a rodeo arena. I ran around the bull and got him out of the way, but not before he chased me a little. Then they had a shot where I had to bulldog some of the bad guys, which was easier. I came out of the shoot without a scratch, but Lee's double did have an accident one night, cutting a finger off.

In 1985, I was inducted into the Texas Sports Hall of Fame at Waco. My fellow honorees were former Houston Astros pitcher Nolan Ryan and Pittsburgh Steelers star defensive end "Mean" Joe Greene, putting me in pretty good company. I came home for the induction festivities in Waco, but I was still an absentee Texas landowner living in California. Since my dad's death, I owned outright 338 acres at Ivan and 518 acres on the Clear Fork of the Brazos. I wanted to do something different with the land, but I didn't yet know what.

Ben Johnson called me that year and said he would be doing a celebrity roping competition to raise money for needy children and asked if I'd take part. I said I'd be happy to. Ben held the event in Houston, and while I was there, I met Ted Long, a rancher and sculptor from North Platte, Nebraska. Ted said he was fixing to lose a lease where he had a bunch of longhorns. I told him that I had been thinking about putting some cattle on my place in Texas and that it might as well be longhorns. We made a deal and I was the proud owner of twelve longhorn heifers.

I guess my appreciation of this breed goes back to my time in the

Ben Johnson and Dean at Ben Johnson's Pro-Celebrity Rodeo, 1985.

Silver Spurs at UT. They're unique animals. They don't have a lot of fat on them, but they're sturdy. Another thing I like about longhorns is that they run together like one big family. If a coyote tries to get a calf, the others in the herd will shish kebob that SOB or run it off. They're just plain tough, which is what made them so popular back in the old days before other breeds took off. I've seen longhorns bitten by rattlesnakes and survive, though that has a lot to do with where a snake bites them.

I sent my old friend Booger Red Nixon, T. Hibbert, and Snuffy Morales to get those cows. They brought them back to Texas in a big trailer. Then Larry Mahan and I went to Happy Shahan's ranch at Brackettville and bought a bull.

With that bull's help, my herd grew steadily. When people ask me why I decided to start raising longhorns, I tell them that longhorns are durable and you damn sure get your picture made better standing with them. It's better to have longhorns than a bunch of cattle you have to feed all the time, especially during droughts. I sell them mostly to ropers or other breeders, but on the marketplace longhorns are a little harder to move than breeds that are hamburgers on the hoof.

In 1987 Dale Robertson gave me a paint horse, a sorrel with four stocking legs and a white blaze face. A magnificent animal, I named him Hollywood. I took him to my old friend Glenn Randall and spent time with Glenn helping train him. All the while I was soaking up Glenn's techniques. The difference between Hollywood and my older horse Sunday was that I could do anything on Hollywood—roping, what they call "team pen" in rodeo, or just working cattle—plus put him through his tricks. Sunday was high-strung, but Hollywood is easygoing. He's getting up in years, but Hollywood's still a delight to ride. Even though both of us have been around for a while, when I ride him into an arena to do tricks for children, or at charity events, every eye is on him. What an exceptional horse he has been.

Another old friend, Chuck Roberson, died of cancer on June 8, 1988. They gave him a stuntman's funeral at the Little Church on the Way at the Warner Bros. studio. They carried his body in a horse-drawn coach, with all us stuntmen and cowboys following behind. Somehow the driver got off the path and we must have walked two miles before we finally got to the church. I could just see old Chuck laughing his ass off at that.

Chuck also would have gotten a kick out of what happened to me one

Dean working with trick horse Hollywood at the ranch,
c. 2004. Courtesy of Mark Engebretson.

day later that summer, but I didn't think it was particularly funny. Headed home after dropping off some pictures and updated résumés at my agent's office, I decided to stop for a Diet Coke at a convenience store on Sunset Boulevard. When I got to the counter with my drink, a black fellow who must have been about six-foot-two and 225 pounds stuck a .38 pistol in my chest. I didn't believe what was happening. It was like a stunt in one of the countless movie scenes I had worked in, but looking down and seeing that fellow's big hand holding that gun up against my heart made me realize this was the real deal. The guy told me he wanted my Rolex and I slipped it off and gave it to him. As I was doing that, he said to give him my diamond horseshoe ring. I was very fond of that ring, which I had bought in New York while making the movie *Stiletto*, where I doubled Alex Cord. Only problem was, he had that pistol.

Then the gunman told the cashier to hand him the cash from the register. That's when I decided to do a little sleight of hand. I dropped my hand while he was looking the other way and took off my old worn-out University of Texas ring and gave him that, not the bigger ring with the rock. He was in a big hurry and never looked. As he ran out the door I thought about running after him, but reality took hold when I remembered that his pistol wasn't loaded with blanks. On top of that, he probably outweighed me by fifty pounds.

It took the police nearly twenty minutes to get to that convenience store, and so far as I know, they never found the robber. I sure never saw that Rolex or my class ring again. I had a friend who had been the football manager for the Longhorns while I was at UT, Jerry Thompson. Jerry and his brother owned the 7-11 chain. I called him, and their insurance bought me a new Rolex within three days. You never know when you might need someone from your past.

By the late 1980s, everything seemed to be going to hell in Hollywood, at least for a guy who had made his living as a cowboy stuntman in Westerns. Westerns were long gone from TV and what few Western movies were being made were shot in Canada, where they didn't have to pay union scale or live up to union rules. That left me and a lot of my actor and stunt friends without jobs. They're still making a lot of movies in Canada, and for the most part they are successful, because that's all we have. But I still like movies made in the United States. A Western looks better here where the West begins and the pavement ends. I am a proud American and I like everything made in America.

I'd still go to the studios looking for projects, but there just wasn't anything happening. I knew a lot of people, but it began to seem like that didn't make any difference. Anita didn't want me to retire, but I kind of wanted to get back to my ranches in Texas. Keeping up a home in California and one in Texas had started getting pretty old. I felt like I was just throwing money in a hole by staying in Woodland Hills. I would rather spend that money making improvements to my property in Texas, where I had already started getting the place built up.

By the time I turned sixty in 1992, the Westerns had pretty much ridden off into the sunset, and my career was trailing along on one of the pack mules. I kept thinking Westerns were going to come back, but they didn't. The work that I loved and enjoyed so much was gone, deader than a bad guy trying to outdraw Marshal Matt Dillon. When they killed the Westerns, they hurt America. Westerns taught strong values to several generations, and I'm afraid that without them, we're gonna end up with a hole in our bucket, big time.

Finally, I decided to hang 'em up and come home to Texas. Anita and I arrived at my ranch on August 15 that year. If business picked up, I figured I could always go back to California. After all those years away, it was good to be home again. We spent the fall of 1992 getting acclimated, and by December we had settled into a comfortable routine. After living in L.A. for so long, the peace and quiet of the country was pretty pleasant.

Not long before I came home, at Occidental College in L.A., I had run in my last official track meet, a senior event for runners forty to sixty years old. I ran in the 100- and 220-yard events. I'm proud to say, I never lost a race after the Olympics. When I first moved back to Texas, I was still running every day. I ran around on my property in white shorts, white T-shirt, and white tennis shoes. Somehow, word got around that I was running in the nude. I guess that rumor's the price I had to pay for living so long in California, the land of fruits and nuts. I assure you, I wasn't out there running naked.

I wasn't doing many stunts anymore, but in a way I was still performing. I received a lot of invitations to speak to civic organizations and other groups about my Hollywood career. On December 6, 1992, I had a speaking engagement at the Ladies Lions Club meeting at the American Legion Hall in Graham. I told Anita we had to be there at 11:00 a.m. She said to go on without her; she'd come later in her own car. She liked to primp and took pride in keeping herself looking good.

I got to the American Legion Hall and was checking out the video player to make sure it would work. Thirty minutes before my talk, I got a call from my cousin Don Smith telling me Anita had been in a bad car wreck. I left immediately for the hospital there in Graham, but when I got there, she wasn't there. They told me the ambulance crew was still trying to stabilize her, so I left the hospital and started down the highway toward the ranch.

When I arrived, Don and his wife, Kay, were already there. The first thing I saw was Anita's car turned upside down in the pasture. She had made it only two miles from the ranch on State Highway 67, the road to Graham. It was a one-car accident. Something had caused her to swerve or had distracted her—we think it was a low-flying air force jet, but we'll never know for sure. She had been thrown from the car. Someone said it looked like she was dead but then I heard her say, "Oh no, I'm not." She was fifty and still had a whole lot of energy, and she was going to need every bit of it from there on out.

After they decided it was safe to move her, the ambulance took her to the Graham Hospital. I left my car on the side of the road and rode in with her. At the emergency room, the doctor said he thought she was paralyzed from the neck down. As soon as she could talk, the first thing she asked was if she was going to live. I assured her she was. They wanted to fly her by helicopter to Harris Hospital in Fort Worth but couldn't because of the weather, so we went by ambulance.

The next morning she had surgery to fuse the vertebrae together in her neck. That left her an incomplete paraplegic from the neck down. She had some movement but not much.

After two months at Harris they sent her to the Dallas Rehab Institute, one of the country's best. Caruth Byrd, whose father had been one of our sports sponsors at the University of Texas, got me an apartment there. While I was gone, my family and friends helped take care of my horses and longhorns. At the institute, they helped Anita quite a bit and taught me how to take care of her—everything from physical therapy and bath-

Dean escorting Dale Evans for her induction into the
Cowgirl Hall of Fame, Fort Worth, Texas, 1995.

ing to giving a catheter. She had to wear a cage on her head to protect her
neck, which was very fragile.

By the summer of 1993 they had done all they could for Anita and
sent us home. It felt like, *Here's your hat, what's your hurry!* But I knew
she'd had the best care possible. Taking care of her at home was a twenty-
four-hour job, exhausting to say the least. I had a hard time finding someone to help care for her. I went through several inept people, but I had two
or three who were wonderful with her. I couldn't have made it without
those women.

One bright spot was a call I got from Cheryl Rogers-Barnett, who
asked if I would escort her mother, Dale Evans, when she was inducted
into the Cowgirl Hall of Fame at the National Cowgirl Museum in Fort
Worth. On the day of the event, I took a few hours off from caring for

Anita and drove to Fort Worth to do the honors. I was very proud to be with the Queen of the Cowgirls and to have known exceptional people like her and Roy, who by this point was eighty-two and in frail health with congestive heart failure. Dale had been raised in Texas and her maiden name was Smith. That made us almost kin.

After Anita's accident, word got back to Hollywood that I needed to work a little to keep my insurance going. My old and good friend James Garner was doing a movie version of *Maverick* with Mel Gibson and got me a small part on it. I went to California to work and enjoyed spending some time with a lot of my old friends who had cameos in the movie. It gave me a much-needed break and I was able to keep my insurance.

When I came home from the West Coast, they had started the *Walker, Texas Ranger* television series in the Fort Worth–Dallas area. Lenny Katzman, the producer, was a friend (we met when I did a bit on *Playhouse 90* back in 1958) and he hired me for some stunt work. I did some fights and little bits, and they used my wonderful trick horse Sunday. My other horse, Hollywood, even starred in one of the episodes. Thanks to Chuck Norris and his son Eric, another pair of Okies, I did stunts for the series through 1995.

In 1994, Dale Robertson called me and asked, "How would you like to have a stocking-legged, blaze-faced trick horse that weighs 2,000 pounds?" I didn't know for sure, but I did know that Dale had given me my best horses ever. I took my truck and trailer and headed off to Oklahoma. I got to Dale's and we pulled his big trailer to Tulsa in the snow. That's where I got Max, whose trainer had died. For a one-ton Clydesdale, he was an amazing animal. He could smile, count, shake his head yes or no, push a rubber ball around, get on a pedestal, and teeter-totter. He was a smooth ride and did dressage, a true gentle giant.

Between stunt gigs, I traveled around quite a bit doing appearances at rodeos, celebrity charity events, and schools with Sunday, Hollywood, and Max, three of the greatest trick horses a man could ever have. I lost Sunday in 1993, way before his time, but I have Hollywood to this day and he is still magnificent. Max passed away too soon also, but not before many kids in the area had seen him perform and sat on his back. I'd usually do about a forty-five-minute show during which I'd get old Sunday, Hollywood, or Max to smile, count, rear, sit, pray, kneel, take a bow, and lie down. On April 29, 1995, I performed at home, appearing in the Stephens County Ranch Rodeo at Breckenridge. Choya, Sunday, and Max are buried on the ranch at Ivan. I have had some great horses and loved them like family. They always made me look good.

In the spring of 1996, I was hired to work on the TNT movie *Michael*, directed by Nora Ephron and starring John Travolta, whom I found to be a very kind and gracious man. I worked with a lot of younger stuntmen, including Corey Eubanks, Johnny Hawk (he was the grandson of John Epper, the third generation of the biggest clan of stunt people in the business), and Ben Scott. I was the oldest guy by twenty years or more. We did a fight scene in a bar, just like old times. I had a lot of fun and the food provided the cast was some of the best I'd ever had during a production.

They shot *Michael* at Gruene Hall in Gruene, Texas, a small town outside New Braunfels, south of Austin. I was supposed to travel to Arizona for a Ben Johnson roping, but I had to cancel since I was working. When Ben passed away the next week, my utter sadness was only a precursor of things to come.

Working on *Michael* made a nice break, but I spent most of my time caring for Anita at the ranch. We both knew this was no movie, that nothing would alter the difficulties or pain we were facing together. Yet in February 1996, her family pressed Anita to return to Connecticut, to a rehab facility there. Anita was persuaded. She missed her mom and brothers and dared to hope that rehab could work. She stayed in Connecticut for a couple of months, but made no progress in rehab. Seeing the toll her rigorous care taking was on her family, she decided to be near her daughters and grandchildren in California; there, she lived with her youngest daughter, Laurie. Anita wanted me to join her, but I just couldn't.

In July 1996, Anita was near Laurie's swimming pool and fell in. By the time they discovered her walker and pulled Anita out, her brain was so damaged that she required life support. I flew out to California. Anita, once so vibrant, so full of life, couldn't respond. Her brain, the doctors explained, had died. In the hardest decision of our lives, Anita's daughters and I decided it was best to let her go.

We held Anita's memorial service in California and buried her in Connecticut next to her father. In the years since Anita's accident, so many family and friends had stood by us, especially my cousin Don and his wife. I will be forever grateful to them all.

After so much tragedy, I felt the Lord took me by the hand and guided me to Debby, the delight of my life. Like me, she was born in Breckenridge, though she didn't come along until 1959. Her parents A. K. and Jo Anna Stoker raised six children—four girls and two boys—in Breckenridge, where A. K. was the water superintendent. In a way, our connection goes back to when I played football against her father, who played for Woodson, a little community about twenty miles north of Breckenridge. I have known the Stokers in Stephens and Throckmorton Counties all my life.

My first meeting with Debby had been a brief encounter at the First National Bank in Breckenridge, where she worked as a teller, in 1977. At that time I never gave her a thought, except for how pretty she was. In the late 1980s I was home for a while working on the ranch and saw her once again at the Quick Six in Breckenridge. By this time she had three small children and I visited with her some about her family. I wouldn't see her again until I came home from Dallas in 1993 after Anita's accident. From then on, it seemed like every time I would go to Graham or Breckenridge I would run into her and her children, mostly at McDonald's. A few years passed and she asked me if she could bring her kids out to see my horses. I said sure, and we had a nice visit. I could tell she was a lot like me and that we had a lot in common. After Anita's death, I went to see Debby and before long we started going out. She's one of the most beautiful human beings I have known, a country girl who's everything a man who owns a ranch would want.

In October 1996 we were in Bandera, where I was working on the TNT television movie *Teddy Roosevelt and the Rough Riders*. On the weekend of the twenty-sixth, Debby and I drove from there to Brackettville, where we got married in the little church on the Bexar set at Alamo Village on Happy Shahan's ranch. Debby's family attended our wedding along with her children, fourteen-year-old Ash, eleven-year-old Mary, and nine-year-old Paul. My old childhood friend Larry Mahan was my best man.

When the preacher asked if there was anything I wanted to say in the

Mary, Paul, Dean, Debby, and Ash a few months
after Dean and Debby's wedding, 1997.

vows, I said, "Yes, Debby will always open and shut the gates and I will always provide them." As long as Debby opens and shuts my gates, I will survive. We raised Ash, Mary, and Paul on the ranch. They are all out on their own now and successful. Ash did a one-year tour in Iraq with the 490th Civil Affairs Army Unit and Paul did one tour in Iraq and one in Afghanistan with the Third Battalion, Sixth Marines.

When I go somewhere with Debby, there's never a prettier girl in the crowd. The nice thing about that is she is not one bit phony; she is real and genuine. I had one more blessing coming. It had always bothered me that I had not been able to raise my son Charles. On top of that, he'd

Left: Dean and Finis Smith, c. 2001. Courtesy of Sargent N. Hill.
Right: 2002 Dean Smith Celebrity Rodeo grand entry.

never fathered any grandkids I could spoil. But the Lord was kind to me. On December 7, 1998, my son Finis Dean Smith II was born. I was ecstatic to have such a fine young son, someone I could raise on the same land I grew up on.

These have been the happiest years of my life, but the steady loss of old friends continues to remind me that life is fleeting. Roy Rogers passed away in 1998. The last time I saw Roy and Dale together was in 1997 when I went out to see them in Apple Valley. By then he and Dale were both in bad health. She lived until 2001.

I put on three Dean Smith Celebrity Rodeos. The first was in October 2002 in Graham, a tribute to Ben Johnson to benefit the local American Cancer Society and the John Wayne Cancer Institute. The second was November 2004 in Abilene, a tribute to the Duke that benefited the John Wayne Cancer Institute and Cancer Services Network of Abilene. And the third was October 2006, a tribute to the singing cowboys that also bene-

Trevor Brazil, Roy Cooper, Dean, August Long, and Buck Taylor at the 2006
Dean Smith Celebrity Rodeo. Courtesy of Mark Engebretson.

fited the John Wayne Cancer Institute and Cancer Services Network of
Abilene.

I couldn't have done my rodeos without the support of rancher-oil-
man John Mecom, Jr., Peter and Julianna Holt, and Ed and Vicki Bass.
They made it all possible, along with the many volunteers from Graham
and Abilene.

Vicki Bass, wife of Ed Bass of the well-known Bass family in Fort
Worth, competed in the rodeos. Vicki and Ed have always been great sup-
porters of our western heritage and countless charities. Vicki is also a
great horsewoman and competitor.

Mecom I met through Dale Robertson, who had introduced us back
in 1959 in San Antonio while Dale was performing there. John and I became good buddies. Seven years after I met him, in 1966, he paid a $7.5
million franchise fee to start a professional football team in New Orleans,
the Saints. Nineteen years later, in 1986, he sold the team for $70 million.
He is one of the nicest guys I know and a very loyal friend.

There's an interesting story behind how I got to be friends with the Holts. One day I got an unusual phone call: a woman who said she was Julianna Holt told me she was fixing to turn fifty and wanted to get a picture of herself on the back of a rearing horse. She said she'd heard I had a horse that could do tricks, and I told her that old Hollywood could rear so high I'd have to feed him up in the trees. She laughed and asked if I could get Hollywood to rear with her in the saddle. I said that would be easy for an old stunt coordinator and a fine horse, but I was a little hesitant, not wanting to get her hurt. But she was persistent and I finally said, OK, come on up to my ranch. On the day she scheduled the photo shoot, she called and said she would be flying to Breckenridge and I said I'd meet her there. Well, Debby and I went to the airport and this private jet taxied up and she and her photographer got out of the plane. Up to then, I didn't know much about her, but I quickly found out that she and her husband, Peter, owned the San Antonio Spurs.

We drove her out to the ranch, where she put on her hat, boots, and chaps. Then I helped her up on Hollywood and she got the shots she wanted without any trouble. She was thrilled. After that, we drove her back to her jet and she flew back to their place at Blanco. A few weeks later, she invited us to her birthday party. That's where I got to meet Peter, a swell fellow. After that, we got to be good friends.

Debby and I took Finis to New York in the spring of 2002 for the fifty-year reunion of the 1952 US Olympic team. We stayed at the New York Athletic Club and attended a dinner at the Waldorf-Astoria and heard Rudy Giuliani speak. This was the same hotel where the Olympic team had been honored in 1952. It was so good to see my old friends, J. W. Mashburn, Thane Baker, Lindy Remigino, Bob Mathias, Malvin "Mal" Whitfield, Charlie Capazolli, Jack Davis, Perry O'Brien, Harrison Dillard, Darrow Hooper, and others. I went with my teammates to Ground Zero, a very moving experience. We took a carriage ride through Central Park, went to a Broadway play, and generally had a great time.

I had done charity rodeos to support cancer research since that disease had claimed so many Western actors, stuntmen, and athletes, many of them friends of mine. What I didn't know was that I would soon be benefiting from the medical expertise already gained in that field.

On Super Bowl Sunday in 2005, I rode my horse for a while, drove to Breckenridge to pick up the Fort Worth paper, and settled in that evening to watch the game. During the game, I started having severe back pain. I made it through the game, but the pain got so bad that I couldn't sleep that night. The next morning Debby took me to see Dr. Pete Brown, my family doctor, who put me in the Graham hospital for observation. I just kept getting worse, running a 104-degree fever and developing pneumonia, but those were just the symptoms. They really didn't know what was wrong with me. Many tests and five days later they finally found that I had a staph infection that had settled in the bone in my lower back. I was the sickest I had ever been and do believe if I had not been in such great physical shape, I would not have made it. With the help of Pete's father, cardiologist Dr. Bobby Brown (a former American League baseball player and later league president, he sat on the board of Baylor Medical), after the first week I had a room in Baylor All Saints Hospital in Fort Worth. While I was there, Dr. Catherine Colquitt, an infectious disease doctor whom Pete had been conferring with, found that I also had shingles. On my last day at the hospital, Dr. Lance Mandell did a bone marrow test and discovered I had multiple myeloma, cancer of the bone marrow. I went home and, thanks to Debby and my doctors, I made it through a two-week period when most people my age probably would have died. After six more weeks on IV antibiotics and home health care I finally got over the staph infection. I then started my treatments of a Zometa infusion every other month for my bones and an IVG (immunoglobulin) infusion each month for my immune system. I do this at the Center for Cancer and Blood Disorders in Fort Worth under Dr. Mandell's direction.

Everyone should have a wife like Debby. Twenty-four hours a day, seven days a week, month after month, she has taken great care of me. If ever anybody has a lust for living, it's me. I want to spend as much time as I can with Debby and I want to watch Finis go through high school and college. If I get to that, I will be blessed more than any man could hope to be. I find it pretty ironic after three charity rodeos for cancer that I would end up with this disease. Having cancer certainly makes you realize how great it is to be alive and be productive on this earth. My advice to people is if you're not feeling well, get checked out—don't mess around.

I can't run like I used to, but I'm still pretty spry for an old cowboy. I belong to a wellness center in Graham and work out there regularly. I sure didn't have anything that great when I left Graham in 1950 to go to

UT. And the athletic facilities at UT today are much better than they were when I went there. I also ride Hollywood and put him through his tricks to keep us both prepared for that next show. I still attend celebrity events for charity and still team rope, team pen, cut, or whatever is asked of me.

Despite my cancer, which Dr. Mandell has labeled as smoldering, my life was rolling along like a stagecoach on flat ground until I discovered that the oil company that leases my river ranch had spilled a lot of saltwater on the place. In the Bible, invaders salted the land to ruin it for others, and that's what happened to my property. Parts of the river ranch are as dead as the face of the moon, and will be for no telling how long. I sued for damages in state district court, a jury trial in my home county, lost in the appeals court in Eastland, and the Texas Supreme Court denied our petition for review. A piece of land that's been in my family since the 1870s was damaged and I'm not happy about it.

A few years before I got bogged down in that legal mess, Al Qualls, a mutual friend of Dale Robertson's and mine, introduced us to a fellow named Jimmy Rane. Jimmy is president and CEO of Great Southern Wood Preserving, Incorporated, the leading lumber treater in the United States. Great Southern's main facility is in Abbeville, Alabama, but they also have plants in Arkansas, Florida, Georgia, Mississippi, Missouri, and Texas.

On May 18, 2006, Debby, Finis, and I were picked up in Jimmy's private plane, and we flew with Dale and Terry Bradshaw to Auburn. As anyone who watches pro football knows, Bradshaw is a natural comedian, and I spent the entire trip laughing.

I was to receive the Jimmy Rane Foundation Lifetime Achievement Award at the Jimmy Rane Charity Golf Tournament. The tournament's banquet was held at the Marriott Auburn/Opelika Hotel and Conference Center at the Grand National golf course. Bradshaw was the keynote speaker. It was an exciting night and a huge honor. The Jimmy Rane Foundation actively works to raise money to fund college scholarships for deserving students.

Jimmy played football for Auburn, and since I played for the Longhorns, we both like the color orange real well and get along fine. Jimmy is also a big fan of Westerns, and he portrays the Yella Fella character in his humorous television commercials. Patterned after the Western serials from days gone by, the commercials promoting Great Southern were filmed as cliffhangers with "To be continued" at the end of each one.

In the fall of 2007 I got to go to Moab, Monument Valley, and Benson to work on some of those commercials. What a thrill it was to be back where I had been, in Westerns, earlier in my career. A group called Riders in the Sky played great western music for the shoot. Surrounded by that beautiful landscape and hearing the music took me back to my days of riding, running, and jumping.

In 2010 we filmed more commercials in Santa Fe, New Mexico. I worked with James Riley, Slats Slaton, Norton Dill, and Jimmy's young daughter Lindsay, who had a horse accident on the shoot and broke her pelvis. One tough cowgirl, she recuperated and went right back to riding.

Jimmy "Yella Fella" Rane originally brought me onto the production crew of those commercials as a stunt coordinator and advisor. Being a seasoned stuntman, I could show the young guys how to take a punch. I had a brief scene as the messenger in the first season, but by the third season, Jimmy decided I should be a regular character in the commercials. I played Mose, the Yella Fella's faithful friend and sidekick. In the commercials, Yella Fella and Mose show how courage forms a bond between two men who want to do what's right. The lead-off commercial for 2011 premiered during the Super Bowl, viewed by multiple millions all around the world.

The "Yella Fella" commercials have been a great success, and they have given me a chance to play cowboy once again. Jimmy is a first-rate guy who, like Duke, wouldn't ask you to do anything he wouldn't do himself. He is a wonderful family man and bedrock honest, the kind of fellow I like to associate with. I have met his lovely wife, Angela, and his parents, Tony and Libba Rane, as well as his children and employees, and have come to feel a part of his team.

In April 2011, Jimmy, the "Yella Fella" producers, and I were awarded a Western Heritage Wrangler Award from the National Cowboy and Western Heritage Museum for "Yella Fella and the Lady from Silver Gulch," which won in the 2010 Outstanding Fictional Drama category.

The next month, Debby and I boarded Jimmy's plane with actor Barry Corbin and Barbara and flew to Callaway Gardens in Pine Mountain, Georgia, for the annual Jimmy Rane Charity Golf Tournament. It was a big success and a very memorable event. I hope to spend even more time with the Yella Fella.

Back in March 2010 Debby, Finis, and I went to San Antonio to be part of the celebration of the fiftieth anniversary of John Wayne's *The Alamo*. I was the only cast member there, which left me feeling like the last man standing. Four of the actors are still around—Linda Cristal, Joan O'Brien, Frankie Avalon, and Patrick Wayne—but none had been able to attend the party.

That October, I was inducted into the Texas Trail of Fame in Fort Worth. There's a bronze star with my name on it embedded in the sidewalk at the stockyards in front of the Coliseum. That was one of my proudest moments, having my star resting between the stars of two of the greatest rodeo cowboys, Yakima Canutt and Casey Tibbs.

When I started in Hollywood, I hoped to become a Western star in my own right. After all, Gary Cooper got his start as a stuntman. But the competition turned out to be just too tough. With so many great Western actors in the 1950s and '60s, you'd have to be outstanding to get top billing. I think if I had been there earlier, I probably could have been a leading man, but I was just a little late. I'm not worried about that, though. I may not have gotten to be as big as Gene, Roy, or Duke, but I knew every one of them by their first name. Now that they are all gone, and I'm a ways down the road to being gone myself, I realize that I was in the movie business at a special time. Unfortunately, it's not a special time there any more. Shoot, even the old Western lots in Hollywood have nearly all been torn down.

I want to be able to go to a movie and enjoy the scenery and a good, action-packed story. What I don't want is all this political crap they put in movies today. To me, Hollywood seems lost. They're wagging their tail but nothing else is moving. I'd dearly love to see them make good Westerns again. Looking back, those old boys wearing the white hats sure made an impression on me. A guy riding across the silver screen on a good horse is something bigger than life. Westerns taught us to use our imagination and dream big. Those movies gave us a sense of fair play, even though real life is not fair. The Old West was never like Hollywood showed it, but I think our Western myth convinced several generations of Americans to stand up and do what's right.

A lot of people thought I was crazy for going to Hollywood and chasing my dream, but I had the ability to ride, run, and jump, and the good Lord let me become one of the industry's top stuntmen. That's what was intended for me to do and I didn't have to take a backseat to anybody. I was that guy from Texas who could run like the devil. Nobody could say he was a faster stuntman.

Mama used to say, "Dean, people are gonna judge you by the company you keep." In sixty years of participating in sports, rodeos, and movies, I met some great guys and gals—cowboys, actors, stunt people, and folks from all walks of life. Like that Johnny Cash song, I've been everywhere. I went through a lot of heartache, yet still came out a champ. My only regret about Hollywood is that it destroyed the part of the business I loved, the Westerns. It's been a great ride and I would do it all again. Not bad for a kid from the Clear Fork of the Brazos who grew up during the Depression.

DEAN SMITH FILMOGRAPHY

1950 – 1960 – 1970 – 1980 – 1990 – 2000 – 2010
An asterisk indicates films starring John Wayne.

STUNTS

Rough Riders (1997) TV movie
Michael (1996)
The Quick and the Dead (1995)
Maverick (1994)
Hot to Trot (1988)
Raw Deal (1986) (Stunt double: Sam Wanamaker)
Cloak & Dagger (1984) (Stunt player)
The Lonely Guy (1984) (Stunt double)
Christine (1983)
Simon & Simon (1981–1982) TV series (Stunt coordinator, 10 episodes)
    "Tanks for the Memories"
    "Double Entry"
    "Earth to Stacey"
    "The Uncivil Servant" (and six more)
The Concorde . . . Airport '79 (1979)
The Legend of the Golden Gun (1979) TV movie
1941 (1979)
FM (1978) (Stunt policeman)
How the West Was Won (1978) TV miniseries (Stunt coordinator)
Black Sunday (1977)
Mackintosh and T.J. (1975) (Stunt double)
Three Days of the Condor (1975) (Stunt double)
The Drowning Pool (1975) (Stunt double)
The Great Waldo Pepper (1975) (Stunt double)
The Towering Inferno (1974)
Earthquake (1974)
Airport 1975 (1974)

The Sugarland Express (1974)

The Sting (1973) (Stunt double)

Westworld (1973)

The Life and Times of Judge Roy Bean (1972)

Ulzana's Raid (1972)

Hickey & Boggs (1972)

Search (1972) TV series

Jeremiah Johnson (1972) (Stunt double)

The Legend of Nigger Charley (1972)

     a.k.a. *The Legend of Black Charley* (USA: TV title)

Evel Knievel (1971)

Big Jake* (1971)

Sometimes a Great Notion (1970)

Rio Lobo* (1970)

The Cheyenne Social Club (1970)

Little Big Man (1970)

Airport (1970)

True Grit* (1969)

The Stalking Moon (1968) (Stunt double: Trooper)

The Outcast (1968) TV series

Ironside (1967) TV series

El Dorado* (1966)

The Iron Horse (1966) TV series (Stunt double: Dale Robertson)

    47 episodes

What Did You Do in the War, Daddy? (1966)

Stagecoach (1966) (Stunt double)

The F.B.I. (1965) TV series

The Great Race (1965)

In Harm's Way* (1965)

Rio Conchos (1964)

Blood on the Arrow (1964)

Cheyenne Autumn (1964)

A Distant Trumpet (1964)

Kings of the Sun (1963)

McLintock!* (1963)

The Birds (1963)

How the West Was Won* (1962)

The Virginian (1962) TV series

*The Comancheros** (1961) (Stunt double)

Gunfight at Black Horse Canyon (1961) TV movie (Stunt double)

Two Rode Together (1961)

*The Alamo** (1960)

The Tall Man (1960) TV series

Bat Masterson (1960) TV series

    "The Pied Piper of Dodge City"

Laramie (1959) TV series

They Came to Cordura (1959)

*Rio Bravo** (1959)

Auntie Mame (1958)

Born Reckless (1958)

Cimarron City (1958) TV series

Cat on a Hot Tin Roof (1958)

Wagon Train (1957) TV series

ACTOR

4TH and Goal (2009) Coach Phillips

Silk Stalkings (1991) J. Henderson Moss (TV series, 1 episode)

Guns of Paradise (1991) The Man (TV series, 1 episode, "The Search for K. C. Cavanaugh")

Three Fugitives (1989) Playboy

Creepshow 2 (1987) Mr. Cavanaugh (segment "Old Chief Wood'nhead")

Timestalkers (1987) (TV movie)

Raw Deal (1986) Patrovita's Double

Rhinestone (1984) Cowboy Doorman

Simon & Simon (1981) Driver (TV series, 1 episode, "The Least Dangerous Game")

Bret Maverick (1981) Jack Danner (TV series, 1 episode, "Welcome to Sweetwater")

The Last Ride of the Dalton Gang (1979) Parker Deputy Sheriff (TV movie)

Fraternity Row (1977) Andy

The Quest (1976) Jess (TV series, 1 episode, "The Captive")

Invisible Strangler (1976)

Three for the Road (1975) (TV series, 1 episode, "Odyssey in Jeans")

Mackintosh and T.J. (1975) Bent

Seven Alone (1974) Kit Carson

Earthquake (1974) Pool Player

The Sugarland Express (1974) Russ Berry

The Six Million Dollar Man (1974) Major Osterman (TV series, 1 episode, "Rescue of Athena One")

Scream of the Wolfe (1974) Lake (TV movie)

Mrs. Sundance (1974) Avery (TV movie)

Ironside (1973) Joe (TV series, 1 episode, "The Ghost of the Dancing Doll")
  (1972) Thaler (TV series, 1 episode, "Find a Victim")

Search (1972) Cowhand (TV series, 1 episode, "The Gold Machine")

The Life and Times of Judge Roy Bean (1972) Outlaw

The Bold Ones: The New Doctors (1972) Sam (TV series, 1 episode, "A Purge of Madness")

Ulzana's Raid (1972) Trooper Horowitz

Hickey & Boggs (1972) Bagman

Squares (1972) Carl

Big Jake (1971) James William "Kid" Duffy

Sometimes a Great Notion (1970) Bit part

Rio Lobo (1970) L/Cpl Bide

The Cheyenne Social Club (1970) Bannister Gang Member

True Grit (1969)

Cimarron Strip (1967) Third Deputy (TV series, 1 episode, "The Legend of Jud Starr")

Hurry Sundown (1967) Hunt Club Member

El Dorado (1966) Charlie Hagan

The Legend of Jesse James (1966) Deke (TV series, 1 episode, "South Wind")

Wagon Train (1964) Jim (TV series, 1 episode, "The Kate Crawley Story")

McLintock! (1963)

Tales of Wells Fargo (1962) Michael (TV series, 1 episode, "Vignette of a Sinner")
  (1962) Guard (TV series, 1 episode, "Reward for Gaine")
  (1961) Second Man (TV series, 1 episode, "New Orleans Trackdown")
  (1961) Wagon Guard (TV series, 1 episode, "Border Renegades")

Have Gun Will Travel (1962) Wagon Driver (TV series, 1 episode, "One, Two, Three")

The Alamo (1960) Bowie's Man

Seven Ways from Sundown (1960) Hanley Gang Member

Gunsmoke (1960) Cowboy Running in Bar (TV series, 1 episode, "Crowbait Bob")

Rio Bravo (1959) Card Playing Burdette Henchman

SELF

100 Years of John Wayne (2007) TV documentary
John Wayne: Working with a Western Legend (2005) Documentary
Thank Ya, Thank Ya Kindly (1991) TV documentary
Dean Smith, Hollywood Stuntman (1963) TV documentary
U.S. Olympic Champions (1952) Documentary

CHRONOLOGY OF HONORS

1980 Inducted into Stuntmen's Hall of Fame, California
1980 Inducted into the University of Texas Hall of Fame, Austin, Texas
1985 Inducted into the Texas Sports Hall of Fame, Waco, Texas
1993 Ben Johnson Award, Los Angeles, California
1997 All-American Cowboy Award, Bandera, Texas
1998 Golden Boot Award, Los Angeles, California
2000 American Culture Award for Western Movies and Television, Lubbock,
    Texas
2002 Head of the Class Alvin Davis Award, Lubbock, Texas
2006 Inducted into the Texas Rodeo Cowboy Hall of Fame, Temple, Texas
2006 The Duke Award, John Wayne Cancer Institute Odyssey Ball, Beverly
    Hills, California
2006 Lifetime Achievement Award from the Jimmy Rane Foundation, Abbeville,
    Alabama
2007 Lifetime Achievement Award from the National Cowboy and Western
    Heritage Museum, Oklahoma City, Oklahoma
    Honorary major in the former Texas Ranger Foundation, Texas
    Silver Spur Lifetime Achievement Award, Los Angeles, California
    American Cowboy from West Quest
2009 Inducted into the National Multicultural Western Heritage Museum and
    Hall of Fame, Fort Worth, Texas
2010 Inducted into the Texas Cowboy Hall of Fame, Fort Worth, Texas
    Saluted by the Alamo Society for spectacular Stunt Career, San Antonio,
    Texas
    Inducted into the Rex Allen Museum Hall of Fame, Wilcox, Arizona.
    Inducted into the Texas Trail of Fame, Fort Worth, Texas
2011 Western Heritage Wrangler Award from the National Cowboy & Western
    Heritage Museum for Actor in "Yella Fella and the Lady from Silver Gulch,"
    2010 Outstanding Fictional Drama
2012 Inducted into the Big Country Athletic Hall of Fame, Abilene, Texas

LETTER FROM BOB MATHIAS

Bob Mathias
Olympic Decathlon Champion
1948 and 1952

The 1948 Olympic Games in London were fast and furious for me since I was only seventeen years old and had only heard what a decathlon was three months before the Games started. The 1952 Olympic Games in Helsinki were even more exciting than London since I was then an old guy of twenty-one years and knew a lot more about the decathlon than I had four years before.

I got a chance to meet a lot of great athletes from all over the world from just about every Olympic sport. I really enjoyed meeting and getting to know all of the great track-and-field athletes on the USA team. One of these newly met friends was a great sprinter from Texas—Dean Smith. It was a real pleasure to watch him run with his graceful and even stride and knowing that his speed was equal to that of the best sprinters in the world. Dean had a wonderful Texas personality that went along with his big Texas smile that made everyone like him from the very start. That included me. So it was a sad time when the 1952 Olympic team left Helsinki, and we all went our separate ways. I went back to Stanford University for my senior year and then spent two and half years in the Marine Corps. I then had a chance to join a Hollywood production company by the name of Batjac. The owner of Batjac was a former USC football player by the name of Marion Morrison—also known as John Wayne. I was getting ready to be in a Batjac movie called *China Doll* that starred Victor Mature when I got a call from my Olympic friend Dean Smith. He was in town, and of course we got together. One day we went to Batjac, and he met all the nice people there, including Bob Morrison, John Wayne's brother, and Michael Wayne, John's son, and many others who were involved in John Wayne's previous cowboy movies. From these contacts and others Dean soon became one of the best stuntmen in Hollywood. He stood in for many of the leading Western heroes doing dangerous and difficult stunts for them.

What I admire about Dean Smith is that he put the same effort, hard work, dedication, and ability into all his work in pictures as he did in competing in the Olympic Games and being one of the fastest men in the world.

Being one of the fastest men in the world and outrunning every horse in Hollywood was no easy task!

LETTER FROM THE JOHN WAYNE FAMILY

Wayne Enterprises
July 2011

Dear Dean,

Over fifty years ago in a tiny town in Texas began a friendship with our family that has transcended generations. On the set of the movie *The Alamo*, we first met a handsome young stuntman by the name of Dean Smith. While working on this movie, he earned a permanent spot in ten John Wayne films and many John Ford movies. He also cemented a place in our hearts and family.

Many times in Hollywood, friendships made on movie sets end with the wrap party, but not our friendship with Dean. Through the years we have appreciated the support and love that Dean has given our family. When our patriarch, John Wayne, passed away, he was there to offer a shoulder for us to cry on and prayers to help us move forward. Dean traveled with the family to Washington, DC, when we were presented with our father's Congressional Gold Medal.

When he left California to live in Breckenridge, Texas, again, he kept in touch with our large family. His charitable activities have always been impressive: he has performed and participated in charities that have benefited children and cancer all of his life. In 2004, Dean put on his Dean Smith Celebrity Rodeo and donated the proceeds to the research being conducted at John Wayne Cancer Institute. Shortly after that when Dean's own battle with cancer began, it was our turn to offer a shoulder and many prayers! The "Big C" is not enough to stop Dean; he put on another of his celebrity rodeos in 2006 for our benefit and is gone at least once a month to appear for the benefit of a charity or civic group. Whenever we need advice Dean is available and always gives us his clear vision.

Debby Smith, his fabulous wife, and Finis Smith, his handsome son, are the reason that he keeps such a positive attitude. Finis is already charming the younger female generation in our family—he is a chip off the old block! We now claim them as part of our family, too.

Dean's life has been exciting; he has met people from all walks of life, been all over the world, garnered many awards and accolades, and faced hardships. Through it all, his faith and love of family have carried him through. Dean has never let his battle with cancer stand in his way and is a shining example of all the values and traditions that have made our country so great and would have made the "Duke" so proud.

We are so proud to be a part of your life, Dean, and part of your amazing story.

Love always,
The Wayne Family
XO

INDEX

ABOUT THE AUTHORS

Retired stuntman and actor **Dean Smith**, an Olympic gold medalist at the 1952 Helsinki Games, lives on a ranch in Ivan, Texas, with his wife, Debby, and young son, Finis. His long list of honors includes membership in the Stuntman's Hall of Fame, the Texas Rodeo Cowboy Hall of Fame, and the Texas Cowboy Hall of Fame and a Lifetime Achievement Award from the National Cowboy and Western Heritage Museum.

The 2010 recipient of the A.C. Greene Award for lifetime achievement, **Mike Cox** is the author of twenty-one nonfiction books. An award-winning former journalist and longtime freelance writer, he lives in Fredericksburg, Texas, and is a spokesperson for the Texas Parks and Wildlife Department.